Baltic Light

Early Open-Air Painting in
Denmark and North Germany

Baltic Light

Early Open-Air Painting in Denmark and North Germany

Catherine Johnston

Helmut Börsch-Supan

Helmut R. Leppien

Kasper Monrad

With contributions by
Stig Miss
Gertrud With

National Gallery of Canada, Ottawa

In association with
Yale University Press
New Haven and London

Published in conjunction with the exhibition *Baltic Light: Early Open-Air Painting in Denmark and North Germany*, organized by the National Gallery of Canada, Hamburger Kunsthalle and Thorvaldsens Museum

Venues
National Gallery of Canada, Ottawa
15 October 1999–2 January 2000

Hamburger Kunsthalle, Hamburg, Germany
26 January–26 March 2000

Thorvaldsens Museum, Copenhagen, Denmark
19 April–18 June 2000

Published by the National Gallery of Canada, Ottawa
in association with Yale University Press, New Haven and London

NATIONAL GALLERY OF CANADA
Serge Thériault: Chief, Publications Division
Lynda Muir: Editor

FOR YALE UNIVERSITY PRESS
Edited by Jane Havell and Adam Freudenheim
Designed by Jane Havell

Translators
From German: Heather Hess, Jenny Marsh,
Hilary Schmalbach; from Danish: Glyn Jones

Typeset in Walbaum
Printed and bound in Singapore by C.S. Graphics

FRONT COVER: Carl Hasenpflug, *View of the Garrison Church in Potsdam*, 1827 (detail). See cat. no. 65.

BACK COVER: C. W. Eckersberg, *The Russian Ship of the Line "Asow" and a Frigate at Anchor in the Elsinore Roads*, 1828. See cat. no. 30.

FRONTISPIECE: Thomas Fearnley, *The Painter and the Boy*, 1834 (detail). See cat. no. 36.

Canadian Cataloguing in Publication Data

Baltic light : early open-air painting in Denmark and North Germany.

Exhibition catalogue.
Issued also in French under title: Lumière du nord.
Includes bibliographical references: p.
ISBN 0-88884-696-7

1. Painting, Danish – Exhibitions.
2. Painting, German – Exhibitions.
3. Painting, Modern – 19th century – Denmark – Exhibitions.
4. Painting, Modern 19th century – Germany, Northern – Exhibitions.
5. Plein air painting – Exhibitions.
6. Light in art – Exhibitions.
I. Johnston, Catherine. II. National Gallery of Canada. III. Title.

ND717 B35 1999   759.89'09'03407471384   C99-986003-8

Contents

Foreword

This occasion marks the first time that the National Gallery of Canada has collaborated with the Hamburger Kunsthalle and Thorvaldsens Museum of Copenhagen in mounting an exhibition. Comprising some one hundred paintings, *Baltic Light* draws not only on works from our partner museums, but also from other Danish and German collections. A principal source has been the Statens Museum for Kunst in Copenhagen, the main repository of Danish Golden Age painting, and collections in Berlin and Potsdam. We are very grateful to our colleagues at the State Hermitage Museum and at the State Museum Reserve "Peterhof" in Russia for their generosity in lending key pictures, as indeed we are to all lenders.

Inevitably, in any such collaborative endeavour, not all loan requests can be approved for all three venues. The National Gallery of Canada greatly appreciates the Louvre's collegiality in allowing a much-asked-for painting, Caspar David Friedrich's *Raven Tree*, to come to Ottawa, because of its particular relevance to the theme of the exhibition. We are also indebted to the Wallraf-Richartz-Museum in Cologne for lending Friedrich's *Ship on the Elbe in the Early Morning Fog*, and to the Fine Arts Museums of San Francisco for sharing the recently acquired and enchanting night sky by J. C. Dahl.

The gestation of this project has been especially long. The idea began with discussions between Kasper Monrad and Catherine Johnston, both of whom were convinced that connections and parallels between German and Danish painting of the period warranted closer scrutiny. Villads Villadsen, former director of the Statens Museum, was supportive from the outset. The National Gallery would like to thank his successor, Allis Helleland, for permitting Kasper Monrad's continued involvement. We are grateful to Stig Miss, Thorvaldsens Museum director, for enthusiastically collaborating in loan negotiations and the catalogue. Our sincere thanks go to Dr Helmut Leppien, former chief curator of the Hamburger Kunsthalle, who warmly embraced the opportunity of exhibiting German artists in the current context. We are also very cognizant of Dr Helmut Börsch-Supan's contribution to the catalogue on Friedrich and on artists from Berlin.

The timeframe of the exhibition is bound by the Napoleonic Wars and the Industrial Revolution. Despite the difficulties of post-war economic recovery, paintings of the period appear tranquil and optimistic. Hardship, nonetheless, brought about emigration to the New World, and many German and Danish settlers came to Canada in search of a better life. One such was William Berczy, a founding father of Canadian painting, who set sail in the 1790s from the Danish port of Altona, near Hamburg, eventually leading a group of German colonists to Markham, Ontario. Berczy's well-known *Woolsey Family* is in our collection, and it is interesting to note that Jean Trudel once compared it to a family group by C. W. Eckersberg, an artist featured here.

Although it is not possible to claim that the Danish and German works in this exhibition exerted any real influence on Canadian art, they are primarily landscapes, the dominant genre in historical Canadian painting. Also, topographical landscapes require an accuracy that comes only from training the eye and hand through making drawings, watercolours or oil sketches on the spot. Thus the earlier military surveyors of this country, or the later school of landscape painters known as the Group of Seven, can be seen to share many of the methods employed by the artists represented here. The resulting directness and spontaneity was a far cry from the more formal or dramatic renderings of nature we might expect from European painting of the period. This exhibition attempts, therefore, to show another face of landscape painting – pure and unencumbered, and produced fully a generation before Impressionism – which was little known beyond the borders of Denmark and Germany until recently, and which is still scarcely represented in North American collections.

PIERRE THÉBERGE, C.Q.
Director, National Gallery of Canada

Lenders to the Exhibition

We gratefully acknowledge the generosity of the
private collectors and public institutions who have
made this exhibition possible.

Denmark
Copenhagen, Den Hirschsprungske Samling
   Det danske Kunstindustrimuseum
   Ny Carlsberg Glyptotek
   Statens Museum for Kunst
   Thorvaldsens Museum
Nivå, Nivaagaards Malerisamling
Odense, Fyns Kunstmuseum

France
Paris, Musée du Louvre

Germany
Berlin, Staatliche Museen zu Berlin, Nationalgalerie
   Staatliche Museen zu Berlin, Kupferstichkabinett
   Stiftung Archiv der Akademie der Künste
   Stiftung Stadtmuseum Berlin
Bremen, Kunsthalle Bremen, Kupferstichkabinett
Chemnitz, Städtische Kunstsammlung
Cologne, Wallraf-Richartz-Museum
Dresden, Staatliche Kunstsammlungen,
   Gemäldegalerie Neue Meister
Düsseldorf, Kunstmuseum im Ehrenhof
Erfurt, Angermuseum
Essen, Museum Folkwang
Frankfurt am Main, Freies Deutsches Hochstift /
   Frankfurter Goethe-Museum
Halberstadt, Städtisches Museum

Halle, Staatliche Galerie Moritzburg
Hamburg, Hamburger Kunsthalle
Karlsruhe, Staatliche Kunsthalle
Lübeck, Museum für Kunst und Kulturgeschichte
Munich, Bayerische Staatsgemäldesammlungen
Oldenburg, Landesmuseum für Kunst und
   Kulturgeschichte – Schloss und Augusteum
Potsdam, Stiftung Preussische Schlösser und Gärten
   Berlin-Brandenburg
Rudolstadt, Thüringer Landesmuseum Heidecksburg
Weimar, Kunstsammlungen zu Weimar, Schlossmuseum

Norway
Oslo, Nasjonalgalleriet

Poland
Poznán, Muzeum Narodowe

Russia
Petrodvorec, The State Museum Reserve "Peterhof"
St Petersburg, The State Hermitage Museum

Sweden
Göteborg, Göteborgs Konstmuseum

United States
San Francisco, Fine Arts Museums of San Francisco

Acknowledgements

First and foremost, it has been a delight to work with the co-authors of this catalogue. Many colleagues were forthcoming in discussing the thesis of the exhibition at its initial stages. Particularly helpful have been Villads Villadsen and Marianne Saabye in Copenhagen; Helmut Börsch-Supan in Berlin, and Peter-Klaus Schuster, whose Blechen exhibition also featured open-air sketches but cut a much wider swathe; Christoph Heilmann in Munich, who organized a noteworthy Dillis exhibition; Torsten Gunnarsson in Stockholm, whose thesis on a similar topic was published in 1989; John Leighton and Jean-Pierre Cuzin, who made early purchases of related material for the National Gallery, London, and the Louvre. Boris Asvarishch in St Petersburg, Gerd Bartoschek in Potsdam and Peter Wegmann in Winterthur gave freely of their time in showing the extensive collections in their care.

The curators of the lending institutions must be thanked: we are grateful to Allis Helleland, director, and Henrik Bjerre, chief conservator, of the Statens Museum for the exceptional number of loans and for arranging conservation treatment of Rørbye's *View from the Artist's Window*, enabling it to travel; Søren Dietz at the Ny Carlsberg Glyptotek for loans by Rørbye and Lundbye; and Tone Skedsmo from the Nasjonalgalleriet in Oslo, who has been understanding of our need for works by the Norwegian artists Dahl and Fearnley, while collections in Berlin and Potsdam have been especially generous; Pierre Rosenberg, Jean-Pierre Cuzin and Olivier Meslay were gracious concerning a late request for a loan, as were Lynn Orr and Steven Nash. Rolf Bothe was kind to supply, at short notice, a transparency of Friedrich's missing painting from Weimar; Stephan Koja in Vienna, Martha Wolf and Hsiu-ling Huang in Chicago, and Matthias Wohlgemuth in Winterthur have all assisted in furnishing illustrations for the introductory chapters, while Elisabeth Foucart-Walter and Madeleine Koch at Verlagsgruppe Bruckmann have been helpful regarding photographs of earlier exhibitions in Paris and Munich. John Ittmann and W. R. Johnston provided information on the early display of German paintings and drawings in Philadelphia, New York and Baltimore. Many discussions on *plein air* painting have taken place with Michael Pantazzi, who also indicated the existence of two pictures by Dahl in a Toronto collection in the mid nineteenth century.

At the Hamburger Kunsthalle, the registrar Anna Barz made a stellar contribution in coordinating the German loans. At Thorvaldsens Museum, Britta Tøndborg compiled the Danish bibliography. Ann Collins and Linda McDonald, successive Consuls General of Canada in St Petersburg, gave prompt assistance with visits to Russia and with loan negotiations; Philip Somerville, Minister at the Canadian Embassy in Bonn, kindly followed through on requests for photographs in Germany. In Canada, Raold Nasgaard was an early supporter of the exhibition. A particular debt is owed to Beate Stock and to Mitchell Frank for their resourcefulness in finding early literature on the subject of German Romantic and Biedermeier painting, and to Liz Smidt Stainforth for collecting material on Danish paintings. At the National Gallery, Anna Kindl was tireless in locating books in both Germany and Denmark that were hitherto lacking in the Library. Karen Colby-Stothart and Julie Hodgson have done an admirable job as exhibition coordinators. Chief of Publications Serge Thériault played an instrumental role in publishing the catalogue, while Lynda Muir displayed her usual care in assembling and pre-editing the manuscript, and Myriam Afriat brought refinement to the editing of the French version of the catalogue. Shirley Proulx showed great diligence in handling correspondence and managing the database. Finally, a word of praise to John Nicoll and Adam Freudenheim of Yale University Press, London, and to Jane Havell, for the excellent editing and handsome layout of the catalogue.

CJ

Contributors

CJ

Catherine Johnston is Curator of European Art at the National Gallery of Canada, Ottawa. She was co-author of *Bolognese Drawings in North American Collections, 1500–1800* (1982) and *Vatican Splendour: Masterpieces of Baroque Art* (1986), both exhibition catalogues for the National Gallery of Canada.

HBS

Helmut Börsch-Supan was formerly Chief Curator of Painting and Sculpture at Verwaltung Preussische Schlösser und Gärten, Berlin. He was author of the catalogue raisonné of the works of Caspar David Friedrich (1973), of *Die deutsche Malerei von Anton Graff bis Hans von Marées* (1988) and of many other publications on German art of the eighteenth and nineteenth centuries.

HRL

Helmut R. Leppien was formerly Chief Curator of the Paintings Department at the Hamburger Kunsthalle. He was author of *Caspar David Friedrich in der Hamburger Kunsthalle* (1993) and curator of *Mit klarem Blick. Hamburger Malerei im Biedermeier* at the Hamburger Kunsthalle (1996), as well as many other exhibitions of nineteenth-century and modern art.

KM

Kasper Monrad is Senior Research Curator at the Statens Museum for Kunst, Copenhagen. He was curator of *The Golden Age of Danish Painting* at the Los Angeles County Museum of Art/Metropolitan Museum of Art, New York (1993–94), and of *Caspar David Friedrich and Denmark* (1991) and *Christen Købke* (1996), both at Statens Museum for Kunst.

SM

Stig Miss is Director of Thorvaldsens Museum, Copenhagen, and author of various essays on Danish and international art of the late eighteenth and early nineteenth centuries, and on modern Danish art.

GW

Gertrud With is Curator at Thorvaldsens Museum, Copenhagen, specialising in Danish art of the late eighteenth and early nineteenth centuries.

CG

Chris Gerbing, University of Karlsruhe, was formerly an intern at the Hamburger Kunsthalle.

KvO

Kristine von Oehsen, University of London, was formerly an intern at the Hamburger Kunsthalle.

Preface

Although much has been written in the last quarter-century on both Danish and German art of the early nineteenth century, traditionally the Danish Golden Age, German Romanticism and Biedermeier painting have been regarded as separate entities. Admittedly, Danish artists were included in the large *Biedermeier* exhibition held in Munich in 1988–89, just as *plein air* sketches by Danish and German artists were displayed side by side in *In the Light of Italy* of 1996–97, but this is the first exhibition to concentrate on and explore the shared interests that existed among artists who stemmed from the Baltic region. Danish and north German painting of this period is characterized by a number of related artistic concerns. Keen observation was common to artists from Copenhagen, Hamburg, Berlin and Dresden, who viewed well-known motifs with fresh eyes and also discovered new motifs with their open and unbiased attitude. Such painters described what they saw with loving attention to detail, although they might base their work on a comprehensive idea. All these artists were greatly interested in light – that is, in carefully observed daylight – which is described with the same precision as other features of their pictures.

The exhibition focuses on landscapes and cityscapes, and explores the early introduction of open-air painting to northern practice. Pictures included here range from small oil sketches quickly and lightly executed in the open to large and carefully worked-out compositions executed in the studio. They encompass works of spontaneous perception and objective registration of the motif, those of suggestive or evocative presentation or, at the other extreme, works with pictorial elements carefully arranged to express the philosophical, religious or artistic view of the artist. This is one of the obvious paradoxes of the period: that behind the apparent realism may hide an ideal concept.

For fifty years, from the late 1790s through most of the 1840s, a lively exchange took place between artists located on the north and south shores of the western end of the Baltic Sea. Not only were the regions they inhabited geographically close but, in the early years of the century, political ties between them were also strong. Though today part of Germany, the region where Caspar David Friedrich was born was then still part of Swedish Pomerania, while Danish borders extended down from Jutland through the duchies of Schleswig and Holstein to the outskirts of the free Hanseatic city of Hamburg, and north-west to include Norway. Given this proximity, and the absence of other art academies in the north, it was logical that artists such as Friedrich, Runge, Kersting and Dahl should have frequented the Royal Danish Academy of Fine Arts in Copenhagen. It was equally likely that, with the realignment of some of these territories following the Napoleonic Wars, they should then gravitate to Dresden, or lend their works to exhibitions in Berlin or Weimar. It was not surprising, therefore, that younger artists such as Morgenstern, Gurlitt and Carmiencke should continue to migrate to Copenhagen, where the Academy had been reinvigorated through the teaching of C. W. Eckersberg, until hostilities broke out between Germany and Denmark in 1848, with a definitive severance of Schleswig and Holstein occurring in 1864. On the other hand, practically all Danish artists visited Germany, maintaining contact with Friedrich and Dahl in Dresden, or frequenting the landscape painters who congregated around Dillis at the Academy in Munich, whose teaching was based on his Italian experience, as was Eckersberg's. Many artists of this period travelled even further south, and Danish and German painters met in the circle that formed around the Danish sculptor Bertel Thorvaldsen in Rome.

For northern artists, the lure of Italy had existed for centuries, but its attraction was renewed through Goethe's trip, his famous *Italienische Reise*, and through Thorvaldsen's long sojourn in Rome, where he flourished as a neoclassical sculptor and portrayer of the cosmopolitan society resident there. Adopting the accepted French precedent, art academies in Germany and Denmark awarded scholarships to Rome, while Danish and German kings and crown princes themselves travelled to Italy, also sponsoring artists who wished to study there. When Constantin Hansen painted a group portrait of artist-compatriots in Rome (cat. no. 63), considerably fewer Danes were reported to be living there than Germans, whose community numbered over a hundred. Not all shared the same outlook or followed the same paths as those trodden by the artists represented in this exhibition, but an Italian trip was deemed a useful formative and liberating experience.

For Eckersberg, one of the earlier Danish artists of the period to benefit from a stay in Italy, the experience meant fulfilling the terms of his history painting scholarship and at the same time producing some thirty vibrant views of Rome and its environs. As Valenciennes had done before him, Eckersberg retained these small pictures on his return to Copenhagen in 1816, and they hung in his apartment attached to the Academy of Fine Arts, where they were seen and studied by his students. Curiously, Corot, whose more famous views of Rome were made a decade later than Eckersberg's, actually leased out his Roman sketches on his return to Paris for French artists to copy. Other artists travelled further afield, to Naples and even Sicily, while Rørbye ventured on to Greece and Turkey.

Of course, not all artists found it necessary to travel south. The Berlin painter Gaertner, although he worked in the same sphere as Schinkel and Blechen for whom Italian journeys had been essential, chose rather to study in Paris with Corot's teacher, Jean-Victor Bertin, himself the pupil of Pierre-Henri Valenciennes, the great French champion of *plein air* painting. Clearly Friedrich's personal perception was so strong that visits to the island of Rügen, the Hartz mountains and Bohemia sufficed to renew his contact with nature and feed his vision of the sublime. In Denmark, the art historian Høyen encouraged artists to remain at home to study their own land, thereby favouring the development of a nationalist school at mid-century. Well before that, however, Dahl regularly returned to his native Norway, his dramatic paintings of its mountains and stormy sea coast evidently holding special appeal for the patrons of German Romanticism; while Gurlitt and Morgenstern also made outdoor sketches there. Friedrich, it is said, even considered going to Iceland; and Carus did travel to Scotland to study the basalt rock formations on the west coast, in the spirit of empirical nature that was the product of the Age of Enlightenment.

The pictures in this exhibition comprise primarily topographical views. These were either painted out of doors or, for the more ambitious works, were based on drawings or sketches made on the spot. In the case of Friedrich, an effort has been made to choose scenes that are clearly rooted in his experience of Pomerania and Rügen. With other artists it is possible that the locale of a setting is no longer identifiable today, but this should not cast doubt on the credibility of specific landscapes in their oeuvre as topographical works. In some images, grasses, plants or rocks are seen at such close range that where they were done is of no relevance, though it is obvious that they were painted directly from nature.

Philip Conisbee and Torsten Gunnarsson have addressed the problems facing artists working outdoors in an age before paints were available in tubes, when necessity dictated preparing for excursions by grinding pigments in advance, suspending them in an oil medium, and then placing them in little impermeable sacks made from the bladders of small animals. Similarly, it was common practice to prepare paper or canvas supports with a ground layer that would have dried before reaching the site to be depicted. A previously executed drawing might underlie this preparatory layer, especially if the subject involved architecture, or might be laid on top of the initial paint layer if the sketch was completed in one sitting. Views that were executed in one go tend to be looser in handling – to take advantage of the coloured ground – and more limited in their colour range, because of the problem of wet paints mixing. Many pictures and drawings record artists actually painting in the open country, habitually seated on folding stools in the shade of large umbrellas, as often as not dressed in the frock coat and top hat of the day (cat. no. 36).

Sometimes a view was made in greater comfort, looking out of an open window. Wasmann shows us a hasty sketch done from a rustic Italian window (cat. no. 108), whereas Hansen indicates a view over the rooftops beyond the figures of Danish artists carefully posed in his Roman studio (cat. no. 63). Friedrich, Carus and Dahl all lived in the same house in Dresden, and we see in Kersting's painting of Friedrich at his easel (fig. 23, page 66) that the master sat close to the window with the light coming over his shoulder, and just how large such windows were, especially in northern climes where light is at a premium in the winter months. Friedrich painted his wife looking out one such window, just as Tischbein had made a watercolour of Goethe, also from behind, leaning out of a window in Rome. Friedrich's evocative sepia drawings of his studio windows are as much about the interior as the view beyond, which is also true of Rørbye's scene of plants on the window ledge (cat. no. 95). In his small painting from Lübeck (cat. no. 12) Carus focused on the window itself, and it must have been from windows in Copenhagen and possibly Norway that Dahl made cloud studies (cat. nos. 16 and 21). Dahl's view of Pillnitz from his window in Dresden even repeats the image by reflecting it in the window panes (cat. no. 17). Such a play is also characteristic of Hummel's painting of the great marble basin still in the polishing shed (cat. no. 67), for it is not the view from the windows that catches our attention so much as the row of window panes reflected on the basin's curved and shiny surface. Light from windows – and the shadows it produced – also occupied the imaginations of such artists as Bendz and Kersting, who produced among the most beautiful and serene interiors in the Biedermeier style, sometimes leading the eye out of the window (cat. no. 72), or confining it to the space defined by the interior walls, but with shadows suggesting windows that lie outside the line of vision.

Panoramic landscapes are represented in the early works of Jens Juel (cat. nos. 70 and 71), in Eckersberg's imitative view of Møn (cat. no. 24), or a later one from the ramparts of Kronborg Castle (cat. no. 31). In a related vein, Blechen's sweeping sketches on a smaller scale capture his fleeting impressions of the Italian coast (cat. nos. 5 and 7), while Gaertner (cat. no. 54) and Gensler (cat. no. 56) portray the flat shoreline of lakes in the March of Brandenburg or of the Baltic coast. Most of Gaertner's scenes of Berlin adhere to the Dutch seventeenth-century tradition of cityscapes or the Italian vedutas brought north by Bellotto. Gaertner's view of Berlin from the roof of the Church of Friedrichswerder (cat. no. 52) belongs to a more recent tradition that places the spectator in the centre of a 360-degree panorama. Decorations made by Købke for the walls of his parents' house in Blegdammen, although taken from the roof of Frederiksborg Castle (cat. no. 78), are more clearly allied with the broad landscape views of Juel and Blechen.

Købke was, in fact, the most faithful practitioner of *plein air* painting in Denmark, for which Eckersberg's luminous scenes of Rome and the excursions he led into the Danish countryside proved the catalyst for a whole generation of artists, fundamentally conditioning their approach to nature and irreversibly changing the course of landscape painting in the north. While not all works featured here can claim to have been painted in the open, as the title of the exhibition might suggest, they all share in a new and heightened interest in nature and in light.

CJ, HBS, HRL, KM, SM

D. = DUCHY
GR. D. = GRAND DUCHY
K. = KINGDOM

//// Swedish Pomerania to 1815
- - - Frontiers, 1815
.... Danish internal frontiers
━━━ Frontier of the German Confederation

KINGDOM OF SWEDEN

NORTH
SEA

Århus

Kalundborg *Copenhagen*

Ödense

Ribe

SCHLESWIG

KINGDOM OF DENMARK

BALTIC
SEA

Altenkirchen

Bergen *Rügen*

Stralsund

Greifswald

Wolgast

Kiel

Heligoland
(Brit.)

HOLSTEIN

Lübeck

Rostock

POMERANIA

LAUENBURG

GR. D. OF
MECKLENBURG-
SCHWERIN

Güstrow

Neubrandenburg

GR. D. OF
MECKLENBURG-
STRELITZ

Stettin

Altona *Hamburg*

R. Elbe

K. OF UNITED NETHERLANDS

Oldenburg

GR. D. OF
OLDENBURG

Bremen

KINGDOM OF
HANOVER

Neuruppin

R. Oder

Berlin

Brandenburg *Potsdam*

Hanover

Brunswick

Magdeburg

P R U S S I A

KINGDOM   O F

D. OF BRUNSWICK

Halberstadt

Harz

D. OF   ANHALT

R. Elbe

Kottbus

Düsseldorf

D. OF
WALDECK

Kassel

Halle

R. Rhine

Leipzig

Riesen
Mountains

Meissen

ELECTORATE
OF HESSE

THURINGIAN

Weimar
STATES

KINGDOM OF SAXONY

Dresden

Saxon
Switzerland

1

A View Through Three Arches: Danish and German Artists in Denmark, Germany and Italy

KASPER MONRAD

During his visit to Rome from 1813 to 1816, C. W. Eckersberg was repeatedly engaged in portraying the Colosseum. The first time he made a drawing in the ruin was in the spring or summer of 1814, and he returned there to paint on several occasions during the course of the next two years. Significantly enough, he did not depict the ancient building in its entirety, seen from the outside. Just as with his other Roman views, he avoided the most traditional angles. Instead, he chose to paint the interior of the Colosseum, with a few figures to indicate the human dimension and therefore the overall proportions. He was at his most original, however, when he positioned himself on the third level of the ruin, looked out across the city, and painted the view as seen through three of the arches (fig. 1).

The painting is evidence of an amazingly sharp power of observation. Eckersberg has examined the ruin with the thoroughness of an archeologist, and the many details in the background are depicted with great precision, presumably with the help of a telescope. But the striking effect of the picture is due first and foremost to the way in which the view is framed by the three arches. Eckersberg has undertaken a classical division of his motif and made use of the arches to create a carefully balanced composition – he had not been the pupil of Jacques Louis David in Paris for nothing. If we seek to unearth his working method, however, it turns out that he has not reproduced one specific view of Rome at all. He has in fact combined three views into one. When standing on the third level of the Colosseum in front of the centre one of the three arches, he had before him the part of Rome that can be seen through this arch. But he could not from there see the views

that we can see through the other two arches. They were partly hidden by the columns in the building. In order to see them, he had to take in the one case two paces to the left and in the other five paces to the right.[1] In other words, he has adjusted visible reality so that every part of the picture could be given a clearly structured character. This painting is a work of great importance in Danish art. The principles on which it was executed were not crucial only to Eckersberg's art, but to early nineteenth-century Danish painting in general. What was being established here was a set of completely new artistic ideals. Painters moved between two opposing poles – on the one hand there was the original, often unexpected, observation, and on the other the conscious selection and structuring of what was seen.

During his stay in Rome, Eckersberg associated with the group surrounding the sculptor Bertel Thorvaldsen, thereby meeting the German artists resident in the city. But amazing as it may seem, he appears not to have had any closer contact with them and not to have had any artistic exchanges with them at all. From his letters it clearly emerges that he was not keen on the aims of the Nazarenes, and he makes no mention of the German landscape artists.[2] With his thorough French schooling, he was not receptive to contemporary German painting. The few examples to which we can point of German influence on Eckersberg's art are scarcely the results of a conscious effort on his part. In this, he was very much an exception among the Danish artists of the time. Virtually all other Danish painters, including his most loyal pupils, took a lively interest in contemporary German art and in many cases received inspiration from it.

In 1818, after his return to Denmark, Eckersberg was appointed professor at the Royal Danish Academy of Fine Arts in Copenhagen, and he came to exercise an enormous influence – greater than that of any other Danish artist before or since. He therefore has a great deal of responsibility for the general course of artistic developments in Denmark over the next few decades.[3] As early as 1824, a Danish critic pointed out that some Academy pupils, including Wilhelm Bendz and Martinus Rørbye, had "all sprung from one school", and he stressed that the quality of their works was "to the credit of both the artists and their teacher, Professor Eckersberg."[4]

Eckersberg's ideas were clearly expressed in his teaching – partly in his strong emphasis on the theory of perspective, partly in practical exercises, in that he regularly took pupils on excursions outside Copenhagen where they had their powers of observation sharpened and where they practised

drawing and painting out in the countryside. On this point, Eckersberg was a pioneer, as the study of nature did not form a direct part of the teaching in any other academy of fine arts in Europe at this time. The flood of painted oil studies from the young Danish painters also derived from Eckersberg's teaching. He encouraged his pupils to paint the first motifs they came across – "no matter what", as he himself said. It was a question of seeing familiar motifs with fresh eyes. Eckersberg himself showed the way when he painted the unprepossessing view across Copenhagen harbour towards the shipyards on Nyholm in 1826 (cat. no. 28), and his pupils eagerly took up the idea: Martinus Rørbye painted the view from his parents' window (cat. no. 95), Wilhelm Bendz the view from a window in the Academy of Fine Arts in Charlottenborg looking across the basin of Nyhavn (cat. no. 1), Frederik Sødring a courtyard to the rear of Charlottenborg (cat. no. 102), and Christen Købke the garden gate to his parents' house (cat. no. 84).

Eckersberg formulated his ideas in 1833 in a brief study, *An Attempt at Guidance for Young Painters in the Use of the Theory of Perspective*. He argued that the value of a work of art lay to a great extent in a precise reconstruction of nature, or – in his own words – in "the exact agreement of the forms with the original picture". The object was to unite "the idea" with "the external form of the object".[5] By "original picture", Eckersberg did not merely mean the natural scene, but rather the fundamental idea behind nature's outward appearance. He was implying an ideal striving to raise nature as it was in fact seen to a higher plane. Eckersberg may well have wanted to portray nature – but only its essence, with none of the chance elements. In practice, Eckersberg's view of art's task found its expression in 1828 when he painted the Russian ship of the line "Asow" (cat. no. 30). He did not paint the ship as he had seen it in reality, but as he would have seen it if he had observed it under optimal conditions – i.e., from an ideal point of view, at a suitable distance, and in the right weather.

Eckersberg's new artistic principles were received with great interest in Copenhagen, not only among the artists, but also among leading writers in the art world. In 1834, the philosopher F. C. Sibbern published the first part of his treatise *On Poetry and Art*, where he touched on some of the points Eckersberg had taken up in his *Attempt at Guidance*. Sibbern argued that "art can and should go beyond nature" in that it should "allow nature to have an effect of greater power and harmony than is seen in nature itself in reality." Art must allow itself to be guided by nature, but "not to remain rooted in what is immediately given by nature"; the artist must nevertheless not "paint anything other than what really *could* occur, and then not paint it differently from how it would then be seen in reality."[6] Sibbern was in close touch with several of the leading figures in artistic life, including the art historian N. L. Høyen and the sculptor H. E. Freund,[7] with whom Eckersberg also associated: the possibility cannot be ignored that in these arguments Sibbern might have influenced Eckersberg when the latter was about to put his own thoughts into words the previous year.

Some years later, Sibbern stressed the importance of being able to enjoy sense impressions: "We must be able to delight in the reflection of the sun falling radiantly on the uppermost part of the roof while the rest is in shade." The philosopher

encouraged his readers constantly to have their eyes about them while walking through the city: "But as we pass houses and courtyards we must let our eyes move along, sometimes looking up to see and absorb the different character and physiognomies of the buildings [i.e. their particular appearance] and the play of light on them, sometimes far down to observe human activities. Looking into grocers' windows, into their shops, into everything they put on show."[8] Thus wrote Sibbern in the second part of his novel *Gabrielis Breve* [Gabrieli's Letters]. There are clear parallels between his view and that of the painters, but this text was not published until 1850; it is therefore possible that the philosopher was allowing himself to be influenced by the painting of the time.

In the Academy of Fine Arts, Eckersberg formed a kind of partnership with the historical and landscape painter J. L. Lund, who was also appointed professor in 1818. To a great extent they supported each other's initiatives, but there was also a clear division of labour between them. Thanks to his striving for idealized art, Lund represented a contrast to Eckersberg's attitude with its emphasis on reality, and thanks to his links with the German Nazarenes and his youthful friendship with Caspar David Friedrich, Lund became a link with contemporary German painting. On the other hand, after his return from Rome in 1816, Eckersberg completely lost touch with art abroad. There was a clear tendency for the young Danish pupils to seek guidance from the Schleswiger Eckersberg (who, incidentally, was bilingual), and for the pupils from Holstein and north Germany to turn to Lund.

The Academy in Copenhagen at this time was a great draw to a large number of north Germans who wanted to be trained as artists; for many of them, it was more natural to go there than to Berlin. Around 1800, first Friedrich and then Philipp Otto Runge spent some years in Copenhagen, and a few years later G. F. Kersting followed. At the end of the 1820s, the Hamburg painters Christian Morgenstern and Adolph Vollmer were pupils at the Copenhagen Academy, and in 1834 Hermann Carmiencke settled in the city. In addition there were the many Holstein artists – principally Ditlev Blunck, Ernst Meyer and Louis Gurlitt – to whom, as subjects of the Danish king, Copenhagen seemed the most obvious choice.

So, around 1830, almost as much German as Danish was spoken in the Academy of Fine Arts in Copenhagen, and many friendships were established across the language barrier. But for the Danish and German pupils at the Academy, life together was not entirely without conflict or free from the establishment of cliques. We can gain an impression of this from the account sent by the Schleswig painter Carl Goos to the sculptor H. W. Bissen in May 1824: "There is now a great deal of tension in the Academy between the Eckersberg School and the Germans. Eckersberg has been told all about the fun with Klees on the north bridge, and he is now very cold towards us, and we are never called anything but the German clique in Eckersberg's studio. Lund, on the other hand, is friendliness itself."[9] Apart from a hint of some student pranks, we have confirmation from this of the impression that J. L. Lund was the professor most receptive to contact with the German painters. In 1828, when Morgenstern painted his study of beech trees near Frederiksdal north of Copenhagen (cat. no. 89), he was undoubtedly influenced by Eckersberg's views on art. But, in more concrete terms, the picture was more likely to have been painted on an excursion with Lund, who was a friend of the German-born poet Friederike Brun and often visited her country mansion of Sophienholm near Frederiksdal, where he himself painted a large number of landscape studies. At the end of the 1820s the pupils in the Academy formed groups that were often based on shared accommodation, but these groups were not determined by nationality. Constantin Hansen, Heinrich Eddelien (born in Greifswald) and Jørgen Roed shared an apartment nicknamed "Gimle" (taken from Norse mythology), and regular visitors there were the students Wilhelm Marstrand, Christen Købke, Gurlitt and the coming architect Gottlieb Bindesbøll. The Holsteiner Adolph Jahn and the Schleswigers Carl Goos and Fritz Westphal occupied another apartment known as "Valhalla".

How much the Danish pupils in the Academy were aware of what was happening in contemporary German art can be difficult to determine. At times the parallels are striking, as is the case with Johan Erdmann Hummel's *Game of Chess* from 1818–19 (Nationalgalerie, Berlin) and Wilhelm Bendz's *A Smoking Club* from 1827–28 (Ny Carlsberg Glyptotek, Copenhagen).[10] Both painters have portrayed an evening gathering with games being played, pipes being smoked, discussion and impressive light effects, and a number of features are common to both pictures. It is difficult to imagine that Bendz should have painted his tobacco-smoking party without knowing Hummel's painting, but it is also difficult to explain how he could have known it. Perhaps on a short, undocumented visit to Berlin?

On the other hand, it is completely impossible that Christen Købke could have seen any of Eduard Gaertner's views of Berlin before painting *Morning View at Østerbro* in 1836 (cat. no. 80). Here, it is a question only of related aims. Just as the German painter did in several paintings, Købke has given a monumental representation of a road lined with fairly anonymous buildings and a number of everyday occurrences. The precise registering of details, the effect of space and the sense of light and air are all found in both paintings. However, Købke was exposed to direct influence from Friedrich before he painted his *Autumn Morning on Lake Sortedam* in 1838 (fig. 2). Friedrich enjoyed great admiration in Denmark at this time, when his star was otherwise sinking at home in Germany. The author and critic Peder Hjort had a painting by him in his home in Sorø, and Crown Prince Christian Frederik possessed two moonlight pieces. Hjort's picture, painted in 1818 and portraying a man and a woman contemplating a very special moonlit scene, might have been *Man and Woman Contemplating the Moon* (cat. no. 47), which Købke could consequently have known.[11] The misty, somewhat melancholy autumn mood, the tree with the extended naked branches and the lonely wanderer in Købke's picture – all these are features that he can scarcely have painted but under the influence of Friedrich, even though he has adapted them to his own artistic temperament. There is not the same reverential, almost religious surrender to nature, and the space effect in the two pictures is fundamentally different: the path along the lake leads to the Copenhagen suburb of Vesterbro, not to eternity.

Rome and Italy were still the principal goal for the studies of the young Danish painters, and it was perfectly natural for them to make stays in the German cities on their way there. But they did not have Eckersberg's blessing on that journey: he sought to persuade them to go via Paris, as he himself had done. When Constantin Hansen left in 1835, Eckersberg wrote to his son Erling: "He is still travelling according to the prejudice so entrenched here to the promised land of Germany to seek wisdom from the famous Germans. It is beyond comprehension that the prejudice still exists among us that there is nothing to see or take note of in Paris – even such an excellent man as Höien seems to have beaten into them a fear of the French nation and French art, and even Rørbye, not to mention the good [but completely incompetent *crossed out*] painter [Christian] Holm could not stand Paris, and so it is understandable that others dare not go there either."[12]

Fig. 2. Christen Købke, *Autumn Morning on Lake Sortedam*, 1838. Ny Carlsberg Glyptotek, Copenhagen

Hamburg and Berlin were only brief stops on the journey for the Danish painters; Dresden attracted them far more. Here they were already assured of contact with artistic life thanks to the Norwegian painter J. C. Dahl. He had settled in the city in 1821, but had maintained close links with artistic life in Denmark, and he exhibited almost every year at Charlottenborg in Copenhagen. So the Danish painters were already familiar with Dahl's art, and he was able to arrange contact with his friend Friedrich. Virtually all the Danes stayed for a time in Dresden on their way to Italy, including Blunck (in 1828), Bendz (in 1831), Hansen (in 1835) and Købke (in 1838), and several of them mention not only Dahl, but also Friedrich in their letters.[13] It is striking, however, that none of them remained there for long. Perhaps they felt that they could gain enough knowledge of Dahl's pictorial universe at home in Copenhagen.

So the Schleswiger Fritz Westphal was an exception when he spent about a year in Dresden in 1829 and 1830. Here he met his friend the Norwegian painter Thomas Fearnley, whom he knew from his time studying in Copenhagen. The portrait Westphal painted of Fearnley at the window of his apartment seems to suggest that he had received influences other than those he had been given in Copenhagen (fig. 3).[14] The picture is in keeping with one of the most popular motifs of the time – the open window, which Dahl especially employed several times. In comparison with the painting Rørbye had made a few years before (cat. no. 95), Westphal has moved away from his Danish starting point in that the symbolism at which

Rørbye merely hinted is here clearly underlined. In Westphal there is no doubt as to the Romantic longing.

During Bendz's stay in Dresden, he could tell that Dahl did not hesitate to recommend young German painters to go to Copenhagen to receive a thorough training: "One of Dahl's pupils has told me that, to the irritation of the Germans, Dahl does not refrain from criticising the shoddy work and actually tells them that they ought to study at the Academy in Copenhagen."[15] Several painters followed Dahl's suggestion, foremost among them being Hermann Carmiencke.

From Dresden the Danish painters went on to Munich, which tempted far more of them to make a lengthier stay.[16] Bendz remained there for a year from 1831 to 1832 and wrote enthusiastically about conditions in the city; apparently, he considered settling there on his return from Italy. In Munich, he met several of his friends from the Academy of Fine Arts in Copenhagen, including Morgenstern and Fearnley. A few years later, Gurlitt and Sødring also went to Munich.[17] The Danish and north German painters revitalized painting there with their fundamentally realistic approach and their fresh view of motifs. But the painters who stayed in the city for longer had in common the fact that their art gradually lost its original special character and adopted a more idealized quality like the rest of painting in Munich. Most of them, however, went on to Italy (Bendz, however, died on his way to Rome in 1832, aged only twenty-eight).

In Rome, the young Danish painters continued to join the circle around Thorvaldsen, but in the 1830s the ageing sculptor no longer seems to have been a meeting point for the Danish and German artists together. The Danes kept increasingly to themselves. It is significant that in 1837, when Hansen set about painting an impression of artistic life in Rome, he chose to portray only Danish artists (cat. no. 63), not Danes and Germans together, as had been the case before.

Eckersberg's pupils followed in their teacher's footsteps in Rome, quite literally, visiting the places where he had painted twenty to thirty years before – but, entirely in his spirit, they did not choose the same motifs for their studies but found their own instead. They too tried to look at familiar motifs with fresh eyes, and this often resulted in unexpected views and surprising ways of cutting the motifs, most originally in Hansen's small study of the Arch of Titus near the Roman Forum (cat. no. 64).

Jørgen Roed painted what was known as the Poseidon Temple in Paestum (now identified as a temple dedicated to Hera) in 1838 (fig. 4),[18] and he appears simply to have followed his teacher's directions, choosing not to paint the entire temple from a representative angle, but selecting a section of the interior of the ruin. The two rows of columns are seen drastically foreshortened, just as Eckersberg would wish. Meanwhile, the viewpoint is not so new and untried as the painter himself might have believed: presumably completely unconsciously, Roed positioned himself so that he was looking at the temple from almost exactly the same place as the Italian Piranesi had done some seventy years before when he selected the motif for an etching (fig. 5). Even the way in which the motif is cut on the right side is the same in the two works. It was impossible to avoid classical models!

In a few cases, however, Danish artists could still unite with the Germans in an artistic community in Italy. Fritz Petzholdt did just that. He was the only one of Eckersberg's pupils who chose landscape painting as his speciality.[19] As the extent to

Fig. 3. Fritz Westphal, *Portrait of Thomas Fearnley*, Dresden, 1829. Private collection, Oslo

Fig. 4. Jørgen Roed, *The So-called Temple of Poseidon at Paestum*, 1838. Statens Museum for Kunst, Copenhagen

which his teacher painted landscapes after returning to Denmark from Rome was limited (apart from studies on excursions with his students), Petzholdt was by the nature of things obliged to seek inspiration elsewhere. He found it in the community of artists in the Casa Baldi in Olevano, where a number of German landscape artists met every summer to paint in the Sabine mountains. It was the Holstein art historian, Baron C. F. von Rumohr, who made this possible by renting a house for the artists from a local innkeeper by the name of Baldi (von Rumohr has since been given a place in German art history, but he was also in close contact with artistic life in Copenhagen). In the Casa Baldi, Petzholdt undoubtedly met the German painter Friedrich Nerly, who was the same age. There is much to suggest that the Dane learned a great deal from his German colleague's landscape studies. At all events, they both painted some quite unusual studies of cliffs seen at close range (figs. 6 and 7).[20] There are some strik-

ing parallels between the two paintings both in conception and the way in which the motif is cut, but there are also differences. Nerly's study has been painted with a relatively flowing use of the brush – in accordance with the international efforts at open-air painting in Italy at this time. Petzholdt, on the other hand, has taken out his pointed brushes and meticulously brought out the details – just as his teacher had shown him at home in Copenhagen.

Until the end of the 1830s, the Danish and German artists lived and worked side by side, perhaps divided up into smaller groupings, but without any fundamental disagreements. But around 1840, the simmering conflict on the national affiliations of the duchies of Schleswig and Holstein and their relations with the Kingdom of Denmark came into the open, and in Denmark it came to bitter disagreement between those with Danish sympathies and those with German. Several younger painters such as Lundbye, Skovgaard and Dankvart

Fig. 5. G. B. Piranesi, *The Interior of the Temple of Poseidon at Paestum,* etching, published 1778. Department of Prints and Drawings, Statens Museum for Kunst, Copenhagen

Dreyer set themselves the aim of turning their pictures of the Danish countryside into part of the national struggle. In the tension between Danish and German sentiments, the painters from Holstein and north Germany who were living in Denmark had to find a standpoint. One of them was Louis Gurlitt.[21]

Gurlitt was born in Altona in the southern part of Holstein and was thus a subject of the Danish king. He received his early training in Hamburg in 1828 to 1832, but for the following three years he studied at the Academy of Fine Arts in Copenhagen, making several study trips to Norway and Sweden. In 1836 he went to Munich, but the following year he was back in Copenhagen to get married. At the end of 1837 he returned to Munich, from where he undertook a study trip to northern Italy the next year. In 1839 he returned to Copenhagen and lived in Denmark for the following three years. At the end of 1843 he moved to Düsseldorf. From 1843 to 1846 he travelled in Italy, and then settled in Berlin. In 1847 he made a final visit to Copenhagen, and from then on he lived in Germany, though undertaking a large number of visits and longer stays abroad.

Depending on whether his career is looked at from a Danish or a German point of view, a different picture emerges of his role in the history of art. In German art literature there is a tendency to view him as a German and count him among the Hamburg painters.[22] From this it might look as though the German area was his starting point and that it was from here that he undertook his study journeys, including the stays in Copenhagen. Although on the whole Gurlitt was not accorded any great role in the history of Danish art, he has neverthe-less been considered a Danish artist in Danish museums, as were the other Holstein painters who were active in

Denmark.[23] The years 1832–42 are consequently considered by several Danish art historians to be his Danish years, when Copenhagen was the starting point from which he made his study journeys, and his visits to Munich are viewed in line with the journeys and visits to this city of other Danish painters.[24] During Gurlitt's lifetime, both the painter himself and the other actors on the Danish artistic stage were for a long time of the same view as later Danish art historians. During his period of studying in Copenhagen, he associated with the Danish pupils, and during his visit to Munich in 1839 he wrote home to his parents in Altona, in German: "Wir sind 18 Dänen hier [We are 18 Danes here]."[25] It was as a Danish artist that he became a member of the Royal Danish Academy of Fine Arts in Copenhagen in 1840, and he was on various occasions proclaimed to be one of the best Danish landscape artists.[26] About 1840, he went so far as to contribute to the incipient passion for the Danish countryside (see cat. no. 59).[27] In 1847 he was appointed a Knight of the Order of Dannebrog. But with the increasing polarization between those with Danish and German sympathies in Denmark in the 1840s, Gurlitt was forced to choose sides, and the excited anti-German mood without doubt played a part in his leaving Denmark in 1842. When the Schleswig-Holstein war broke out in 1848, Gurlitt sided with the rebels – or, if preferred, the freedom fighters – and declared himself in favour of a united Germany.[28] The reaction in Copenhagen was swift and unam-biguous: the paintings by him that had been hanging in the Royal Gallery of Paintings were simply taken down![29] In 1860, Gurlitt was given the status of a foreign member of the Royal Academy of Fine Arts in Copenhagen, and more than a hundred years were to elapse before he was again given a place in the history of Danish art.

Fig. 6. Friedrich Nerly, *Cliffs at Olevano*,
c. 1830. Angersmuseum, Erfurt

Fig. 7. Fritz Petzholdt, *A Road in Italian
Mountains with Overgrown Cliffs*, 1830/36.
Private collection, Denmark

1. I am indebted for this information to the Danish painter Lars Physant, who pointed out this very important aspect of the picture's genesis to me.
2. See Bjarne Jørnæs, "Tyske kunstnere i Rom", in Dyveke Helsted et al., *Eckersberg i Rom*, exhibition catalogue, Thorvaldsens Museum, Copenhagen, 1983, pp. 69–73.
3. For a general view of artistic trends in Denmark at the beginning of the nineteenth century, see Kasper Monrad, *Hverdagsbilleder. Dansk Guldalder – kunstnerne og deres vilkår*, Christian Ejlers Forlag, Copenhagen, 1989; also Kasper Monrad, "The Copenhagen School of Painting", *The Golden Age of Danish Painting*, exhibition catalogue, Los Angeles County Museum of Art and The Metropolitan Museum of Art, New York, 1993–94, pp. 11–19. For landscape painting in particular, see Kasper Monrad, "Die dänische Landschaftsmalerei des soganannten Goldenen Zeitalters", *Aus Dänemarks Goldener Zeit. Landschaftsmalerei des früheren 19. Jahrhunderts aus dem Statens Museum for Kunst, Kopenhagen*, exhibition catalogue, Wallraf-Richartz-Museum, Cologne, 1995, pp. 29–40.
4. See *Literatur-, Kunst- og Theater-Blad*, 24 April 1824.
5. C. W. Eckersberg, *Forsög til en Veiledning i Anvendelsen af Perspectivlæren for unge Malere* [An Attempt at Guidance for Young Painters in the Use of the Theory of Perspective], Copenhagen, 1833; repr. 1973, p. 4.
6. Frederik Christian Sibbern, *Om Poesi og Konst* [On Poetry and Art], Copenhagen, 1834–69, I, pp. 363 ff.
7. See Kasper Monrad in *Caspar David Friedrich og Danmark / Caspar David Friedrich und Dänemark*, exhibition catalogue, Statens Museum for Kunst, Copenhagen, 1991, p. 76; German translation, pp. 145 ff.
8. Quoted in Monrad 1989, pp. 133.
9. Author's translation of Carl Goos, letter to H. W. Bissen, dated Copenhagen, 5 May 1824, The Royal Library, NKS 3341: "Bey der Akademie ist jetzt eine große Spannung zwischen der Eckersbergschen Schule und den Deutschen, denn den ganzen Witz bey Klees auf der Nordertorbrücke haben sie Eckersberg erzählt, welcher jetzt sehr kalt gegen uns ist, und wir werden in Eckersbergs Malerschule nicht anders als die deutsche Klike genannt. Lund ist dagegen die Freundlichkeit selbst." Jürgen Hoppmann, Schleswig, has kindly drawn my attention to this letter.
10. See Monrad 1989, pp. 105 ff., figs. 79 and 80.
11. See Kasper Monrad in Copenhagen 1991, pp. 77 ff.; German translation, pp. 146 ff. However, it must be pointed out that Helmut Börsch-Supan believes for stylistic reasons that Hjort's painting cannot be identical with the painting in the Nationalgalerie in Berlin; see cat. no. 47.
12. C. W. Eckersberg to Erling Eckersberg, draft of a letter dated 11 July 1835; quoted in Agnes Guldbrandsen, *Jens Christian Holm 1803–1846. En guldaldermalers skæbne*, Bogan, Copenhagen, 1988, p. 68.
13. See Kasper Monrad in Copenhagen 1991, pp. 98 ff., 113 note 42; German translation, pp. 154, 161 note 42.
14. See Ulrich Schulte-Wülwer, *Fritz Westphal und Josef Petzl. Gezeichnete Tagebücher zur Zeit des Biedermeier*, Heide, 1993, p. 29, frontispiece.
15. Wilhelm Bendz's travel accounts, quoted in Marianne Saabye, ed., *Wilhelm Bendz 1804–1832. A Young Painter of the Golden Age*, exhibition catalogue, The Hirschsprung Collection, Copenhagen, 1996, p. 215.
16. On the Danish painters in Munich, see Ejner Johansson, *De danske malere i München. Et ukendt kapitel i dansk guldalderkunst*, Spektrum, Copenhagen, 1997.
17. On Sødring's relations with painting in Munich, see Kasper Monrad, "Tyske forbilleder. Frederik Sødring og Christen Købke og Münchenskolens malere", *Meddelelser fra Thorvaldsens Museum*, 1994, pp. 61–65; summary in English, "The German Example. Frederik Sødring and Christen Købke and the painters of the Munich School", p. 199.
18. See London 1984, cat. no. 39, and Paris 1984–85, cat. no. 173.
19. On Petzholdt, see Erik Drigsdahl, *Fritz Petzholdt 1805–1838*, exhibition catalogue, Kunstforeningen, Copenhagen, 1985, and Kasper Monrad in Cologne 1995, pp. 46 ff.
20. See Monrad 1989, p. 212, fig. 205, and Philip Conisbee et al., *In the Light of Italy. Corot and Early Open-Air Painting*, exhibition catalogue, National Gallery of Art, Washington, D.C., Brooklyn Museum, New York, and Saint Louis Museum of Art, 1996–97, cat. no. 119.
21. See Ulrich Schulte-Wülwer and Bärbel Hedinger, eds., *Louis Gurlitt 1812–97. Porträts europäischer Landschaften in Gemälden und Zeichnungen*, exhibition catalogue, Altonaer Museum, Hamburg, Museumsberg Flensburg and Nivaagaards Malerisamling, Nivå, 1997–98.
22. See Hamburg 1996, pp. 17 ff., 116–18.
23. Thus in Statens Museum for Kunst Gurlitt is registered as a Danish painter in line with Holsteiners such as J. L. Lund, Ernst Meyer and Ditlev Blunck: see *Ældre dansk malerkunst. Katalog*, museum catalogue, Statens Museum for Kunst, Copenhagen, 1970.
24. See Monrad 1989, pass., and Ejner Johansson, *De danske malere i München. Et ukendt kapitel i dansk guldalderkunst*, Spektrum, Copenhagen, 1997, pp. 124–27.
25. Quoted in Ludwig Gurlitt, *Louis Gurlitt*, Berlin, 1912, p. 177.
26. See exhibition reviews in *Kjøbenhavnsposten*, 4 May 1842, 5 May 1843 and 4 May 1846.
27. Monrad 1989, pp. 242–45, 251 ff.
28. Hamburg, Flensburg & Nivå 1997–98, p. 90.
29. See C. L. le Maire, *Fortegnelse over den Kongelige Malerisamling paa Christiansborg Slot*, Copenhagen, 1839, cat. nos. 526 and 527 and idem, *Fortegnelse over den Kongelige Malerisamling paa Christiansborg Slot*, Copenhagen, 1853; trans. into German as *Verzeichnis der Gemälde der Königlichen Bildergalerie in Kopenhagen*.

Friedrich and Pomerania

HELMUT R. LEPPIEN

Caspar David Friedrich was born in Greifswald in Pomerania on 5 September 1774. The country on the Baltic Sea east of Mecklenburg had been divided between Sweden and Brandenburg in the Peace Treaty of Westphalia in 1648 (only in 1815, after the Congress of Vienna, did the whole of Pomerania become part of Prussia). From 1720, Swedish Pomerania was approximately equivalent to today's West Pomerania, including the towns of Stralsund, Greifswald and Wolgast as well as the island of Rügen. It was a province under Swedish sovereignty and still a part of the Holy Roman Empire. The country was to a large extent independent, since the royal provincial administration co-existed with a body of representatives of the knighthood and the seven towns. The eighteenth century was a period of economic prosperity and intellectual freedom, but with the occupation in 1806 by Napoleonic troops this period of peace came to an end. Like the poet and professor in Greifswald, Ernst Moritz Arndt, and many others, Friedrich regarded rule by the French as oppression.

Before he had turned twenty, Friedrich had sought distant climes, first in Copenhagen, where he studied at the Academy until spring 1798, and then in Dresden, where he lived until his death in 1840. But he was noticeably influenced by the knowledge and experience he had acquired in his Pomeranian homeland. Fourteen years old when he was sent to be taught by the academic draughtsman Johann Heinrich Quistorp of the University of Greifswald, he learned more than one might have expected in this province at the end of the eighteenth century. Quistorp, for example, travelled with his students in areas surrounding the town as far as the island of Rügen. Thus, in his early years, Friedrich learned to perceive nature and to sketch immediately in front of the motif. It was through Quistorp that he met his close friend the theologian Ludwig Theobul Kosegarten. From 1792, Kosegarten lived in Wolgast (Philipp Otto Runge's native town) where he was a school headmaster, so Friedrich probably first read his work and then got to know him personally when he was a provost in Altenkirchen on the island of Rügen. We know that he visited him in Altenkirchen; the personal contact was presumably revived when Kosegarten did his doctorate in theology in Greifswald in 1793 and was elected consistorial counsellor. While a minister on Rügen, Kosegarten preached to fishermen on the beach in the midst of nature.[1] His teaching – that nature should be regarded as a revelation of God – must have made a strong impact on Friedrich.

As well as staying in touch with his parents and siblings, Friedrich also visited Rügen from Dresden for walking tours. On his return from Copenhagen in May 1798 he was in Greifswald, then again in 1801/2, presumably in 1806 and definitely in 1809. A drawing from the autumn of 1815, *Meadows near Greifswald* (private collection, Hamburg) must have originated during a fourth journey to his homeland. He married in 1818 and introduced his bride to his homeland on their honeymoon. He was at home for the last time in 1826. According to Helmut Börsch-Supan, "Greifswald remained his actual place of residence. It was the nearby sea that gave the town its special quality."

The island of Rügen was equally important to Friedrich. His visit home in 1801/2 lasted approximately seventeen months, of which little is known; what we do know is gleaned

from the dated nature studies he made on Rügen. These were the basis for the large sepia compositions that he showed in Dresden at an Academy exhibition in the spring of 1803; they were well received, and his compatriot Runge bought a *Morning* and an *Evening* from him. The visit to Pomerania in the summer of 1806 lasted over three months; apart from seeing his family – his stay in Neubrandenburg is proven – his main reason for this journey was to draw on Rügen.

In the years from 1808 until 1810, Friedrich painted the two major works *Monk on the Sea* and *Abbey in the Oakwood*, which are pictures of his homeland. In the summer of 1809, he again travelled north, especially to draw the mighty old oaks in the surroundings of Neubrandenburg. He made many drawings during his 1815 visit, including the ruins of the Gothic church of Cloister Eldena near Greifswald. His honeymoon in July and August 1818 took him not only to his family but also to Stralsund and Rügen. In the picture *On the Sailboat* (cat. no. 41) we may see the recollection of this experience. In accordance with these powerful influences, he executed one of his most famous paintings, *Chalk Cliffs on Rügen* (fig. 8), as well as *Woman on the Beach of Rügen*, showing the cliffs of Cape Arcona in the distance. *Rural Plains* (cat. no. 44) and *Landscape with Windmills* (cat. no. 45) also show views of Rügen and of the country around Greifswald. In 1826

Friedrich drew very little, since he was recuperating after a severe illness, but the same coastal images occupied his fantasy.

Friedrich's pictures teach us what he learned from his homeland – a feeling for nature that goes beyond the seen. An exact observer, he used a sharpened pencil to draw trees, rocks, churches and ships and, not least, the flat land and outlines of the coast. But he indissolubly connected the world he perceived with what he had experienced. Certainly, his pictures of Bohemian and Saxon mountain ranges are the ones most imprinted on our minds, but his paintings of the Baltic coast are neither rare nor casual. One can even ascertain in his oeuvre a polar relationship between the motifs of mountain and of coast.

That elementary experience of the coast, the border between land and sea, made an impression in his adolescence that influenced Friedrich for the whole of his life. And from the coast he also got to know another boundary – that between water and sky, the horizon. Initially, Friedrich tried to express his vision in sepia ink, as was the contemporary fashion. His sepias are pictorial in format, in technique (brush instead of pen) and in intention: they should be regarded as monochrome paintings. One may go so far as to suggest that it was the sensation of light on water that may have led him to overcome his hesitation to paint in oil colour, bringing to an end his almost

Fig. 9. Caspar David Friedrich, *Fog*, c. 1807. Österreichische Galerie Belvedere, Vienna

monastic sacrifice of the richness and colour of life. He was at this time thirty-three years old. In *Fog* (fig. 9), one of his first oil paintings, executed probably in 1807, the light above the water merges with the fog – the fog is more than an interesting meteorological phenomenon, it is the constituent element of the picture. Not only the mixture but also the transparency of the colours result in something quite different, something new – a sailing boat is perceptible through the fog, both vague and clear at the same time. Within a light tonality of little contrast, the eye is led from the tangibly near to the merely suspected far, which is even beyond the ship and goes into the depths of the sea. Shortly after this, Friedrich began *Monk on the Sea*, a work of great drama, with its stark contrasts between land and water. Although this great painting is in poor condition (much of the differentiation between sea and sky and within the sky can only be guessed at), the same polarity can be seen between light and dark, low and high tension, the nearly serene and deep solemnity.

Friedrich was remarkably determined in his preference for the moonlight in his pictures of the Baltic coast. He even depicted the harbour in moonlight. This was in connection with his Christian view of the world – he regarded the moon, which captures and reproduces the light of the sun, as a symbol of the Son of God, who allows human beings to perceive, indirectly, the brightness of divine light. The philosopher of nature Gotthilf Heinrich von Schubert once interpreted a moonset over the sea by his friend Friedrich as indicating that the journey of life, commencing in the mild light of the moon, will not end in darkness but on the coasts of a distant country in the bright light of the next world.[2] The coastal pictures

therefore all have a common meaning, but each painting is a new and individual phenomenon. Friedrich does not change only the composition, but also the depiction of light. The way he paints evening and even night, as well as clouds, is based entirely on observation, and light is always the dominant characteristic. The warm afterglow of the sun that has just set, the light of the dawning moon, the cool light of the moon reflected in water, the clouds that are coloured by the evening or night light – these phenomena of light that belong to the northern coast had never been depicted before.

Friedrich shares this exact observation of light with the other painters represented in the present exhibition. What differentiates him from the others, however, is his attitude, which led to his statement, at once apodictic and paradoxical: "Close your physical eye, so that you can first see your picture with your spiritual eye." The young artists in Copenhagen, Hamburg and Berlin at this time would have been irritated by this injunction: they wanted to see, to open their eyes, and not to "know" beforehand how nature looks. But Friedrich continued: "Then bring up what you have seen in the darkness so that it reacts upon others from the outside to the inside."[3]

What did Friedrich see "in the darkness"? No pictures of hell or horror, no monstrous products of the fantasy, but pictures recollecting the seen and the experienced. Despite his oil studies of clouds in Vienna and Mannheim, and despite his three studies of ice floes on the Elbe in Hamburg – despite, that is, some impressive exceptions – Friedrich decided against the direct method of painting from nature. One can imagine how he must have watched his fellow-lodger and friend

Fig. 10. Caspar David Friedrich, *Meadows near Greifswald*, 1821/22. Hamburger Kunsthalle

J. C. Dahl set off in the morning to study nature, and how he must have viewed Dahl's sketches when he returned in the evening – what he accepted or even approved of for the other artist he refused categorically to accept for himself. We learn from Friedrich's pictures that he did not say "no" because he was blind, but because he had seen. Basically, he used his visual memory instead of the oil study. His pictures are saturated with visual experience. One is tempted to say that nothing is invented, everything is based on observation: he portrayed in pencil the outlines of a cliff or the structure of a sailing boat, but the changing light of the sky and the reflection of the sunset in the clouds he saw "in darkness".

Helmut Börsch-Supan has indicated the change that Friedrich underwent in 1818. He married Caroline Bommer in January. Johan Christian Dahl and Carl Gustav Carus had entered his circle. His pictures became brighter. Whereas in

1816 or 1817 he painted *View of Greifswald in the Evening Light* (Nasjonalgalleriet Oslo), in 1821/22 he painted *Meadows near Greifswald* (fig. 10). According to Börsch-Supan, "few of Friedrich's pictures are so serene" – his home town now appears in a haze, the promised homeland in paradise. In this picture of a sunny day it is once again the light that gives it its special character, with a cloudless sky of pure colour, a colour that merges gradually from a soft yellow to a bright blue. The man who in Dresden was always "different" and who regarded himself as a stranger was at home in Pomerania. His relationship with Pomerania is evident in his ties to his parents, his native town, the landscape and the Baltic Sea; it culminates in his relationship with the land edging the sea with which he was connected since his first conscious observations, his experience of the light in which the world appears to us and which is the creation of God.

1. Katharina Coblenz, ed., *Hier ist gut sein. Aus den Uferpredigten Ludwig Gotthard Kosegartens*, Evangelische Verlagsanstalt, Berlin, 1988.
2. G. H. von Schubert, *Ansichten von der Nachtseite der Naturwissenschaft*, Dresden, 1808, quoted in Börsch-Supan and Jähnig 1973, p. 71.
3. Caspar David Friedrich, *Was die fühlende Seele sucht. Briefe und Bekenntnisse*, ed. Sigrid Hinz, Henschel Verlag, Berlin, 1991, p. 78.

Between Copenhagen and Dresden: Berlin

HELMUT BÖRSCH-SUPAN

Brothers are often less aware of each other than friends are. And the ends of branches become ever further away from the trunk as a tree grows. Thus, although nineteenth-century landscape painting in north Germany and Denmark shared a common source in the Netherlandish tradition of the seventeenth century (in particular, the "golden century" of Danish painting looks like a repeat, two hundred years later, of the "Golden eeuw" in Holland) and despite many obvious similarities between the two neighbouring countries, not just in painting, we can nevertheless discern a curious distance. More intensive attempts to overcome this by means of a new awareness have been made only during the last fifty or so years, and this is also the aim of the present exhibition.

Unlike the situation with sculpture – Bertel Thorvaldsen was recognized as a key figure of supranational rank, not least because of the monuments he created for Germany – a significant painter like Christoffer Wilhelm Eckersberg received no equivalent appreciation. Interest in the heyday of Danish painting was not aroused in Germany until the beginning of the twentieth century, following a revised assessment of art from the period around 1800. A clear sign of this was the book *Arbeit, Brot und Friede. Dänische Maler von Jens Juel bis zur Gegenwart* [Work, Bread and Peace: Danish painters from Jens Juel to the present day], which appeared in 1911 in the popular Blaue Bücher series in an edition of 30,000 copies. A statement in the foreword read: "This book is the outcome of the wish to make the European – and particularly the German – public more familiar with Danish painting of the last 150 years, as artistically able as it is humanly likeable." But the German museums which at that time were making urgent attempts to

acquire German paintings of around 1800 and the following decades collected virtually no Danish art.

When Germans looked north in the nineteenth century, their gaze was directed at Norway and Sweden rather than Denmark. What they sought in the north was naturalness – the rugged, unspoilt nature that maintains a healthy humanity.[1] Denmark was considered too cultivated. And it was a Norwegian, Johan Christian Dahl, who gave landscape painting in Dresden a lively boost from 1818 and who in 1822, when he exhibited in Berlin for the first time, encouraged Carl Blechen to adopt a fresh view of nature and cultivate an impulsive hand. It is true that Dahl had trained in Copenhagen, but he nevertheless tried to retain spontaneity and vitality, which is what differentiates his work from the controlled manner of working of the Danes. Dahl trained many landscape painters in Dresden, and quite a few of them travelled to Norway at his suggestion.

There were renewed encounters between Scandinavia and Germany from 1837, when greater numbers of Norwegian and Swedish painters started to attend the Düsseldorf Academy, the second most important in Prussia after Berlin.[2] Danes who wanted to study in Germany preferred Munich around that time; only a few of them sent pictures to the Berlin Academy's exhibitions.

In the late eighteenth century, however, Berlin had attracted Danish artists – not as a place of study but as a place to work. The copper engraver to the Copenhagen court, Johan Frederik Clemens, was active in Berlin from 1788 to 1792. The engraver Meno Haas, also from Copenhagen, had arrived in Berlin two years earlier, probably at the same time as his brother Peter, who practised the same trade. The art embroiderer of Italian descent, Joseph Genelli, entered the service of Frederick the Great in 1774; he was accompanied by his talented sons Janus (born 1761, landscape painter), Hans Christian (born 1763, architect) and Frederik (born 1765, engraver), all born in Copenhagen. The history painter Asmus Jakob Carstens, celebrated as an innovator of German art, and his brother Frederik, mainly active as an engraver, although born in St Jürgen near Schleswig in 1754 and in Schleswig in 1762 respectively, were students at the Copenhagen Academy of Fine Arts before going to Berlin in 1787 and 1790. In 1792 the elder of the brothers went to Rome, where he died in 1798; the younger remained in Berlin until his death that same year. Caspar David Friedrich, who had studied in Copenhagen from 1794 to 1798, arrived in the Prussian capital in 1798 but after a few weeks moved on to Dresden, obviously partly because Berlin offered him too little inspiration with regard to landscape painting.

This genre of landscape painting developed in Berlin only with difficulty and in a particular manner, namely under the strong influence of the landscape garden. The reason for this was that Berlin's surroundings were considered bleak and devoid of attractions for painters. Travellers arriving in the city always emphasized how surprising they found its beauty after their journey through the boring regions around it. This is also why the orientation of Berlin's painting towards the Dutch model in the seventeenth century had negligible consequences for landscape painting in general.

Not until around 1740, for a brief period under Frederick the Great, was there a development in landscape art, inspired by Watteau and his circle, that tried to capture atmosphere.[3] This was done by means of light brushwork, a palette restricted to bright colours and careful attention to the effects of light. Antoine Pesne and Georg Wenzeslaus von Knobelsdorff were the first to find beauty in the Mark Brandenburg region, and they produced the most enchanting works of this all-too-brief flowering. Even at that time, painters' endeavours were linked with the king's attempts to wrest a garden paradise from the sandy soil by means of cultivation. It was pride in the human achievement, not gratitude for nature's gifts, that was involved. At Schloß Rheinsberg, located north of Berlin on Lake Grienerick, Crown Prince Frederick of Prussia (before he became known as "the Great") made an initial attempt between 1736 and 1740 to translate the dream world painted by Watteau

into reality and to conceive of the local landscape as an asset that enriched the spirit. This idea was repeated in a more splendid form in the park of Sanssouci, with its vineyard palace nestling amid hilly terrain, but from around 1750 this early phase of enthusiasm for nature was over as far as the king was concerned. Knobelsdorff and his friend, the landscape painter Charles Sylva Dubois, died in 1753, Pesne four years later.

A new approach to landscape art, typically in pictures of the Tiergarten park district and the environs of the royal residence at Charlottenborg, was initiated around 1760 by Jakob Philipp Hackert, who originally came from Prenzlau in the Uckermark region. As early as 1762 Hackert travelled to Stralsund, then Sweden, then Paris and finally in 1768 to Italy.[4] From Stralsund he visited Rügen, setting down his impressions in a series of etchings, so he is considered to be the artist who discovered the scenic beauties of the island that would later primarily be associated with the name of Caspar David Friedrich. In Italy, Hackert laid essential foundations for nineteenth-century German painting. The fact that he was unable to do so in his native land typifies the barrenness of this soil for landscape painting.

When in 1799 the Prussian king Friedrich Wilhelm III called for his country's artists to create "patriotic" themes, he meant not just scenes of episodes from the history of Brandenburg and Prussia but also landscapes on Prussian themes.[5] However, the pictures submitted to the Academy exhibitions, with the exception of two vedutas of Potsdam, displayed merely mountainous landscapes of Silesia and the Harz, as well as the Giebichenstein near Halle. The flat land in the vicinity of Berlin occurred as a theme only when some striking building provided the main subject matter.

Nevertheless it was at that time, during a stay in his Pomeranian homeland, that Caspar David Friedrich discovered the charm of the lowland plains of north Germany, expressed purely through barely fluctuating lines, and of the coastal region with its high skies. From 1802, in addition to sepia washes systematically worked up from the white of the paper into darker tones, he also painted a few gouaches, thereby following the contemporary predilection for this technique, which captures the light with its dull, chalky colours. These observations were developed in Dresden into evidence of a new view of nature.[6]

Even under the pressure of the political conditions of the time, Friedrich soon developed paintings in which symbolic encoding communicated the religious in combination with the occasional patriotic message. People were susceptible to this in Berlin, where opposition to Napoleon was gradually gaining strength. At the 1810 exhibition, therefore, Friedrich's most famous paintings, *Monk on the Sea* and *Abbey in the Oakwood*, caused a sensation as a radical expression of his beliefs and they were acquired by the king. In his *Berliner Abendblätter* Heinrich von Kleist wrote a congenial text about *Monk on the Sea*, "Perceptions before Friedrich's Seascape", which was a memorable testimony to the intellectual unrest shortly before the outbreak of the Wars of Liberation.

In Saxony, landscape painting that was close to nature had a tradition dating back to the early eighteenth century and was based on the beauties of nature in the vicinity of Dresden. In the third quarter of the century it underwent a strong revival through the Swiss painter Adrian Zingg. Zingg trained numerous students who made local themes well known, especially through drawings and coloured prints. This was the foundation on which Romanticism flourished after 1800.

At the end of the eighteenth century, this broad-based production inspired Berlin artists to try something similar, but it did not lead to comparable successes in either quantity or quality. Berlin artists, with a greater leaning towards the functional and the practical, preferred architecture to landscapes, and this gave rise to an enthusiasm for perspective as a tool for mastering space through a measured way of seeing things: the spirit of the Enlightenment had little feeling for the impenetrable mysteries of nature. This pleasure in comprehending space was also fostered by scene painting, which in Berlin was closely associated with architectural painting from the second half of the eighteenth century. The city, both real and imagined, became a central theme. Friedrich Gilly (who died in 1800 at the age of just twenty-eight), Karl Friedrich Schinkel's brilliant teacher, worked himself up into what was a veritable passion for designing urban space, taking the ancient world – and especially Greece – as his model.[7]

Schinkel allowed himself to be swept along by this example, and his absolute mastery of perspective enabled him to realize his architectural visions, generally combined with landscape, in paintings with complete conviction.[8] In 1807 the Berlin Academy wanted to appoint him as teacher of geometry and perspective. He declined, however, and the post was instead assumed by Johann Erdmann Hummel from Kassel, who had arrived in Berlin in 1800. The latter specialized in this field

with such scientific fervour that he became known as "Perspective Hummel". For him, the puzzles of nature were to be resolved through precise observation of perspective, light, shade and reflections. Much of his work is reminiscent of that of Eckersberg. Hummel was not on close terms with the Romantics.

Only in 1816, following the Wars of Liberation, when people were hoping for a new flowering in Prussian art, was landscape drawing introduced as a subject at the Berlin Academy. The task was entrusted to Peter Ludwig Lütke (born 1759), one of Hackert's students. Lütke had returned to Berlin from Rome in 1787 and initially painted Italian landscape views, servicing the public's pronounced interest in the natural world of the south, which grew even stronger in the nineteenth century. At the Berlin Academy exhibition in 1795 he showed a German subject – a Harz landscape from the region around Goslar – for the first time. He also tackled theoretical problems. Thus in 1816, according to the catalogue, he exhibited "A landscape in oil; an ideal in the patriotic style. An essay into the question: to what extent can the local green colours of nature be used in a landscape work regardless of effect and illusion, and where may the limit of this use lie?" Lütke had expressed patriotic beliefs in earlier landscape pictures. But, combined with a feel for landscape gardens, he also had a tendency to mix the local with the exotic. The landscape was, so to speak, dressed up, the local terrain made unfamiliar. Thus in 1795 he had created a cabinet, a small room, in the Schlößchen on the Pfaueninsel (Peacock Island) near Potsdam in the form of a bamboo hut with painted views of its surroundings enlivened by palm trees and exotic birds. The intention was to transform the Pfaueninsel into Tahiti. In his memoirs, Johann Gottfried Schadow remarks of Lütke that he was "the teacher of the landscape class and, as it were, its founder. Types of trees, depicted individually and drawn by himself, founded the elements of this field of art in the most appropriate manner and many a landscape painter from his school has demonstrated the good results of this. An amateur in the art of landscape gardening, he also had an excellent eye for the details of the plant world. Blechen became his first follower; the latter had a more poetic orientation, which aroused admiration, as a result of which his predecessor's merits were forgotten more than was proper."[9]

For the landscape painters of the north, as for landscape gardeners, the tree was the most important design tool. Water was also a necessity. The landscaping of the environs of Potsdam which had begun under Frederick the Great at Sanssouci continued under Friedrich Wilhelm II in the Neuer Garten, influenced by the example of Wörlitz, and was completed under his two successors Friedrich Wilhelm III and Friedrich Wilhelm IV: from 1816, in Peter Joseph Lenné, they had the most notable German landscape gardener at their disposal. This had a marked influence on landscape painting, since the latter had the additional task of glorifying, in pictures, the Prussian kings' achievements in cultivating the land.

Architecture, as the solid core, is part of the landscape garden, with its balance of free nature and cultivation in the service of man. This was the dominant art in Berlin, and as such it also had a considerable influence on landscape painting, primarily thanks to the varied talents of Schinkel. Gustav Friedrich Wagen, Schinkel's friend and biographer, believed the meeting with Gilly meant that Schinkel cultivated his talent for architecture more strongly than that for painting: "The circumstance that the only person in Berlin at that time with an artistic temperament intellectually akin to Schinkel's was an architect thus became decisive for the main direction that he was to follow in his art. If this person had been a sculptor, or a painter, he [Schinkel] would equally as well have developed in one or other of these arts by preference."[10]

Karl Friedrich Schinkel became the central figure in Berlin's art world from about 1810. The sheer versatility of his talent, his broad intellectual horizon and his clear awareness of the purpose of art in the life of a nation equipped him for this role. In no other German city did a single artist have such a great, and at the same time beneficial, influence during the nineteenth century as Schinkel did in Berlin. Not even Peter Cornelius in Munich had such a strong and lasting impact. Schinkel the architect pictured his buildings within their setting, and Schinkel the painter saw a creative power working to constructive effect in his landscapes. His art was always political in the sense that it was intended to have an educational effect on the community. In this he differed from the inwardness, rooted in Christian faith, of Caspar David Friedrich. It is no surprise that architecture usually plays an essential role in Schinkel's paintings. In the trees, too, which he always drew or painted as fully mature, splendid examples of their type, we sense the architectural principle of growth regulated by laws. He liked to juxtapose trees and buildings. Damaged or dead trees – like ruins – appear only exceptionally in his work.

Between 1806 and 1815 – between Prussia's defeat and its victory in the wars against Napoleon – Schinkel, unable to obtain architectural commissions, as a supporter of patriotic Romanticism placed his painting totally at the service of people's reformation through aesthetic education. Although many of his paintings from that time and the following years survive, the forty or so dioramas that he created between 1807 and 1815 can now only be reconstructed from preliminary studies and contemporary descriptions.[11] The strong impact of these gigantic distemper paintings, presented like stage sets without a play, was not least due to effects achieved by changes in lighting. The light, so to speak, acted as a substitute for the plot. There were also nocturnal pieces and scenes of illuminated architecture. From 1815 to 1828 Schinkel developed further in his stage sets the methods he had worked out for the dioramas.

A very important component of the visual experience, apart from the constant form of things, was the variable factor of the changing light and thus of time. Among Schinkel's paintings and drawings therefore we find pairs depicting morning and evening. The seasons, on the other hand, play no role in his work. This is also largely true of the other Berlin landscapists, unlike their counterparts in Dresden. Winter landscapes are relatively rare in Berlin. The exception is Carl Blechen, who felt the transitoriness of nature very keenly and, like Caspar David Friedrich, emphasized the beauty of the play of colour as something ephemeral.

With only a very few exceptions, Schinkel's creations spring from his imagination; however, this had first been fed by observation and, coupled with his excellent memory and gift of depicting what is shown as though it were real, he is able to convince the viewer. The situation is quite different in the case of three paintings that resulted from a trip to Rügen. Two of these were lost during World War II. In the third, *Rugard on the Island of Rügen* (fig. 11), Schinkel can be seen to have reproduced his observations very faithfully: the eye moves in a north-easterly direction from the church tower in Bergen. The light of the sun low in the sky concerned him just as much as the myriad indentations of land and sea in this panorama-like vista. It is as though Schinkel were overcome by his experience of the coastal landscape, with its sheer expansiveness that defied composition. Otherwise, there is no artistic vision in his work that did not involve a process of formative reflection.

Carl Blechen, Schinkel's junior by seventeen years, was a very different kind of artist.[12] It speaks for Schinkel's tolerance and far-sightedness that he valued and understood this artistic soul who was driven by quite different forces, who was extremely one-sided and destroyed at an early age by mental illness. Blechen's destiny as an artist ran its course in the brief space of time between around 1822 and 1837 – in other words, during the period in which architecture, and with it architectural painting, blossomed in Berlin. Blechen, with his feel for the demonic powers within nature, did not believe these could be tamed by mankind, and he typically ignored the subject of gardens. His trees generally appear to be under threat.

His heightened sensitivity enabled Blechen to capture novel sensations in landscape: temperatures, humidity, even smells. His contemporaries commented on this and found he could make them feel the musty chill of stagnant swamp water or the searing heat of a summer's day in Italy. Even when he painted from nature, however, his perceptions of the nature around him are always expressions of a state of mind; he did not by any means depict the full range of natural manifestations but only what corresponded to his inner condition. He succeeded in combining the internal and the external through a mysterious and unerring sleight of hand – his grasp of reality was spontaneous and his assurance instinctive, not achieved through some process of laborious analysis and reproduction. This is where the magic of Blechen's works lies, in this sense of an uncanny power. Architecture, even when he allowed its inclusion as a motif, was unable to give his pictures any solidity. He saw it as in a state of developing or decaying. His buildings are often ruins. Of the Berlin painters, Blechen was the one who tackled the subject of the sea most intensively. He depicted it in all manner of forms – as a deep blue, peaceful surface or in a high swell, in radiant sunshine or in the depths

of the night. As an incomprehensible, menacing element it preoccupied him continually.

In the few years from 1831 to 1837 that Blechen was active as a teacher he had many students who tried to imitate him but through them it becomes evident how uniquely profound was his understanding of nature. Wilhelm Schirmer (born 1802), for example, who took over the landscape class in 1839, attempted to use similarly dramatic effects in his compositions but he did not penetrate to the elemental.[13] Schirmer remained firmly fixed to the idea of the landscape garden – in other words, to the taming of the primeval. On Schinkel's recommendation, he provided the lithographs for a book by Prince Pückler which appeared in 1834, *Andeutungen über Landschaftsgärtnerei, verbunden mit der Beschreibung ihrer praktischen Anwendung in Muskau* [Hints on landscape gardening, combined with the description of their practical application in Muskau]. Schirmer's career can also be used to elucidate another feature of Berlin landscape painting of the time – the link with painting on porcelain. Before he started painting in oils, Schirmer worked for the Berlin porcelain manufactory, initially as a flower painter and then drawing landscapes that were used as models for vedutas on porcelain wares. The depiction of "patriotic" landscapes and buildings on vases, plates and other objects was popular in Berlin: serving as royal gifts, such products promoted both the country and its ruling house.

In Eduard Gaertner, Berlin's most important architectural painter, who had also started out as a porcelain painter, one senses clearly how the white ground of the porcelain, the detailed depiction using a fine brush, the neatness and the smooth, glossy surface had a contributing influence on Berlin landscape and architectural painting.[14] The other domain that had a formative influence with regard to the shaping of space was the theatre. Friedrich Wilhelm Klose, Carl Hasenpflug and Carl Graeb all began as scene painters and in this way reinforced their knowledge of perspective.

If we compare the work of Blechen and Gaertner, it becomes obvious how wide the divergence could be between the concepts of painting held by artists of almost the same age in the Berlin of the 1820s and 1830s. Gaertner, three years younger than Blechen, was totally different from the latter as regards work discipline. In this respect he was more like Schinkel, his senior by twenty years, whom he revered, but his orientation towards the visible and his curbing of the imagination nevertheless led to a parting of the ways, not just because of the age difference but also because of the demands he made of art. Despite his ability, Gaertner did not achieve the standing that he perhaps deserved. His name was scarcely mentioned in the circles that determined Berlin's artistic life. In 1833 he became a full member of the Academy but did not

take up any further tasks there. He seems merely to have played the role of a keen observer, as was later the case with Adolph Menzel, fourteen years his junior, who saw things in even greater depth.

Architectural painting in Berlin,[15] which was making very rapid advances in the early 1820s, found fertile ground not so much in the existing building stock as in the new buildings in which the vitality of the Prussian capital manifested itself. Schinkel's architectural achievements definitely made a contribution. This can easily be discerned from the effect that his theatre on the Gendarmenmarkt, inaugurated in 1821 as the first major construction following the Wars of Liberation, had on Carl Hasenpflug (born 1802) and on Gaertner, a year older. The former made his debut at the Academy exhibition in 1822 with a view of the Gendarmenmarkt, the latter at the same time with a watercolour of the painters' room at the

Schauspielhaus. This was followed in 1824 by Gaertner's first oil painting, an interior view of Berlin's cathedral, which had been altered by Schinkel. That was also the year in which the architectural painters Friedrich Wilhelm Klose (born 1804) and Heinrich Hintze (born 1800), both made their appearance. They were just as capable as Hasenpflug and Gaertner but a bit pedantic, Klose with watercolours of the Sophienkirche and the Klosterkirche, Hintze with a landscape that was followed in 1826 by a number of urban views. Wilhelm Brücke (born c. 1800), similarly talented, submitted five architectural subjects to the exhibition in 1826, including a view of the Marienkirche in his home town of Stralsund. Another who embarked on his career around this time was Eduard Biermann (born 1803), who belonged to the same circle.

This simultaneous emergence of architectural painters coincided with a high point in Schinkel's architectural creativity. After his second journey to Italy in 1824 he had attained a serene composure; shadows began to fall two years later,

however, following a trip to England and the insights he gained there into the consequences of industrialization. The artistic climate changed rapidly during those years.

If Gaertner outshone his colleagues of the same age, this was not due just to a greater sensitivity in the perception of natural phenomena and his ability to communicate this in painting but also because of his deeper understanding of the reasons for effects. He also understood that the city was the creature of its inhabitants. The characterization of people and accessories was no less important to him than the depiction of buildings and their surroundings. He knew how to reproduce the atmosphere of a town, including the play of the changing light on masonry that spoke not only through its form but also its age. His skies are not devoid of significance: they are what buildings are most usually set against. Gaertner does not link this with philosophical reflections like the Romantics but is content to state the facts. From the 1840s the lighting in his works becomes more dramatic, and at the same time an

Fig. 15. Adolph Menzel, *The Berlin-Potsdam Railway*, 1845. Staatliche Museen zu Berlin, Kupferstichkabinett

increasing landscape genre can be discerned. Conscientious recording of what is seen does not exclude atmosphere. Carl Graeb (born 1816), a student of Blechen, took this a step further. Like Gaertner he always based his painting on precisely constructed drawings, a framework that demonstrated his discipline. The world, as Graeb painted it, often appears to be threatened but is nevertheless still intact.

On the other hand, Adolph Menzel (born 1815), a year older, adopted a more critical attitude towards the world out of a sense of deep mistrust.[16] He had no need for a drawn framework – the skeleton, as it were, of the body of a picture – but relied completely on his keenness of eye and his excellent ability to reproduce everything that he saw quickly and with a practised hand. With the use of a broad pencil he was able to reproduce the consistency of any material, including light and air, completely convincingly. And he observed what others did not see or did not wish to see – for example, the mistakes that were made in the development of the rapidly growing capital. He painted no pictures of Berlin that its inhabitants could take pride in.

Schinkel and Menzel were both geniuses of the highest order. Menzel began his rise as an artist in 1834, although Schinkel did not recognize this; conversely, Schinkel, with his strenuous endeavours to shape the environment, could no longer serve as an exemplar for Menzel, although like him he worked as one possessed. This – and not just the fate of Carl Blechen – highlights the fact that something began to break apart in Berlin in the 1830s.

1. See *Wahlverwandtschaften. Skandinavien und Deutschland 1800–1914*, Deutsches Historisches Museum Berlin, Nationalmuseum Stockholm and Norsk Folkemuseum Oslo, 1997.
2. See *Düsseldorf und der Norden*, Kunstmuseum Düsseldorf, 1976.
3. See Irmgard Wirth, *Berlin und die Mark Brandenburg. Landschaften. Gemälde aus drei Jahrhunderten*, Hamburg, 1982; *Berliner Malerei im 19. Jahrhundert. Von der Zeit Friedrichs des Großen bis zum ersten Weltkrieg*, Berlin, 1990.
4. See Claudia Nordhoff and Hans Reimer, *Jakob Philipp Hackert 1737–1807. Verzeichnis seiner Werke*, 2 volumes, Berlin, 1994.
5. See Helmut Börsch-Supan, "Vaterländische Kunst zu Beginn der Regierungszeit Friedrich Wilhelms III", *Aurora. Jahrbuch der Eichendorff Gesellschaft 39*, 1979, pp. 79–100; ed., *Die Kataloge der Berliner Akademie-Ausstellungen 1786–1850*, 3 volumes, Berlin, 1971.
6. See Hans Joachim Neidhardt, *Die Malerei in Dresden*, Leipzig, 1976.
7. See *Friedrich Gilly 1772–1800 und die Privatgesellschaft junger Architekten*, Berlin Museum, 1987.
8. See *Karl Friedrich Schinkel. Architektur, Malerei, Kunstgewerbe*, Schloss Charlottenburg, 1987.
9. Johann Gottfried Schadow, *Kunst-Werke und Kunstansichten*, Berlin, 1849, p. 260; repr. Berlin, 1980.
10. Gustav Friedrich Wagen, "Karl Friedrich Schinkel als Mensch und Künstler", *Berliner Kalender 1844*, p. 317; repr. Düsseldorf, 1980.
11. See Mario Zadow, *Karl Friedrich Schinkel*, Berlin, 1980, pp. 51–56.
12. See *Carl Blechen. Zwischen Romantik und Realismus*, Nationalgalerie Berlin, 1990.
13. See *August Wilhelm Schirmer (1802–1866). Ein Berliner Landschaftsmaler aus dem Umkreis Karl Friedrich Schinkels*, Stiftung Preussische Schlösser und Gärten Berlin-Brandenburg, 1996.
14. See Wirth 1979.
15. See *Stadtbilder. Berlin in der Malerei vom 17. Jahrhundert bis zur Gegenwart*, Berlin Museum, 1987.
16. See *Menzel 1815–1905. Das Labyrinth der Wirklichkeit*, Nationalgalerie Berlin, 1996.

"Light, Colour and Moving Life": Hamburg

HELMUT R. LEPPIEN

The painters in the present exhibition from Hamburg and nearby Altona – Hermann Carmiencke, Jacob Gensler, Louis Gurlitt, Georg Haeselich, Christian Morgenstern, Adolph Vollmer and Friedrich Wasmann – had a great role model in Philipp Otto Runge. These young painters came of age artistically between 1827 and 1834, whereas Runge had died in 1810, at only thirty-three years old. It was therefore only his works that they could meet, although those who had known Runge, those who thought and spoke highly of him, would also have had some significance.

None of these artists had grown up in the atmosphere of Runge's artistic thought; perhaps none of them was truly interested in it, either. But in their effort to capture reality in the light of nature, they came upon Runge's intensive study of light. The influential art patron Johann Michael Speckter (whose son Erwin, a figurative painter, was one of the young artists drawn to Runge) wrote in 1815 that it must have been "clear and certain" to Runge what his task had been – namely, the artistic composition of "light, colour and moving life".[1]

A study of Runge's portrait of the daughter of his friend Friedrich Perthes, a publisher and bookseller, reveals what must have drawn the young painters to his work. In *Louise Perthes*, usually known as "Die Kleine Perthes" (fig. 16), it is the light, directed through the window-frame and the drawn-back curtain, that makes the child and the world inside and out visible to us – it makes it ascertainable and tangible in a figurative sense. The light does not only display a girl, perched on her chair in front of the window, in all her "heightened plastic corporeality" (Hanna Hohl), it also fills the nature seen through the window – the Binnenalster seen from Jungfern-

stieg which leads over Lombard Bridge to the dam where a windmill stands, and behind that the Aussenalster. Rays of light pour into the room, along the chair and the cabinet, and Runge makes these rays visible. Light, our young artists could see with their own eyes when standing in front of this painting, does not only become visible through reflection, it can even take shape itself.

Whether Morgenstern or Wasmann, Vollmer or Gensler, had ever read Runge's book *Farben-Kugel* [Colour-Sphere] (published by Friedrich Perthes in 1810), or whether they had quickly put it aside as too abstract, cannot be known. But Runge's example shines through his paintings, from *Louise Perthes* to *The Rest on the Flight to Egypt* (1805) and *The Hülsenbeck Children* (1806), and not least in the large version of *Morning* (1809; all three in the Hamburg Kunsthalle).

Many young Hamburg painters, including Vollmer, Morgenstern, Gurlitt and Gensler, were supported by the art theoretician Baron Carl Friedrich von Rumohr (1785–1843),[2] a wealthy landowner from the old nobility. After five years in Italy, Rumohr returned to his estate of Rothenhausen near Lübeck in 1822, where he wrote his book *Vom Geist der Kochkunst* [The Essence of Cookery]. Rumohr was an important figure in Hamburg artistic life, especially within the Kunstverein. He was a friend of the Danish heir to the throne Christian Frederik, and well known to the Prussian crown prince Friedrich Wilhelm. In Lübeck he was renowned through the acquisition of Overbeck's *Entry of Christ into Jerusalem* as an altarpiece for the Church of St Mary. He encouraged the young artists to paint from nature, and perhaps it made an impression on them that a person of his standing saw as fundamental something that most of them were already doing from their own initiative and for pleasure. However, even for him, their results were nothing more than studies; paintings, for which he arranged buyers, still had to conform to tradition.

A native of Hamburg at this time who wanted to become an artist went to study in Copenhagen, Munich, Dresden or Vienna. Of our seven Hamburg painters, three went to the Copenhagen Academy (like Caspar David Friedrich and Philipp Otto Runge before them), three to the Munich Academy, and Morgenstern to both. When in Copenhagen from 1827 to 1828, Morgenstern probably did not meet compatriots of any significance. Gurlitt was enrolled there later, for quite a long time, from 1832 to spring 1835; he certainly encountered Vollmer there, who left Copenhagen in 1833, and Carmiencke, who was there in 1834. Nothing, however, is known of any close relationship between the three. By 1830, Morgenstern was at the Munich Academy where he knew the Danish painter Wilhelm Bendz, but did he also associate with his compatriot Haeselich? Haeselich and Gensler belonged to a group of six Hamburg painters who met regularly in the evenings in 1828–29 to draw portraits; Wasmann was also in Munich in 1829, but he took no part in these evening sessions nor in the group's outdoor painting trips in the spring. The conclusion is sobering: each went his own way from the beginning and, in any case, they parted ways later. It would be quite inaccurate to speak of anything like a Hamburg school. Although there are certain similarities between their work — a love of precision, a down-to-earth sense and a clear view — these are the character traits typical of their generation.

Christian Morgenstern, born in 1805, is represented here by three pictures, from 1828, 1829 and 1831 (cat. nos. 89, 90, 91). Whether his gaze is concentrated on the close-up or the very distant, it is completely fresh. What occupied him was the transformation of local colour through changes of light into highly differentiated shading from light to dark. Friedrich Wasmann, born the same year as Morgenstern but slightly older, began open-air painting when he went to the Tyrol in 1830, two years later than his colleague. Along with two studies from the Tyrol (cat. nos. 106, 107) are two views of the Roman Campagna from 1832 (cat. nos. 108, 109). His skills in tonal differentiation and in translating light into painting through colour and shading are not what distinguish him from Morgenstern; it is rather his greater spontaneity, which helped him to capture light and air — thus the intangible — with a quick brush. And he combined originality with strict pictorial composition. Two studies by Jacob Gensler, from 1829 and 1842 (cat. nos. 55, 56), indicate the work of a beginner and of a mature artist. As talented as Wasmann in capturing atmosphere, Gensler was a free-handed draughtsman who even tended towards sketchiness and yet remained precise. More than all the others, Gensler adhered most strongly to his homeland for his subject matter, in his pictures of people and his studies of water, air and light. Louis Gurlitt, the youngest of the seven, is represented by two pictures from his student days in Copenhagen (cat. nos. 59, 60), and by one a decade later, a painting from 1845 of the Campagna (cat. no. 61). The two pictures from the north, although so different, have in common the fact that both were painted with a fine brush. In one the land is captured in all its breadth and depth; in the other, a motif painted from close up apparently attracted the artist by its very ordinariness. Gurlitt's landscapes from the south, freely painted, are characterized by changes of light and shadow.

The qualities these painters have in common — precision, rationality and clarity — were certainly shared by the craftsmen and merchants of the time. They are bourgeois values, widely valid at this time but perhaps especially so in north Germany. Behind their meticulousness lies more than just the requirements of the profession — it also has something to do with an ethical view: what is precise is right, thus precision leads to truth. For painters striving to capture reality in the light of nature, this attitude led to the desire to record exactly what they saw with their eyes, and *everything* that they saw — even the inconspicuous, and motifs that until then were thought unworthy of being painted (what those educated in art called the "picturesque") as well as the intangible light of the sky, the clouds and the haze. They painted more than the painters who preceded them and with whom they perhaps had studied, and their painting was directly connected to the act of seeing. One may assume that the same attitudes were shared by painters such as C. F. Gille (cat. nos. 57, 58) and J. U. Jerndorff (cat. no. 69), as well as by many others both in Berlin and Copenhagen.

It should not be overlooked, however, that the work of these seven artists is more complex than this account, and the choice of works for this exhibition, might suggest. Since Alfred Lichtwark's rediscovery of them around 1900, they have been more highly regarded for their nature studies than for their compositions, but this was neither their own judgement nor that of their contemporaries. However, they did regard the studies as worthy of public display: in their own exhibitions staged by the Kunstverein they wanted to demonstrate the breadth of their range. But Jacob Gensler, for example (about whom we know the most through Silke Reuther's monograph, published in 1995), clearly saw himself as a genre painter: he draughted idealized fishermen and craftsmen in his composed pictures, which readily found middle-class buyers. Louis Gurlitt had a longer career than Gensler (who died at only thirty-seven), and was the most successful of the seven. As a rule Gurlitt painted pure landscapes, but his large, representative paintings, though often based on nature studies, are far from rationally objective – they are full of drama, and character-ized by excess effect. Similarly, there is a great difference between the mood landscapes with which Morgenstern garnered success in Munich and the studies chosen for this exhibition. Wasmann had to turn to portraiture in order to earn a living.

The discrepancy between the paintings that were highly regarded by the members of the Kunstverein in Hamburg and the buyers, and the small, inconspicuous studies that the artists painted from nature was probably more spectacular among these artists than for those in Berlin, Copenhagen or Dresden. Carmiencke, Haeselich and Vollmer, like Gurlitt and Morgen-stern, apparently regarded their open-air paintings as mere groundwork, yet these are their real contribution to the devel-opment of European landscape painting in the nineteenth century. They seemed unable, however, to transfer this uncon-ditional sense of reality to the larger task of the representa-tive picture, whereas Gaertner and Købke were able to do so. If this counts as a failure, it is one that applies also to other painters, including the great J. C. Dahl.

Gensler, Gurlitt and the others obeyed the conventions of bourgeois taste, and were themselves part of a society in which, outside the artistic profession, a clear view was apparently not particularly appreciated. A master craftsman who achieved some degree of prosperity became part of the bourgeoisie, and he then restrained his love of precision to work just as the merchant did with his rational sense. Art was something that belonged in the domestic sphere, to the life of family and friends; paintings were the stuff of comfort, and played the same role as furniture in creating cosiness. We can recognize in this the conflict that characterized the Biedermeier years between 1815 and the revolutionary events of 1848 – a fluc-tuation between the open and the reserved, between objective rationality and petty bourgeois conformity.

It took less than one generation for an artist to appear in another country who did not bend to the conventions of bour-geois taste – Gustave Courbet. In 1855 he staged his own exhi-bition in Paris, and over the entrance he wrote a word that has been part of the discourse on art ever since: realism.

1. Philipp Otto Runge, *Hinterlassene Schriften*, II, Hamburg, 1841; repr. 1965, p. 526.
2. See Pia Müller-Tamm, *Rumohrs "Haushalt der Kunst". Zu einem kunsttheoretischen Werk der Goethezeit*, Hildesheim, 1991.

The Rediscovery of Danish and North German Painting of the Early Nineteenth Century

CATHERINE JOHNSTON

In 1972, the American art historian Robert Rosenblum commented on the modern perception of nineteenth-century art as being exclusively focused on France. He remarked that neither the Louvre nor the National Gallery in London, museums renowned for their extensive collections of European painting, owned a work by the great master of the German Romantic movement, Caspar David Friedrich.[1] The same could have been said about the representation of Danish artists of the Golden Age outside Scandinavian museums. In the intervening years, this situation has been remedied through a considerable number of exhibitions, which have brought works from both schools to public attention, and by enlightened acquisitions of such material, not just by the two institutions mentioned (though they have taken the lead), but by some North American museums as well. Why north European painting of the early nineteenth century should have escaped international consciousness for most of the twentieth century can be explained largely by the initial impact and continuing popularity of French Impressionism. This eclipsed all that went before it, a bias that is still reflected today in the price a Renoir fetches at auction or in the attendance records of a Monet exhibition. This essay intends to outline the recovery of interest in works by earlier Danish and German artists – first in their own countries, then, somewhat belatedly, abroad.

Within Friedrich's own lifetime (1774–1840), critical opinion switched attention from the Dresden Romanticists to the Munich and Düsseldorf schools, and Friedrich died forgotten and destitute.[2] Later art historical writing tended to focus more on the Catholic revivalist painting of the Nazarenes in Rome rather than on landscape. It was thus possible at the turn of the century for Alfred Lichtwark, a highly important director in the history of the Hamburger Kunsthalle (from 1886 to 1914), who was noted for his acquisition of works by Monet, Courbet, Manet and Liebermann, and for his rival Hugo von Tschudi, director of the Nationalgalerie in Berlin (from 1896 to 1909), to acquire from Friedrich's heirs pictures that remained unsold, which today form the major concentrations of works by this master.[3] Ironically, it was the investigation by the Norwegian art historian Andreas Aubert of Friedrich's contemporary Johan Christian Dahl that had sparked this renewed interest – especially the translation into German of Aubert's chapter on Friedrich.[4]

In 1906, just ninety-six years after Friedrich had exhibited two early paintings at the Berlin Academy which provoked different reactions,[5] Lichtwark, Tschudi and the art critic Julius Meier-Graefe organized a large exhibition in Berlin, the famous *Jahrhundertausstellung*, examining German painting of 1775–1875 from a new perspective.[6] All three were progressive personalities, who recognized the important innovations of modern painting in France and pioneered its acquisition by German museums. The show introduced the public to works by a number of the artists included in the present exhibition, with paintings by Friedrich and Blechen meeting with an especially positive critical response. The change in attitude to such artists brought about by that exhibition was subsequently reflected in the collecting activity of German museums, the character of whose holdings had hitherto been determined largely by their local history.

Later, several notable collections of German art were formed by private collectors. The first of these was begun in the 1920s

Fig. 17. Caspar David Friedrich,
Landscape with Rainbow, c. 1810.
Formerly Staatliche
Kunstsammlungen, Weimar

in Switzerland by an enlightened businessman from Winterthur, Oskar Reinhart, who, on the advice of Meier-Graefe, acquired works by French and German nineteenth-century artists. These included several outstanding pictures by Friedrich (see fig. 8, page 13), along with *plein air* paintings by Carl Blechen, Eduard Gaertner, Christian Morgenstern and Friedrich Wasmann, as well as by exponents from the Munich, Vienna and Swiss schools.[7] In Germany, the industrialist Georg Schäfer began to collect in the 1920s, and amassed from 1951 a large and varied representation of German nineteenth-century paintings (to be exhibited in the new Georg Schäfer Museum in Erbach, near Schweinfurt, due to open in 2000).[8] The distinguished collection of drawings formed by Alfred Winterstein in Munich demonstrates a sensitivity to the refined and linear character of German drawings of this period.[9]

The renewed interest in this movement was reflected in an important loan exhibition of over a hundred works, held in 1931 at the Munich Glaspalast (fig. 19, page 31). The disastrous fire that broke out, utterly destroying the premises, scored an irreparable loss for German Romantic painting, taking with it nine Friedrichs, including one of Greifswald at sunset from the Hamburger Kunsthalle, and three Runges from the same museum, plus many works by Blechen, Cornelius, Koch and Schnorr von Carolsfeld.[10] It was many years before another attempt was made to exhibit similar material. Further losses were incurred during World War II: among those pertinent to the current context are Friedrich's painting on the island of Rügen (fig. 17), stolen at the end of hostilities, and parts of the version of Gaertner's panorama of Berlin that the artist had taken to Russia in 1836 (cat. no. 52).

Except for Karl Friedrich Schinkel whose reputation, primarily as an architect, had never faded, scholarly appraisal of these artists essentially began only in the 1960s. Modern museum practice lent impetus to this process, when more expansive catalogues brought critical definition of holdings, and exhibitions became more frequent. Central to the rediscovery of early nineteenth-century painting were the bicentennial celebrations of the birth of Friedrich, inspiring not only an exhaustive catalogue raisonné but also exhibitions in Hamburg and Dresden.[11] At the same time, there was a growing recognition that Romanticism and Biedermeier should be viewed as separate stylistic entities. The Select Bibliography (pages 218–20) indicates the specialized literature of the last forty-odd years. Three general publications deserve to be singled out: the very appealing volumes compiled by Marianne Bernhard on German drawings of the period, accompanied by handy biographies of the artists;[12] Herbert von Einem's survey, *Deutsche Malerei des Klassizismus und der Romantik 1760 bis 1840*;[13] and Helmut Börsch-Supan's important *Die Deutsche Malerei*, defining the character of the different schools of painting, with a summary of the cultural life of each centre and highly useful lists of exhibitions held at the local academies and Kunstverein.[14]

Essentially, awareness of contemporary Danish painting had faded from German consciousness with Prussian expansionism and the separation of Schleswig-Holstein from Denmark. The proverbial Germanic predisposition for practicality and rationality – which expressed itself, for example, in guide books and art historical lexicons of exceptional quality – necessitated addressing the question of a Danish school of

art. Histories compiled by Richard Muther, professor of art history at the University of Breslau, viewed nineteenth-century Danish painters as partaking in a nationalist movement, and gave credit to C. W. Eckersberg as its founder and teacher.[15] Naturalism and clarity were deemed the dominant characteristics of Eckersberg's style, while its weakness was a lack of "pictorial conception". Muther also acknowledged the contribution of Eckersberg and Dahl to German landscape painting (although he mistakenly stated that Friedrich had studied under Eckersberg in Copenhagen). Their contribution is also noted in the 1921 edition of Adolf Rosenberg's *Handbook of Art History*,[16] in which the underlying thesis of the present exhibition was already divined: "In northern Germany a movement began which took as its task and goal the true observation and honest reproduction of reality." This movement, led by Eckersberg, was seen as spreading from Denmark to Hamburg and Dresden. In a more popular vein, a small volume on Danish art was included in the *Blaue Bücher* series.[17] Here, however, the beginning of a national school was seen as commencing with Jens Juel, although Eckersberg was credited with introducing a naturalism reflected in his "crystal-clear love of truth".

Danish painters of the Golden Age were never quite as forgotten as their German contemporaries. The nationalistic sentiments of art historian Niels Laurits Høyen, who urged artists to remain at home to paint the Danish landscape rather than seek stimulus abroad, inspired the pastoral landscapes of a generation of artists beginning with Johann Thomas Lundbye and Peter Christian Skovgaard, and influenced the development of a school of figurative painting focusing on poor rural folk. Despite this, works by Golden Age artists remained on public display in Copenhagen. The royal collection had been accessible in galleries at Charlottenborg Palace

since 1827; with the proclamation of a constitution in 1849, it became the property of the Danish State, with funds assigned for further purchases. It is noteworthy that in this first year, these resources were used to acquire works from the estate of Nicolai Abildgaard, but a rare opportunity was missed when the State failed to buy what are today the most prized paintings by Eckersberg, his brilliant views of Rome, when his personal effects were dispersed in 1853. Annual exhibitions were held at Charlottenborg until the royal fine arts collections were transferred in 1896 to the new Statens Museum for Kunst. A retrospective of paintings by Christen Købke was arranged by his nephews in 1884, while the Art Association organized shows devoted to Lundbye in 1893, to Eckersberg in 1895 and to Constantin Hansen in 1897.

In 1838 Bertel Thorvaldsen, the renowned Danish sculptor, returned from Italy and donated to the City of Copenhagen his sculptures, along with a collection of paintings he had acquired by German and Danish artists who had gathered about him in Rome. The following year, construction began of a building in which to display them – designed by M. G. Bindesbøll, it was an extraordinary testimony to Egyptianizing taste. The severe economic crisis that Denmark suffered for having sided with the French during the Napoleonic Wars initially prevented the formation of any great collection of Golden Age paintings. Demonstrative both of recovery and of the continued appreciation of these artists, however, were the collections created in the second half of the century by two industrialists, the brewer Carl Jacobsen (1842–1914) and the tobacco merchant Heinrich Hirschsprung (1836–1908). A number of paintings belonging to Jacobsen were given to the Ny Carlsberg Glyptotek, set up in 1882 to house his collection of ancient and nineteenth-century sculpture; these formed the nucleus of the display of Golden Age

paintings, to which many judicious purchases were later added.[18] Hirschsprung's collection was publicly exhibited in 1888, and it is possible that he influenced collecting at the Statens Museum for Kunst. When Hirschsprung bequeathed his collection to the Danish State in 1904, it could be said that it comprised the most distinguished representation of Golden Age painting on public view.[19]

Monographs by the art critic Emil Hannover on Købke (1893), Eckersberg (1898) and Hansen (1901) furthered public awareness of these artists. However, it was the inclusion of Eckersberg's oil sketches (essential to the formation of his students but hitherto unknown to the public at large) among the more than one thousand paintings on display at the Copenhagen Town Hall exhibition of 1901 that changed the modern perception of Golden Age painters. Exhibitions were devoted to Martinus Rørbye in 1905 and 1930. Dahl's paintings continued to be exhibited with those of both Danish and German artists; exhibitions of his work took place in Bergen in 1880 and in Christiania in 1888, with a retrospective in 1937 (the catalogue was by J. H. Langaard). Karl Madsen, himself a painter, had published a monograph on Lundbye in 1895 and collaborated on the influential Town Hall exhibition of 1901 before becoming director of the Statens Museum in 1911. In 1928, he organized for the Jeu de Paume in Paris a comprehensive exhibition of Danish painting drawn from public and private collections, along with a smaller representation of sculpture and drawings (see fig. 18). This first manifestation of interest in Golden Age painting outside Denmark included a number of pictures that appear in this exhibition (cat. nos. 26, 32, 33, 77, 78, 79, 94). It did not apparently have any immediate effect on collecting outside Denmark; except for portraits by Eckersberg, Købke, Jensen, Lundbye and Skovgaard being shown in the nineteenth-century retrospective that was part of the Venice Biennale of 1934, interest in Danish painting of the period remained for a time largely an internal matter. It was not until Fritz Novotny's 1960 overview of European painting that Danish artists were viewed as partaking in larger Classicist and Naturalist movements.[20] The great neoclassical exhibition in London of 1972 was perhaps even more important in introducing works by Abildgaard, Juel, Eckersberg, Bendz and Købke in a larger context.[21]

The interest of Sturla Gudlaugsson (1914–71) in preparing a book on Biedermeier painting and organizing an exhibition of the Danish Golden Age is forgotten today. Born in Skagen, the son of an Icelandic poet, he studied in Berlin before settling in the Netherlands, where he is best remembered for his book on Ter Borch. It is known that paintings by Vermeer and other Dutch masters had been in the Danish royal collection, and no doubt it was Gudlaugsson's familiarity with this aspect of seventeenth-century painting from Holland that drew him to find parallels with the cool stillness of interiors by Bendz and Kersting – what Novotny called their "palpable silence". Gudlaugsson's papers have yet to be studied in this regard, but may reveal more information on the Danish contribution to early nineteenth-century art than has hitherto been realized.[22]

Exhibitions held in Copenhagen during the 1970s and '80s brought to light the research of such scholars as Dyveke Helstead, Eva Henschen, Bjarne Jørnæs and H. E. Nørregård-Nielsen. But it was the towering personality of Erik Fischer, for many years chief curator of the Kongelige Kobberstiksamling (Royal Print Collection) that, through his catalogue of drawings celebrating the bicentennial of Eckersberg's birth and his role as external lecturer at the University of Copenhagen, influenced a younger generation to see the Golden Age as part of a larger spectrum.[23] A direct result can be found in

Kasper Monrad's doctoral thesis on the subject and in his Friedrich exhibition, which concentrated on the painter's early career and connections with Denmark.[24]

Large monographic exhibitions mounted by the Thorvaldsen and Statens museums and the Hirschsprung Collection have provided extensive catalogues on artists such as Rørbye, Hansen, Købke, Bendz, Juel and Lundbye, while the Dahl show marking the artist's bicentenary in Oslo was followed by the publication in English of a catalogue raisonné by Marie Lødrup Bang. Complementing these endeavours have been the three Golden Days Festivals held in Copenhagen in 1994, 1996 and 1998, which have greatly added to popular awareness of the architecture, decorative arts, literature and music of the period.[25]

International recognition of German Romanticism began only in 1959 with the exhibition *The Romantic Movement*,[26] and of the Danish Golden Age in 1972 with the landmark *Age of Neo-Classicism*. Both these events took place in London, but they were held under the aegis of the Council of Europe and the organizing committees were international in structure. Their impact was far-reaching, affecting not only the teaching of these movements but also museum purchases outside the countries of origin, prompting a flurry of publications and exhibitions touring abroad. Kermit Champa's exhibition of German nineteenth-century painting that circulated from New Haven to Cleveland and Chicago in 1970 had already provided the occasion for a symposium held at Yale featuring papers by German émigré art historians and their former students.[27] The Tate Gallery presented a Friedrich exhibition in 1972,[28] the first of its kind. Jointly co-ordinated by the English scholar William Vaughan (who had studied under Leopold Ettlinger and Nikolaus Pevsner) and the German specialists Helmut Börsch-Supan and Hans Joachim Neidhardt, it provoked a debate with Charles Rosen and Henri Zerner who, while admitting to the presence of a new Romantic language, challenged the interpretation of symbols in Friedrich's landscapes as excessive.[29] It was this exhibition that occasioned the remarks of Robert Rosenblum referred to at the beginning of this essay. Rosenblum's groundbreaking 1975 book on northern painting of the nineteenth and twentieth centuries redressed the previous neglect of Danish and German artists.[30]

France held an exhibition on the German Romantic era in 1976,[31] and Italy, the spawning ground for so many of the artists

under discussion, displayed Classical and Romantic paintings from museums in the former East Germany in 1977.[32] A book on the subject by William Vaughan appeared in 1980,[33] and several exhibitions on the topic toured the United States. The most important of these, organized by Stephan Waetzoldt, was held at the Metropolitan Museum of Art in New York and in Toronto at the Art Gallery of Ontario (with a catalogue contribution by Gert Schiff).[34] A new perspective was introduced when paintings by Caspar David Friedrich from Russian collections were brought to America, with a catalogue essay by Boris Asvarishch expanding on the patronage of Alexandra Fedorovna, daughter of Friedrich Wilhelm III of Prussia, and her husband Grand Duke Nicolai, the future Czar of Russia.[35] Notable for its exploration of the contextual aspects of German art of both this and later periods was the exhibition of 1994–95 in Edinburgh, London and Munich, *The Romantic Spirit in German Art, 1790–1990*. The accompanying catalogue offered chapters on "The Sublime", "The Crystalline", "Elemental Forces" and "Empirical Studies of Nature". It dealt with a religious view of nature – pantheistic, even theosophist, in origin – such as is found in the works of Friedrich and Runge, and an opposing view that had its roots in science.[36] For in the period in which our artists were active, Alexander von Humboldt's findings in the spheres of botany, geology and meteorology became universally recognized; it was Goethe who brought to the attention of a German audience Luke Howard's classification of clouds, published in England in 1802. This avid curiosity about the natural world may have inspired Blechen and Dahl to paint cloud studies, just as it drew Carl Gustav Carus to travel to the Hebrides to examine the rock formations on the island of Staffa.[37]

Interest in Danish painting was made evident through various exhibitions travelling abroad, one in Rome (1977),[38] another mounted by the National Gallery in London (1984), followed by a similar show in Paris at the Grand Palais (1984–85), the last two with catalogue entries written by Kasper Monrad.[39] These exhibitions presented portrait painting and a distinctly Danish type of conversation piece with cool light and play of shadows, as well as landscapes and marine painting. In his introduction to the Paris publication, Henrik Bramsen highlighted the early contribution of French painters, sculptors and architects to the Royal Danish Academy (founded in 1754), and commented on the young Eckersberg's association with Jacques-Louis David when in Paris. Several of

Eckersberg's paintings and elaborately finished drawings of Paris were introduced, which revealed the artist's already highly developed sense of light, as he exploited the possibilities of white page in contrast to the delicate rendering of architecture and foliage in pen and wash. Also on view in Paris were Eckersberg's academic studies in the guise of classical subjects that showed the direct influence of David's teaching.

The 1988 Biedermeier exhibition in Munich[40] featured works by Eckersberg (cat. no. 28), Bendz, Hansen, Jensen, Købke and Rørbye, shown in the company of German paintings of the period by Hermann Carmiencke (cat. no. 10), Deppe (cat. no. 22), Gaertner (cat. no. 50), Hasenpflug (cat. no. 65), Jerndorff (cat. no. 69), Kersting, Klose and Adolph Vollmer (cat. no. 104), and by the Austrians Rebell and Waldmüller. A departure from the usual manner of viewing Golden Age painting in isolation as a purely Danish phenomenon, here the context gave form to Novotny's classification of it as Biedermeier painting (a point of view presumably shared by Gudlaugsson). In fact, the author of the catalogue, Georg Himmelheber, maintained: "In no other city did Biedermeier painting emerge in such pure form as in Copenhagen," going on to say that "the finest achievements of Biedermeier painting were undoubtedly in landscape." A major exhibition organized for the Los Angeles County Museum of Art and the Metropolitan Museum in New York (1993–94) brought a comprehensive view of Danish Golden Age painting to American viewers for the first time.[41] The catalogue offered essays on the Copenhagen School by Monrad, on the character of Golden Age painting by Philip Conisbee, on Thorvaldsen's collection of painting by Bjarne Jørnæs, and on the socioeconomic situation in Denmark during that era by Hans Vammen.

As Danish and German painters, especially of the Dresden school, became known and appreciated and assumed their rightful place in the history of art, their work was sought by the principal museums of the western hemisphere. In 1975, Michel Laclotte and Pierre Rosenberg secured for the Louvre Friedrich's *Raven Tree* (cat. no. 43), in time for it to be featured in the 1976 Orangerie exhibition. As early as 1919, an Eckersberg marine scene had been given to the Louvre at the instigation of Karl Madsen in response to the French having honoured the bequest to the Statens Museum of Eckersberg's well-known *Portrait of the Nathan Sisters*, which had been seized as alien property during World War I. For a time, lacking

a context in the Louvre itself, this was exhibited at the Musée de la Marine. On the occasion of the state visit of Crown Princess Margrethe in 1965, a celebratory exhibition brought Danish paintings once again to French eyes.[42] Acquisitions began in earnest in 1980 with four Golden Age works (another Eckersberg marine, a Jensen portrait, and landscapes by Købke and Roed), followed in 1981 by a larger, finished painting by Fearnley, *Chasse au gibier d'eau*.[43] More significant purchases by the Louvre included an Eckersberg nude (1988), a Hansen scene of two boys playing (1994), a landscape by Lundbye (1996), and two important works by Købke, a portrait of a delightful candour of the artist's sister, and a small outdoor scene with a tobacco seller (1995).[44]

As if taking a cue from Robert Rosenblum, Neil MacGregor and John Leighton were active in pursuing northern pictures for the National Gallery, London. Købke's *View from the North Bridge of the Citadel* was acquired in 1986, then *Winter Landscape* by Caspar David Friedrich in 1987,[45] followed by a wonderfully luminous scene of Berlin's back streets by Eduard Gaertner in 1988, a small portrait of Wilhelm Bendz by Købke in 1992, and a view of the Roman Forum by Eckersberg. The National Gallery of Scotland also invested in Købke's *View of the Square in the Citadel Looking towards the Citadel Ramparts* and a family group by Bærentzen.

In North America, the first picture by Friedrich to enter a public collection was the Kimbell Art Museum's *Mountain Peak with Drifting Clouds* in 1984,[46] while in 1993 the J. Paul Getty Museum bought at auction a late work, *A Walk at Dusk*.[47] It is interesting to note that the Louvre's *Raven Tree* by Friedrich was in a private collection in New York following World War II, while his small *Shipwreck*, currently on loan to the Neue Pinakothek in Munich, was found a decade ago with a family in Utah that had emigrated from Germany in this century.[48] The Art Institute of Chicago purchased in 1996 a rediscovered variation by Blechen on the theme of the *Palm House* (fig. 20), the exotic greenhouse on the Pfaueninsel near Potsdam that housed the collection of palms acquired in Paris for Friedrich Wilhelm III of Prussia by Alexander von Humboldt. In 1989 the National Gallery of Canada purchased an oil sketch of a young oak tree by the same artist;[49] meanwhile, the Cleveland Museum of Art added works by Wilhelm von Kobell, J. P. Hackert and Catel to its collection.[50] These acquisitions have been relatively few and far between, however, and they represent a departure from the norm in

Fig. 20. Carl Blechen, *Interior of the Palm House on the Pfaueninsel near Potsdam*, 1834. The Art Institute of Chicago

Fig. 21. Christoffer Wilhelm Eckersberg, *Two Russian Ships Setting Sail*, 1827. National Gallery of Canada, Ottawa

collecting, especially from a North American standpoint. Although very few works by the German artists in this exhibition have been traced to America in the specialized literature,[51] it is interesting that their presence is nonetheless documented through early exhibition records.[52] Whether this presence was indicative of active collecting and even commerce in works of art of German origin, as opposed to private ownership of a painting reminiscent of the homeland, requires further study.[53]

Purchases of Danish painting of this period include the Cleveland Museum of Art's acquisition of Købke's diminutive *Portrait of Dr Johann Henning Kjetil Hjardemaal* in 1987. In 1990, the Metropolitan Museum purchased another fine portrait by Købke of his brother Waldemar. The J. Paul Getty Museum acquired a *View of the Forum in Pompeii* by the same artist as early as 1984 (see cat. no. 82), and in 1993 the Toledo Museum of Art bought a similar subject by him, *View of the Bay of Naples*: both scenes were executed later in Denmark on the basis of sketches the artist had made while he was in Italy. Also in 1993, the California Palace of the Legion of Honor acquired a small but vibrant cloud study by Dahl (cat. no. 16), and the National Gallery of Canada purchased Eckersberg's *Two Russian Ships Setting Sail* (fig. 21). Danish material in private collections includes paintings belonging to John Goelet, who donated to the Boston Museum of Fine Arts Købke's *Marina Piccola, Capri*, and to John L. Loeb, Jr. in New York;[54] while Charles Ryskamp, former director of the J. Pierpont Morgan Library and Frick Museum, made a point

of collecting Danish drawings of the period. Fewer works by Danish artists can be traced in North American exhibition records of the nineteenth century, and perhaps Louis Gurlitt was considered a German artist when his *Sunset View, near Naples* was exhibited at the Crystal Palace in New York in 1853. Similarly, in 1858, two views of Norway by Dahl were shown in a loan exhibition in Toronto, and in 1883 a marine scene by Vilhelm Melbye, an artist of the next generation, was one of the first gifts made to the newly founded National Gallery of Canada.[55]

Modern recognition of northern artists of the early nineteenth century coincided with a developing interest in the origins of *plein air* painting. With the important catalogues raisonnés that appeared in the 1960s on Poussin and Claude, the two great seventeenth-century landscape artists in the South, came general awareness of the excursions they made into the Roman Campagna to draw directly from nature. This was found to be true also of their Dutch contemporaries living in Rome, and a close observation of nature can equally be divined in the paintings of the German artists Elsheimer and Wals. Sandrart's claim that both he and Claude actually painted out in the open became more credible (in the absence of works to attest to this) with the discovery that Richard Symonds, an English traveller to Italy of the time, had designed a paint box for this specific purpose. The box had separate compartments for the pigments which were pre-ground in the studio and for the oil to bind them, a place for his palette, with the lid of the box serving as a cradle on to which the canvas was already

stretched. In the eighteenth century, the development of view painting compelled the artist to make studies out of doors, but the architectural complexity of a scene might mean that drawings were achieved with mechanical aids – a ruler at the very least, and sometimes a form of *camera obscura*. An enlarged painting would then be executed in the studio. Nevertheless, the conscious endeavour to represent the effects of light – particularly evident in works by the Dutch topographical painter Gaspar van Wittel, and by Canaletto, who began his artistic career painting Venetian theatre sets (just as Blechen and Gaertner would do in Berlin) – go far beyond the mechanical replication on canvas of a specific cityscape, and testify that these artists had spent long hours in the open, contemplating their intended subject.

By the eighteenth century, open-air sketching in oils had become a common practice in Rome, especially for students at the French Academy there, but the result usually served only for reference in composing more elaborate landscape compositions in the studio. Despite the advocacy of Vernet and Valenciennes, it was not until 1816 that landscape painting gained official recognition by the Academy in Paris, with the establishment of a Prix de Rome for study in this discipline. And it was only in the 1970s that a critical appraisal of these artists' contribution to open-air painting came about, with the Valenciennes exhibition organized by Geneviève Lacombe at the Louvre. In England, study of the two most famous exponents of landscape painting in the nineteenth century, Constable and Turner, revealed that they, too, practised open-

air painting on home soil, independent of formative experiences in Rome. It can be stated that the whole English watercolour tradition clearly adhered to this practice, and that two Welsh painters, Richard Wilson and Thomas Jones, set an obvious precedent in this regard when working in Italy.[56]

In 1976 the Kunsthalle in Hamburg organized an impressive Turner exhibition. Although not primarily devoted to *plein air* painting, the show offered paintings, watercolours and drawings by Turner liberally supplemented with works in various media by such German landscape artists as Schinkel (cat. no. 99), Friedrich, Blechen and Dahl (cat. no. 21).[57] The following year's presentation at the Kunsthalle in Bremen drew primarily on its own exceptional collection of oil sketches, highlighting a range of later nineteenth-century works, but also including several by Blechen, Dahl (cat. no. 19), Gille and Friedrich Nerly.[58] For the most part, these were acquisitions made in the post-war years by the Kunsthalle director Günter Busch,[59] whose son Werner Busch pursued this interest in several important articles on oil sketches. In 1979, Philip Conisbee's definitive article on the subject, "Pre-Romantic Plein-Air Painting", was published.[60]

Although Danish landscapes were not admitted into the company of works by French, Dutch and German artists featured in the 1977 Bremen show, this was accomplished in 1981 with Peter Galassi's brilliant exhibition *Before Photography* at New York's Museum of Modern Art,[61] which was not only the first occasion open-air painting was shown in America, but which brought together oil sketches by artists as varied as Valenciennes, Jones, Granet, Eckersberg, Dahl (cat. nos. 18, 21), Wasmann (cat. no. 108), Corot, Constable, Købke, Gaertner (cat. no. 51) and Meyer (cat. no. 88). Galassi claimed that, in the directness of their vision, such works possessed "the intuitive norm of authentic representation, unburdened by the responsibilities of public art," and they served his purpose "to mark the emergence of a new norm of pictorial coherence that made photography conceivable."[62] They were seen to introduce a new pictorial logic which, though cognizant of linear and aerial perspective, was based on a realistic, seemingly uncomposed view of nature. In this way a building or tree might occur close-up in the picture plane, distracting the eye from immediately focusing on the distance (cat. no. 15), or an object might be illogically truncated due to the vantage point of the artist (cat. nos. 21, 88), or cast in deep or partial shadow (cat. no. 51). The importance of *plein air* sketches was recognized by Himmelheber when, in the context of the Biedermeier exhibition, he included landscapes by Carmiencke (cat. no. 10), Dahl, Eckersberg (cat. no. 28), Gaertner (cat. no. 50) and Vollmer (cat. no. 104), observing: "Toward the end of the Biedermeier period, a number of artists from the north came to Munich: Thomas Fearnley, from Norway, Christian Morgenstern, Friedrich Wasmann and Louis Gurlitt from Hamburg . . . they brought a refreshing breath of Copenhagen *plein air* painting to Munich. It was they who recognized the innovative importance of Dillis's oil sketches and who subsequently raised this genre to a valued art form in its own right."[63] The Blechen exhibition organized by Peter-Klaus Schuster in Berlin in 1990 united many of the artists who had been part of the Turner exhibition in Hamburg, but Blechen occupied centre stage with almost a hundred paintings and nearly double that number of drawings and sketches, augmented by a further two hundred oil sketches by German and foreign artists of the time.[64] Meanwhile, the Whitworth Art Gallery in Manchester and the Fitzwilliam Museum in Cambridge mounted a small exhibition with oil studies, drawings and watercolours by Dahl and Fearnley,[65] and the Kunsthalle in Hamburg presented the work of the local group of *plein air* artists, many of them featured here.[66]

Broader in its scope, a major loan exhibition was held in Washington, D.C., and Brooklyn, coinciding with a large retrospective on Corot to mark the two-hundredth anniversary of his birth. The loan show concentrated on Italy and the brilliant light of the South, with *plein air* sketches forming its core.[67] Here, Eckersberg's paintings came into their own, predating by about ten or fifteen years those of Corot. Comparison revealed that Corot's brushwork was more in evidence and that his sketches were more schematic than Eckersberg's. There were also works by Dahl, Blechen, Fearnley (cat. no. 36), Wasmann (cat. no. 108), Roed (fig. 4, page 8), Købke and Hansen. The catalogue includes a tribute to the late John Gere, who collected pictures of this kind (the collection he and Charlotte Gere formed is now on long-term loan to the National Gallery, London).[68]

Finally, the work of Torsten Gunnarsson cannot be overlooked for his thorough analysis of the methods and purpose of *plein air* painting, but also for his important physical examination of the works themselves. His doctoral thesis on Scandinavian open-air painting appeared in 1989;[69] in 1998, a book on Nordic landscape painting was aimed at a larger public.[70] The first two chapters are devoted to Danish Golden Age *plein air* painters and to Swedish practitioners such as Gustaf Sødering and Gustaf Wilhelm Palm. Gunnarsson draws a distinction between studies made entirely in the open and those begun out of doors but finished in the studio; he defines the intent of the former as capturing the immediate, even ephemeral, at the cost of the timeless and classical aspect of the latter. He has made microscopic examinations of works of both types, distinguishing areas that have been added, since they can be seen to overlap the main portion of the landscape that had dried in the interim; or determining where added touches of paint have united with a still wet underlayer, causing a blurring of image and potentially of colour. Because of the risk of blurring, studies executed entirely *alla prima*, in one sitting, take full advantage of the brownish underground as part of the final image. The colour illustrations and the details of these sketches are seductive in themselves, but also highly informative in demonstrating his case.

1. Robert Rosenblum, "Caspar David Friedrich: A Reappraisal", *Studio International*, CLXXXIV (September 1972), pp. 73–75.

2. I wish to acknowledge my debt to Mitchell Frank for many stimulating discussions and for his help with the translation of material regarding the early reappraisal of German Romanticism and the German view of Danish painting. Dr Frank wrote his doctoral thesis on Friedrich Overbeck at the University of Toronto and is currently preparing a book, "Nazarene Tradition and the Narrative of Romanticism".

3. On this question, see Helmut R. Leppien, *Caspar David Friedrich in der Hamburger Kunsthalle*, Hamburg, 1993; for Lichtwark's overall activity in Hamburg, see the catalogue of the anniversary of his appointment as director, *Kunst ins Leben, Alfred Lichtwarks Wirken für die Kunsthalle und Hamburg von 1886 bis 1914*, Hamburg, 1986–87. See also Johann Georg Prinz von Hohenzollern and Peter-Klaus Schuster, eds., *Hugo von Tschudi und der Kampf um die Moderne*, Nationalgalerie Berlin and Neue Pinakothek, Munich, 1996–97.

4. Aubert 1893.

5. See Philip B. Miller, "Anxiety and Abstraction: Kleist and Brentano on Caspar David Friedrich", *Art Journal*, 33 (1974), pp. 205–10.

6. *Ausstellung deutscher Kunst aus der Zeit von 1775–1875*, Nationalgalerie Berlin, 1906.

7. See Franz Zelger, "Images of a Golden Age Connoisseurship: Oskar Reinhart and his Concept of Collecting", in Peter Wegmann, ed., *Caspar David Friedrich to Ferdinand Hodler: A Romantic Tradition*, exhibition catalogue, 1993–94; travelled to Los Angeles County Museum of Art; The Metropolitan Museum of Art, New York; National Gallery, London, and Nationalgalerie Berlin.

8. *Klassizismus und Romantik in Deutschland. Gemälde und Zeichnungen aus der Sammlung Georg Schäfer, Schweinfurt*, 1966, and *Deutsche Malerei im 19. Jahrhundert*, 1977; see also *Der frühe Realismus in Deutschland 1800–1850*, 1967: all three Germanisches Nationalmuseum, Nuremberg.

9. *Deutsche Zeichnungen 1800–1850 aus der Sammlung Winterstein*, exhibition catalogue, Lübeck, 1969; *Fuseli to Menzel: Drawings and Watercolours in the Age of Goethe from a Private German Collection*, exhibition catalogue, 1998; travelled to Busch-Reisinger Museum, Harvard University; Frick Collection, New York, and The J. Paul Getty Museum, Los Angeles.

10. G. J. Wolf, *Verlorene Werke deutscher romantischer Malerei*, F. Bruckmann, Munich, 1931.

11. Börsch-Supan and Jähnig 1973; *C. D. Friedrich und sein Kreis*, Albertinum, Gemäldegalerie Neue Meister, Dresden, 1974; Werner Hofmann, *Caspar David Friedrich 1774–1840*, Kunsthalle Hamburg, 1974. Hofmann also edited a series of essays examining how the artist came to be linked with questions of German identity and nationalism: *Caspar David Friedrich und die deutsche Nachwelt*, Suhrkamp, Frankfurt am Main, 1974; in 1992 Hofmann organized *Caspar David Friedrich: Pinturas y dibujos* for the Prado, Madrid.

12. Marianne Bernhard, *Deutsche Romantik: Handzeichnungen*, Rogner & Bernhard, Munich, 1973; afterword by Petra Kipphoff.

13. Herbert von Einem, *Deutsche Malerei des Klassizismus und der Romantik 1760 bis 1840*, Munich, 1978.

14. Helmut Börsch-Supan, *Die Deutsche Malerei von Anton Graff bis Hans von Marées, 1760–1870*, C. H. Beck & Deutscher Kunstverlag, Munich, 1988.

15. Richard Muther, *Geschichte der Malerei im Neunzehnten Jahrhundert*, 3 vols., G. Hirth, Munich, 1893; trans. into English as *The History of Modern Painting*, Henry and Co., London; revised edn. J. M. Dent, London, 1907, and as *Geschichte der Malerei*, Konrad Grethleins Verlag, Leipzig, 1909, pp. 118–20.

16. Adolf Rosenberg, *Handbuch der Kunstgeschichte*, Velhagen & Klasing, Bielefeld and Leipzig, 1921, p. 554.

17. Vagn Poulsen, *Arbeit, Brot und Friede: Dänische Maler von Juel bis zur Gegenwart*, Karl Robert Langewiesche Nachfolger, Düsseldorf and Leipzig, 1911; repr. as *Dänische Maler*, Karl Robert Langewiesche Verlag, Königstein im Taunus, 1961; texts in English and French, p. iv; Emil Hannover, *Dänische Kunst des 19. Jahrhunderts*, E. A. Seemann, Leipzig, 1907.

18. See H. E. Nørregård-Nielsen, *Danish Painting of the Golden Age*, exhibition catalogue, Ny Carlsberg Glyptotek, Copenhagen, 1995.

19. Several early nineteenth-century painters were at that time better represented in the Hirschsprung Collection than in the Statens Museum, see C. V. Petersen, *Den Hirschsprungske Samling 1911–1936*, Copenhagen, 1936 (offprint from *Tilskueren*, July 1936), pp. 8 ff.; see also Kasper Monrad, "Privatsamlingernes betydning for kunstmuseerne – historisk set", *Kunst og Museum*, vol. 19 (1984), pp. 11–13.

20. Fritz Novotny, *Painting and Sculpture in Europe 1780–1880*, Penguin, Harmondsworth, and Baltimore, 1960.

21. Hugh Honour et al., *The Age of Neo-Classicism*, exhibition catalogue, Royal Academy and Victoria and Albert Museum, London, 1972.

22. Gudlaugsson's interest in Golden Age painting was first brought to my attention by Pierre Rosenberg. Obituaries by A. B. de Vries, *The Burlington Magazine*, CXIII (December 1971), pp. 744–45, and C. Müller-Hofstede, *Weltkunst*, XLI:7 (April 1971), refer to the book Gudlaugsson had been preparing on early nineteenth-century painting.

23. Copenhagen 1983b. Demonstrative of Fischer's teaching is the catalogue introduction: using drawings and the illustrations to Eckersberg's own *Linearperspektiven anvendt paa Malerkunsten* [On Linear perspective and its employment in the art of painting] (Copenhagen, 1841), Fischer reveals that beyond the naturalism hitherto seen as its essence, Eckersberg's art displays a "remarkable combination of philosophical idealism and experimental science".

24. Monrad 1989; Copenhagen 1991.

25. Papers given at the first two festivals were published in *Thorvaldsens Museum Bulletin 1997*, ed. Stig Miss, Copenhagen. See also Bente Scavenius, ed., *The Golden Age in Denmark, Art and Culture 1800–1850* and *The Golden Age Revisited, Art and Culture in Denmark 1800–1850*, Gyldendal, Copenhagen, 1994 and 1996.

26. Kenneth Clark et al., *The Romantic Movement*, exhibition catalogue, Tate Gallery and the Arts Council Gallery, London, 1959.

27. "Correlations between German and Non-German Art in the Nineteenth Century", symposium chaired by E. Haverkamp-Begemann with papers by H. W. Janson, R. Rosenblum, V. H. Miesel, H. Schwarz, L. D. Ettlinger and G. Schiff, *Yale University Art Gallery Bulletin*, 33:3 (October 1972).

28. William Vaughan, Helmut Börsch-Supan and H. J. Neidhardt, *Friedrich and Romantic Landscape Painting in Dresden*, exhibition catalogue, Tate Gallery, London, 1972.

29. Their observations, expressed in various reviews and essays, were gathered together in Charles Rosen and Henri Zerner, *Romanticism and Realism, The Mythology of Nineteenth-Century Art*, W. W. Norton & Co., New York, 1984.

30. Robert Rosenblum, *Modern Painting and the Northern Romantic Tradition: Friedrich to Rothko*, Harper & Row, New York, 1975.

31. Laclotte, Hofmann, Neidhardt and Kouznetsov, eds., *La Peinture allemande à l'époque du Romantisme*, exhibition catalogue, L'Orangerie, Paris, 1976–77.

32. G. C. Argan, M. Cacciari and C. Keisch, *Classici e Romantici Tedeschi in Italia*, Ala Napoleonica, Venice, 1977.

33. William Vaughan, *German Romantic Painting*, Yale University Press, New Haven and London, 1980.

34. Gert Schiff, ed., *German Masters of the Nineteenth Century*, exhibition catalogue with entries by Stephan Waetzoldt, Charles S. Moffett, Alan Salz and graduates of the Institute of Fine Arts, New York, The Metropolitan Museum, New York, and Art Gallery of Ontario, Toronto, 1981; Schiff also supervised a doctoral dissertation on Hummel, see Marsha Lee Morton, "Johann Erdmann Hummel. A Painter of Biedermeier Berlin", New York, 1986.

35. New York & Chicago 1990–91.

36. T. F. Mitchell, *Art and Science in German Landscape Painting 1770–1840*, Clarendon Press, Oxford, 1993, is of interest on this subject.

37. *The Romantic Spirit in German Art, 1790–1990*; exhibition catalogue, Royal Scottish Academy, Edinburgh; Hayward Gallery, London, and Haus der Kunst, Munich, 1994–95. This exhibition also brought to wider attention Friedrich's and Schinkel's painted transparencies, a late eighteenth-century invention also used by Hackert in Naples, Gainsborough in London and Carmontelle in Paris. Schinkel's examples, on a larger scale, evolved into dioramas that were regularly presented at Christmas time in Berlin.

38. *I Pittori Danesi a Roma nell'ottocento*, exhibition catalogue, Palazzo Braschi, Rome, 1977.

39. London 1984 and Paris 1984–85.

40. Munich 1988–89b.

41. Los Angeles & New York 1993–94.

42. *Le Danemark: Ses trésors, son art*, exhibition catalogue, Musée du Louvre, Paris, 1965.

43. This was originally a gift from Charles XV of Sweden to the French Ambassador Hugues Fournier who served in Stockholm 1862–70; it was acquired at a sale of his descendants' property.

44. *Nouvelles acquisitions du département des peintures 1991–1995*, Musée du Louvre, Paris, 1996, pp. 50–58; articles by Bjarne Jørnæs and Elisabeth Foucart-Walter, signalling some of these acquisitions, were in *Revue du Louvre*, 31 (1982), pp. 56–60, and 46 (1996), pp. 88–100.

45. John Leighton and Colin J. Bailey, *Winter Landscape*, exhibition catalogue in the series *Painting in Focus*, National Gallery, London, 1990; the chapter by Aviva Burnstock on materials and technique gives further bibliography on the make-up of pictures by Friedrich and Dahl.

46. Börsch-Supan and Jähnig 1973, no. 449, *Hochgebirgsgipfel mit treibenden Wolken*.

47. Börsch-Supan and Jähnig 1973, no. 407, *Spaziergang in der Abenddämmerung*; "Acquisitions", *J. Paul Getty Museum Journal*, 22 (1994), p. 79, no. 28.

48. Galerie Arnoldi-Livie, Munich, 1987, no. 15 (Börsch-Supan and Jähnig 1973, no. 233). I am grateful to Bruce Livie for clarifying the provenance of this picture.

49. National Gallery of Canada, no. 30398; Rave 1940, no. 233.

50. A 1994 acquisition, Catel's *View out a Window in Naples*, was exhibited in Washington and Brooklyn, *In the Light of Italy*, 1996, no. 79.

49. National Gallery of Canada, no. 30398; Raington with a descendant of the artist.

52. J. Yarnell and W. Gerdts, *Index to American Art Exhibition Catalogues from the Beginning through the 1876 Centennial Year*, 6 vols., G. K. Hall & Co., Boston, 1986. Apart from the many Hudson River scenes painted by Carmiencke after he emigrated to Brooklyn, two Danish landscapes, a Swedish coastal view and two Italian scenes, *Aqueduct near Rome* and *Lago di Gardi* [*sic*] are mentioned as having been exhibited at the Maryland Historical Society (1856) and Maryland Institute (1857), at the International Art Institution in New York (1861), and the Brooklyn and Long Island Fair (1864). Paintings listed as exhibited in 1851 at the Reading Academy in Pennsylvania include *Acropolis* by Schinkel and several works by Friedrich. Although forenames are not quoted, the subjects – *Landscape – Sunset* and *The Brothers*, two works titled *Portrait of a Gentleman*, one *Portrait of a Lady*, and two called *Portrait of an Artist* – suggest works that might well have been painted by Caspar David Friedrich. Hasenpflug's *City Gate* was exhibited by F. J. Freer at the Philadelphia Great Central Fair (1864), Morgenstern's *Italian Coast* in the Cincinnati Industrial Exposition (1872) and Elsasser's *Scene in Calabria* is indicated as belonging to the Carey collection in Philadelphia (de-accessioned by the Pennsylvania Academy in 1951). Two works by Gaertner listed without initial, but indicating that the artist lived in Berlin, were for sale at the International Art Institution in New York between 1859 and 1861. The subjects, *Landscape in the North of Germany* and *Ruins of the Nunnery Leheim in Brandenburg*, are such as to suggest late works by the Berlin architectural painter, the second picture seemingly related to Wirth no. 95, pl. 180. Drawings by Blechen, Gensler, Hasenpflug, Krause, Morgenstern and Schoppe were exhibited (1845?) at the Philadelphia Artists' Fund Society by Alexandre Vattemare (1796–1864). It is not clear

whether the large number of works he exhibited on this occasion actually belonged to him or had been lent for the purpose of exhibiting abroad. Born in France, Vattemare was taken prisoner in 1814 in Prussia, where he commenced a career as a ventriloquist, travelling in Europe and even the United States. The *Dictionary of American Biography* indicates that he frequented museums and libraries, proposing a system of exchanges among them. He is considered one of the founders of the Boston Public Library, and also proposed a building to house a library and museum in Montréal (1841). It is interesting to note that one of the most important collections of German prints outside Germany was compiled around the same time from sources in Germany by John S. Phillips (1800–76) of Philadelphia. Bequeathed to the Pennsylvania Academy, it is now part of the collection of the Philadelphia Museum of Art and includes a number of etchings by Fearnley and three by Dahl. I am grateful to Ann Percy and John Ittmann for this last information.

53. In New York, for instance, works from the Düsseldorf Academy were exhibited and sold from 1849, see R. L. Stehle, "The Düsseldorf Gallery of New York", *The New York Historical Society Quarterly*, vol. 58 (1974), pp. 305–8. Since a number of North American landscape artists had studied at the Düsseldorf Academy, it was logical that paintings from this school would have crossed the Atlantic at an early date. As indicated by Stephan Waetzoldt in his introductory essay to *German Masters of the Nineteenth Century*, exhibition catalogue, New York and Toronto, 1981, the Art Associations or Kunstverein often owned stakes in works of art and actively marketed them at a time before dealers were firmly established in Germany. See also Yarnell and Gerdts, *Index*, op. cit., pp. xxvii–xxx.

54. The Loeb pictures were exhibited at the Busch-Reisinger Museum, Harvard University, in 1994 with a hand list and small catalogue by Peter Nisbet, *Danish Painting of the Nineteenth Century from the Collection of Ambassador John L. Loeb, Jr.*

55. The first is listed by Yarnell and Gerdts, while I owe to my colleague Michael Pantazzi the information regarding the pictures by Dahl. These belonged to a Mrs Briscoe and were exhibited in Toronto in 1858: *Catalogue of oil paintings, water colours, engravings and photographs: from the private collections of gentlemen of Toronto exhibited in Romain's Buildings, King St. West, in aid of a building fund for St Paul's Church, Yorkville*, nos. 203 and 207; the same owner lent two landscape drawings, nos. 88 and 271, but neither the artists nor the precise scenes were identified.

56. Although no sketches of this type by Wilson appear to survive, he did make two paintings of Tivoli showing artists engaged in this activity (National Gallery of Ireland, Dublin). His pupil Thomas Jones. on the other hand, chose to remain in Italy and is known for the *plein air* sketches he made of the rooftops in Naples. An important exhibition of paintings and watercolours by Jones was organized by Francis Hawcroft for the Whitworth Gallery, Manchester, in 1988.

57. W. Hofmann, ed., *William Turner und die Landschaft seiner Zeit*, exhibition catalogue, Kunsthalle Hamburg, 1976.

58. Günter Busch et al., *Zurück zur Natur*, exhibition catalogue, Kunsthalle Bremen, 1977.

59. *Katalog der Gemälde des 19. und 20. Jahrhunderts in der Kunsthalle Bremen*, 1973.

60. Philip Conisbee, "Pre-Romantic *Plein Air* Painting", *Art History*, 2 (December 1979), pp. 413–28, sums up the activity and the relevant literature on the topic.

61. Peter Galassi, *Before Photography: Painting and the Invention of Photography*, exhibition catalogue, Museum of Modern Art, New York, 1981.

62. Ibid., p. 18.

63. Munich 1988–89b; English edn. 1989, p. 32.

64. Berlin 1990; see also Klaus Herding, "Les paysages italiens de Carl Blechen et la lutte du peintre pour la modernité", in *Corot, un artiste et son temps, Actes des colloques organisés au musée du Louvre et par l'Académie de France à Rome (1996)*, Paris, 1998, pp. 542–72.

65. A. Smith, S. Helliesen and E. Haverkamp, *"Nature's Way": Romantic Landscapes from Norway*, exhibition catalogue, Whitworth Art Gallery, Manchester, and Fitzwilliam Museum, Cambridge, 1993.

66. Hamburg 1996.

67. Philip Conisbee, S. Faunce and J. Strick, *In the Light of Italy: Corot and Open Air Painting*, exhibition catalogue, National Gallery of Art, Washington, and Brooklyn Art Museum, New York, 1996.

68. Catalogue forthcoming by C. Riopelle, 1999. Here, the contribution of Jack Baer in championing a taste for *plein air* oil sketches must be acknowledged; see particularly *The Lure of Rome: Some Northern Artists in Italy in the Nineteenth Century*, exhibition catalogue, Hazlitt, Gooden and Fox, London, 1979.

69. Torsten Gunnarsson, *Friluftsmåleri före friluftsmåleriet. Oljestudien i nordiskt landskapsmåleri 1800–1850*, Acta Universitatis Upsaliensis. Ars Suetica 12, Uppsala, 1989 (English summary, "Open-Air Sketching in Scandinavia 1800–1850").

70. Torsten Gunnarsson, *Nordic Landscape Painting in the Nineteenth Century*, Yale University Press, New Haven and London, 1998.

List of Artists

Artists' Biographies

Wilhelm Bendz
(Odense 1804–1832 Vicenza)

Wilhelm Bendz participated in classes in the Academy of
Fine Arts in Copenhagen from June 1820. He became a private
pupil of C. W. Eckersberg in 1822 and again from 1827 to 1831.
In addition to portrait painting, Bendz was particularly adept
at painting groups of figures in interiors, either as portrait
groups or as a result of his pronounced interest in reproducing
complicated light and shade effects with artificial light as the
source of light. These major compositions from his early years
in Copenhagen demonstrate very clearly a desire on Bendz's
part to experiment with his painterly potential in works that
appear to be thought through and composed down to the least
detail. He must certainly have had a good knowledge of
German art during these years. In 1831 he went via Hamburg,
Berlin, Dresden (visiting J. C. Dahl) and Nuremberg to Munich,
where he stayed for a year and enjoyed considerable success.
He might possibly have settled permanently in Munich after a
visit to Italy, but he died prematurely in 1832 in Vicenza on his
way south. His last great painting, representing a gathering of
artists in Finck's coffee house in Munich, was bought by Bertel
Thorvaldsen.

SM

Carl Blechen
(Cottbus 1798–1840 Berlin)

Blechen grew up in a region with a rugged landscape and
devoid of art, and in 1814 went to Berlin to begin a bank
apprenticeship. However, in 1822 his desire to paint became
so strong that he gave up his profession and attended the
Academy of Art. His talent was soon recognized by Schadow
and Schinkel. They recommended him to the Königsstädtisches
Theater in Berlin as a scene-painter. His knack for creating
effective sets and the transmission of ideas and feelings through
painting were thus encouraged. In 1826 he became prominent
as a painter of easel-paintings, and in 1827 he gave up his
theatre work and in 1828–29 undertook a journey to Italy.
This led him as far as Naples, widened his artistic horizon and
developed his ability to reproduce spontaneously the atmosphere
of an original landscape and taught him a new way of drawing
and managing colour. From 1831 Blechen taught the landscape

class at the Berlin Academy and as such had a great influence
on other painters. In 1833 he went on a journey to the Harz,
and in 1835 made a short trip to Paris. Shortly after this, he
was struck by mental illness; his exceptional irritability and
sensitivity were linked to his illness. Shortly after Blechen's
death, the Academy of Art acquired works from his estate.
An élite group of connoisseurs has long admired his work.

HBS

Hermann Carmiencke
(Hamburg 1810–1867 New York)

After an apprenticeship to an interior painter, Carmiencke
moved to Dresden, where he studied under J. C. Dahl. He
went to Copenhagen to study in 1834 and was a student of
C. W. Eckersberg, who introduced him to Danish landscape
painting. Afterwards he entered the service of the Countess
Schönburg in Wechselburg, Saxony, and gave her drawing
lessons. In 1838 he returned to Copenhagen and became the
court painter to King Christian VIII. Study trips led him to
Sweden, the Tyrol and Italy. Carmiencke emigrated to America
in 1851 and was one of the founders of the Brooklyn Academy
of Design. His painting is characterized by its special interest
in north German and northern landscapes, which also brought
him success in New York. He was especially recognized for his
series of landscape etchings.

CG

Carl Gustav Carus
(Leipzig 1789–1869 Dresden)

Carus is certainly the most extraordinary artistic personality
among the Dresden landscape painters. In addition to studying
medicine, he was a natural scientist, a natural philosopher and
an art theoretician. From 1814 to 1824, he worked on *Nine
Letters on Landscape Painting*, published in 1831, in which
he attempted to unify art and scientific theory in poetic form,
modelled on Schellings's ideas of natural philosophy. He was
a self-taught painter. C. D. Friedrich's influence helped him
develop a freer approach to landscapes, affecting his selection
of subject and execution, but their ten-year friendship was
mutually rewarding. This is especially evident in the scenes of
Dresden, which were the result of their shared tours throughout

the environs of the city and were probably painted at Carus's prompting. Dahl's oil studies decisively influenced Carus's artistic development. Their generous freedom of composition, connected with casual choice of motif, approached Carus's yearning for an objective sense of reality, and helped him to achieve greater artistic independence. However, we certainly must take into consideration the clouding over of his friendship with Friedrich after 1828, which led to a more critical dialogue and greater expressive independence in Carus's own art. He maintained a lively correspondence with Goethe, which possibly contributed to his estrangement from Friedrich. Carus travelled to the Riesen Mountains and to Rügen, and also to England, Scotland, Switzerland and Italy. This travel trained his eye for landscape and, following Dahl's example, he prepared studies. Carus was, above all, a scientist. He accepted a professorship of gynaecology in Dresden, and his appointment as court physician in Saxony restricted his artistic life to his friendship with Dahl.

CG

Johan Christian Dahl
(Bergen 1788–1857 Dresden)

As a fully trained journeyman painter, J. C. Dahl moved to Copenhagen from his birthplace in Norway in 1811. Here he was admitted to the Academy of Fine Arts, where he became a pupil of, among others, the landscape painter C. A. Lorentzen. In Copenhagen, Dahl was particularly interested in seventeenth-century Dutch landscape painting, especially Jacob van Ruisdael, whom he could study in the Academy collections, but he was also interested in C. W. Eckersberg's views of Rome. He himself painted studies of the countryside around Copenhagen and other selected areas of Zealand, as well as motifs from Norway partly painted from memory. Through Dahl's eyes, natural scenery was revealed as something august and powerful. Behind his interpretation of the motifs, however, there was often a thorough study of both composition and detail. In 1818, Dahl set out on his grand tour, which took him to Dresden where he made the acquaintance of the German painter C. D. Friedrich and the community of artists in Dresden, who were keenly interested in landscape painting. At the invitation of Prince Christian Frederik, later King Christian VIII of Denmark, in summer 1820 Dahl went from Dresden via Rome to Naples, where he spent a lengthy period and made a number of paintings of the Bay of Naples with Vesuvius in eruption. After this, Dahl settled permanently in Dresden in 1821, living in the same house as Friedrich. From his base in Germany, he painted many poetic depictions of the landscape in and around Dresden, in addition to a large number of

Norwegian and a few Danish landscapes. As had been the case when Dahl was in Copenhagen, the former were based partly on memory and partly on sketches made during visits to Norway in 1826, 1834, 1839 and 1850. He maintained close contact with Denmark and was represented almost every year in the Charlottenborg exhibitions. In Denmark, thanks to his lyrical and dramatic landscapes, Dahl came to represent the diametrical opposite of Eckersberg; he was of great significance to the following generation – Købke, Lundbye and Sødring – and for the further development of landscape painting.

GW

Ludwig Deppe
(dates and places unknown)

Little is known about this artist. In 1820 he entered the exhibition of the Berlin Academy in the section "dilettantes" with three "studies from nature in oil" under the name "Mr Private Secretary Deppe", one of which was bought by King Friedrich Wilhelm III of Prussia and has therefore been preserved. Apart from this, there is a copy by him of a painting by Carl Friedrich Zimmermann, a painter known from Schinkel's circle. His extreme precision as a draughtsman is apparent in the care he took in registering a visual impression as well as in the reproduction of light and colour; it has parallels with the work of Peter Ludwig Lütke (a student of Hackert), Johann Erdmann Hummel and Frédéric Fregevice from Geneva, and also with porcelain painting in Berlin, which liked to insert vedutas. Deppe was in the service of Prince August of Prussia and lived in his palace in Wilhelmstrasse; he is last mentioned in the Berlin city directory of 1855.

HBS

Christian Dankvart Dreyer
(1816 Assens–1852 Barløse)

When only fifteen, Christian Dankvart Dreyer moved from his birthplace at Assens on the island of Funen to Copenhagen to attend the Academy of Fine Arts. Here, together with a group that included J. T. Lundbye and P. C. Skovgaard, he was the pupil of J. L. Lund. In addition he attended C. W. Eckersberg's classes in perspective, and in all probability was also a private pupil of Christen Købke. Although Dankvart Dreyer was responsible for a small number of figure compositions, landscape painting was his preferred genre. Like his friends Lundbye and Skovgaard, he became absorbed in the national liberal sentiments sweeping the country and in the desire to depict characteristic Danish features in his landscape studies. It was these ideas that moved him to become the first landscape artist to paint the countryside of Jutland. In his pictures from various parts of Jutland, he reproduced a natural scenery that was less idyllic than the Zealand landscape that had been mainly favoured by painters. In 1843, when he painted his *Shoreline with Sand Dunes: The West Coast of Jutland*, Dankvart Dreyer encountered severe criticism in Copenhagen because he had not painted the North Sea in stormy weather but as it had looked in the summer when he was staying at Bovbjerg and Trans. Interest in the Jutland landscape was later taken up by several painters, including Georg Emil Libert and Louis Gurlitt. Dankvart Dreyer also painted a number of motifs from his native island of Funen. He was represented in the Charlottenborg exhibitions between 1834 and 1848, but he applied in vain for the Academy's travelling bursary. In 1848 he bought a farm near Barløse on Funen and to some extent laid painting aside. After his death in 1852, he was almost forgotten. However, exhibitions in 1901 and 1912 and later, for instance in 1989, have helped reveal the significance of his landscape painting and reinstate him in the history of Danish art.

GW

C. W. Eckersberg
(Blåkrog 1783–1857 Copenhagen)

Christoffer Wilhelm Eckersberg was born in Schleswig near the present Danish–German border. He was first taught in Åbenrå and Flensburg, coming to Copenhagen in 1803 as a pupil of Nicolai Abildgaard. He appears not to have been particularly close to his teacher, but could nevertheless have derived his interest in perspective from him. Jens Juel was his most important source of inspiration. There is a notable romantic quality in his first landscapes, but this disappeared while he was in Paris to continue his studies in 1810–13. A year spent as a pupil in J. L. David's studio had very far-reaching effects on him. However, it was only during his stay in Rome in 1813–16 that he found his real artistic self. He had little contact with the German painters in Rome at the time. After his return to Denmark he was appointed Professor at the Academy of Fine Arts in Copenhagen in 1818, and from then until about 1850 he exerted an influence on almost all pupils at the Academy. He quickly lost contact with foreign art and advised his pupils not to visit Germany. After 1820, landscapes came to play a lesser role for him, while seascapes gradually became his preferred mode. He placed great emphasis on perspective and published a couple of works on the theory of perspective.

KM

Friedrich August Elsasser
(Berlin 1810–1845 Rome)

Elsasser entered the Berlin Academy in 1825 at the age of fifteen, where he was influenced by painters as different as Johann Erdmann Hummel and Carl Blechen. At the exhibition of the academy in 1830 he stood out with fourteen paintings, showing vedutas of the Pfaueninsel, interior views of medieval buildings in Berlin, and also fantastic architecture. Even when Elsasser went to Rome in 1831 he still felt indebted to Blechen and occasionally rivalled him in the dramatic effect of his sketches. In Rome he joined up with Franz Catel, another painter from Berlin. On his expeditions through Italy and Sicily he executed studies from nature and with these tried above all to record the transient effect of light. He was elected a member of the Berlin Academy in 1841. Like many other German artists in Italy, Elsasser was not able to cope with the strain of working outdoors and died of tuberculosis. Approximately four hundred of his drawings were lost from the Kupferstichkabinett in Berlin during World War II.

HBS

Thomas Fearnley
(Frederikshald 1802–1842 Munich)

Fearnley travelled a great deal during his life, rarely staying in one place for more than a couple of years before moving on. As a result he derived his artistic inspiration from many sources. He was first trained in the Royal School of Drawing in Christiania (present-day Oslo), and in 1822–23 he studied at the Academy in Copenhagen as a pupil of the landscape painter J. P. Møller and apparently also of Lorentzen, but not of Eckersberg. From 1823 to 1827 he studied at the Academy of Fine Arts in Stockholm under Carl Johan Fahlcrantz. In 1827–28 he was again in Copenhagen. In 1829 he went to Dresden, where he became a pupil of Dahl, whom he had met during a journey to Norway in 1826, and was also influenced by Friedrich. He moved on again the following year, but maintained close contact with Dahl. He was in Munich for the next couple of years, mixing in a circle that included his painter friends from Copenhagen, Morgenstern and Bendz. At the end of 1832 he went to Rome, where he associated with both Danish and German painters, and for the next three years he travelled in Italy. In 1835 he travelled via Switzerland to Paris, proceeding the following year to London, where he lived until 1838.

KM

Caspar David Friedrich
(Greifswald 1774–1840 Dresden)

Friedrich, the son of a soap refiner, was born in the part of
Pomerania that then belonged to Sweden. From 1794 to 1798
he studied at the Academy in Copenhagen and then continued
his studies in Dresden. His development as a painter was also
inspired by repeated trips to his native Baltic coast during
the years 1801–2, 1806, 1809, 1815, 1818 and 1826. He also
travelled to Bohemia in 1807, 1808 and 1828; to the Riesen
Mountains in 1810, and to the Harz Mountains in 1811.
Inspired by his visit to the Baltic Sea of 1801–2, he discovered
his own particular artistic style, at the same time as his fellow-
countryman Philipp Otto Runge. The differences between his
homeland of Greifswald and Dresden influenced his art, which
conceives of nature as a creation and therefore as a divine
revelation. He saw it as the artist's task to decipher this symbolic
language, which includes atmospheric visions. By 1810,
Friedrich's status as a landscape painter was established. He
was made a member of the Berlin Academy in 1811 and of the
Academy in Dresden in 1816. He met Carus in 1817 and Dahl
in 1818, both of whom proved important sources of inspiration.
He was appointed professor at the Academy in Dresden in 1824.
But from about 1830 he was ignored and his work considered
old-fashioned; he died in poverty in 1840. He was rediscovered
at the end of the nineteenth century by the Norwegian art
historian Andreas Aubert who was doing research on Dahl,
but he achieved wider international fame only with a London
exhibition in 1972 and one in Hamburg in 1974.

HBS

Eduard Gaertner
(Berlin 1801–1877 Zechlin)

Gaertner grew up in Kassel but returned to Berlin in 1813
where he began to learn porcelain painting at the Berlin
manufactory. This determined specific characteristics of his
art: exactness in drawing and coloration as well as transparency
in his colour application. In 1821 he joined Carl Gropius's studio
to become a decorative painter. In the same year he travelled
to Rügen and West Prussia. Shortly thereafter he turned to
oil painting, and the court bought one of his paintings as early
as 1824. An extended stay in Paris from 1825 to 1828, where
he was a student of Jean-Victor Bertin, sharpened his vision for
light and atmosphere. After his return he rose to become the
leading architectural painter in Berlin with his oil paintings,
watercolours and lithographs. As "chamber painter", he
depicted views of interiors in watercolour. Friedrich Wilhelm III

and Friedrich Wilhelm IV bought his works regularly, but even
so he remained in the background of Berlin society. In 1833 he
became a member of the Academy of Arts. In 1837 and 1838 he
travelled to St Petersburg and Moscow; in 1841–42, 1844 and
1858 to Bohemia and Prague, and in 1848 to Silesia. In 1870 he
moved to Zechlin and afterwards painted very little. Gaertner
can be regarded as the most important German architectural
painter of the nineteenth century. The figurative details in his
pictures capture local characteristics and his narrative powers
go far beyond those of most genre painters. His importance has
been recognized only in recent years.

HBS

Jacob Gensler
(Hamburg 1808–1845 Hamburg)

At the age of thirteen, Gensler drew a portrait of his brother
Martin. He was initially taught by Bendixen and Hardorff, who
advised his father to send the young artist to Wilhelm Tischbein
in Eutin. Through his connections with the Speckter circle,
Gensler met Baron C. F. von Rumohr in 1822. Rumohr
supported Gensler and encouraged him to concentrate on
the study of nature. In 1828 he travelled by way of Meissen,
Dresden and Nuremberg to Munich, where he studied figure
painting at the Academy. That summer he painted out of
doors with a circle of painters from Hamburg, with a view
to becoming a genre painter. In 1830 he moved to Vienna, but
his hopes of finding work as a genre painter there were not
fulfilled. After returning to Hamburg, he taught and travelled
throughout northern Germany. Primarily from economic
considerations, he painted genre scenes with an individual
touch and with crowd-pleasing themes, his series of fisherman
pictures satisfying the desire for a popular idyll. Conscientiously
transcribed details from nature lend his paintings credibility. He
increased their appeal with allegorical and mythological subjects
decorated with alluring feminine figures, and had considerable
success. He died young, from a lung infection.

KvO

Christian Friedrich Gille
(Ballenstedt 1805–1899 Wahnsdorf)

Gille was one of the few artists of his era who did not
spend time in Italy studying ancient ruins. The inspiration
for his subjects came from the environs of Dresden. He came
to Dresden from his home in the Harz in 1825 to train as
a landscape engraver, but switched to become a student of
painting with J. C. Dahl. In order to earn his living, he worked

as an engraver of reproductions, a graphic illustrator, a
portraitist and a porcelain painter, all of which distracted him
from his painting studies. From the time of his apprenticeship,
he found Dahl a faithful mentor. Gille died an old man,
impoverished. The few paintings he exhibited apparently
did not establish him successfully in the art market and are
conventional in their composition and execution. However, the
oil studies and sketches of landscapes, made from the 1820s
until late in his life, strike the viewer with their immediacy and
their ability to evoke new painterly inspiration even from minor
details. His studies from nature were never designed to be used
in the studio as the basis for composition, but were for him the
rendering of impressions of reality seen in nature.

CG

Louis Gurlitt
(Altona 1812–1897 Naundorf, Erzgebirge)

During four years spent as an apprentice with Bendixen, Gurlitt
learned all aspects of decorative painting. His first paintings
reveal the influence of Morgenstern and Dahl. From 1832 he
studied at the Academy in Copenhagen under Eckersberg, who
tried to convey to him the joy of painting from nature and a
talent for colour. During a two-year stay in Munich in 1836–37,
he turned to Rottmann's theories of ideal landscapes. His travels
led him to Norway, Sweden, Italy, Hungary, Greece, Spain and
Portugal. In spite of his success, which in addition to providing
a secure income also led to his being honoured with the Order
of Dannebrog, he never became a professor. He lived and
worked in Copenhagen, Düsseldorf, Berlin, Rome, Vienna,
Gotha and Dresden, selling his own works. In addition to
creating carefully composed heroic landscape paintings, he also
dabbled in lithography, etching and portraiture. His southern
landscapes were particularly influential among younger artists.

CG

Georg Haeselich
(Hamburg 1806–1880 Hamburg)

Haeselich served an apprenticeship under Gerdt Hardorff and
afterwards continued his artistic training in Berlin and Dresden.
During a six-year stay in Munich from 1830 to 1836 he finally
arrived at his richly contrasted style. He was particularly
interested in atmospheric depictions of nature through different
effects of light.

CG

Constantin Hansen
(Rome 1804–1880 Copenhagen)

Constantin Hansen was the son of the portraitist Hans Hansen,
who taught at the Academy of Fine Arts in Copenhagen,
and from 1815 had an official residence there. Hansen began
training as an architect in the Academy in 1816, but gradually
became more interested in painting, although he did not break
off his studies in the School of Architecture until 1825, when he
enrolled in the School of Visual Art. From 1829 he was a pupil
of C. W. Eckersberg. In his early years in Copenhagen
he painted mostly portraits, but by this time he was already
interested in figure painting and in painting inspired by
classical antiquity. In July 1835 he set out on his grand tour, not
returning to Copenhagen until January 1844. He spent most of
this time in Rome, painting a series of Roman views and thus
continuing the kind of studies that Eckersberg had brought
home to Copenhagen after his years in Rome in 1813–16. In
addition, he painted several large-scale figure compositions with
motifs from everyday life in Italy, but always emphasizing the
evidence that remained of classical culture in contemporary
Italian life. Here he gained the qualifications that enabled him,
on his return to Copenhagen, to take part in the embellishment
of recently constructed buildings with motifs inspired by
antiquity; between 1844 and 1853 he collaborated with Georg
Hilker in decorating the large entrance area to Copenhagen
University. During succeeding years, he undertook a great
number of portrait commissions in order to provide for his
large family, but the creation of large-scale figure painting
with motifs from history or mythology remained his dominant
artistic theme.

SM

Carl Hasenpflug
(Berlin 1802–1858 Halberstadt)

After an apprenticeship as a shoemaker with his father,
Hasenpflug became apprenticed to the decorative painter Carl
Gropius, who was closely associated with Schinkel. In 1822 he
gained notice as an architectural painter, and soon concentrated
on accurate renderings of important medieval German
churches. Following Schinkel's example, he also painted pictures
of imaginary cathedrals. Often preservation measures were the
reason for executing exterior and interior views of German
cathedrals. He depicted the cathedrals of Magdeburg and
Halberstadt many times, and in 1828 settled in Halberstadt
where the arts flourished under the local Kunstverein. From
1837 he painted mostly ruins in snow in which he mixed

fantasy with observed details, in order to make the case that his own times could no longer fill these masterpieces of old architecture with life. These often large-scale pictures were very popular and some were sold to America.

HBS

Johann Erdmann Hummel
(Kassel 1769–1852 Berlin)

Hummel entered the academy in Kassel in 1780 and in 1786 became a student of Wilhelm Böttner. In 1792 he received a grant from the Court to go to Rome, where he became affiliated with the circle around Reinhart, Koch, Bury, Carstens and Weinbrenner. He executed landscapes in a rather doctrinaire and theoretical classical style. Due to the French invasion, Hummel was forced to return to Kassel. From there he went to Berlin in 1800 where he initially worked for the theatre. In 1801 he participated in competitions organized by the Friends of Art in Weimar and in 1808 visited Weimar and later Bohemia and Holland. In 1809 he began teaching architecture, perspective and optics at the Berlin Academy, and concentrated on the scientific foundations of painting. This interest led him to make occasional subtle optical experiments in art. As a teacher he had a major impact on the development of architectural painting in Berlin, and he published several manuals. His works were shown at the Berlin Academy until 1842, but he remained true to his classical ideals and died outmoded.

HBS

Just Ulrich Jerndorff
(Copenhagen 1806–1847 Oldenburg)

Jerndorff trained as a landscape painter at the Academy of Fine Arts in Copenhagen from 1823 to 1836, where he also completed training as a conservator. He travelled for several years in Italy with Georg Hilker and Købke, to whom he was extremely close. From 1840 to his death he was the curator and conservator of the ducal Kunstkammer and court painter to the Duke of Oldenburg, where he founded the Kunstverein in 1843.

CG

Jens Juel
(Balslev, Funen 1745–1802 Copenhagen)

Denmark's leading portraitist in the last decades of the eighteenth century, Jens Juel received commissions from the bourgeoisie, the nobility and the royal family. He trained in

Hamburg under the painter Michael Gehrmann in a portrait style that was characterized by a certain realism and inspired by both north German and Dutch painting from the seventeenth and eighteenth centuries. He continued training at the Academy of Fine Arts in Copenhagen from about 1765 until 1771, when he was awarded the prized gold medal. The sophisticated sense of colour of the Swede Carl Gustav Pilo and the portrait style of the Frenchman Louis Tocques were particularly important to him. In the autumn of 1772, Juel was able to embark on a grand tour lasting eight years. It took him through Germany to Italy, with a prolonged stay in Rome, and then to Paris, Switzerland and home via Germany. It was, however, the stay in Switzerland that was of crucial importance to him, since it was there that he became acquainted with Jean-Jacques Rousseau's view of nature and man. Juel himself translated these ideas into practice by sometimes portraying his subjects surrounded by natural scenery, though this was definitely only a decorative framework for his portraits. At the same time, he changed his portraiture style from rather distant rococo portraits to those with greater emphasis on the sitters' human qualities. Juel became a member of the Academy in Copenhagen in 1782, began to teach there in 1784, and became a professor in 1786. In addition to his many portraits, there are also a number of landscapes by Juel, an area in which he became increasingly interested as he grew older. His landscape motifs include romantic mountain scenes and views of specific Danish countryside localities, in addition to the backgrounds for portraits. Juel's landscapes were for many years not valued very highly in the context of Danish art history; however, in recent years, this view has been partly revised. Both as a painter and a person, Jens Juel belonged to the age of absolutism. The realistic character of both his portraits and landscapes, however, points the way forward to the Golden Age, when the bourgeoisie became the dominant social class.

GW

Georg Friedrich Kersting
(Güstrow 1785–1847 Meissen)

From 1805 to 1808, after his first training in Güstrow, Kersting studied at the Academy in Copenhagen. His early style is tentative, striving for individuality in portraiture, landscape and genre painting. In 1809 he was admitted to the freemasons' lodge Phoebus Apollo in Güstrow. He may have arrived in Dresden at the end of that year, where he became acquainted with Friedrich; the two visited the Riesen Mountains together in 1810. He was inspired by Friedrich, and from 1811 acquired fame with his interior paintings, which sometimes included portraits. As a member of the Lützow corps he participated in the War of Independence in 1813/14. From 1815 to 1818 he was art tutor to the Duchess Sapieha in Warsaw and subsequently became head of the painting department at the Meissen porcelain manufactory, where he worked thereafter. Apart from his interiors, he executed portraits, flower pieces, genre scenes and history paintings with a Nazarene touch, all of which add up to a small and uneven oeuvre.

HBS

Friedrich Wilhelm Klose
(Berlin 1804–c. 1874 Berlin)

Like Gaertner and Hasenpflug, Klose was a student of the decorative painter Carl Gropius, who introduced him to architectural painting. He first gained attention in 1824 with a cityscape. In his oil paintings and watercolours he mainly depicted the architecture of Berlin, focusing primarily on its new buildings. He was also active as a chamber painter – a portrayer of private interiors painted in watercolour. In 1828 he went on a study trip to Paris and Italy, but this had little influence on his works. He also painted some pure landscapes. After 1840 he called himself Kloss and earned his living primarily as an art teacher.

HBS

Christen Købke
(Copenhagen 1810–1848 Copenhagen)

Købke was the son of an affluent master baker and was therefore financially well off until his father's death in 1843. He started as a twelve-year-old in the Academy of Fine Arts in Copenhagen; in 1825 he became a pupil of Lorentzen and, after Lorentzen's death, of Eckersberg; he showed himself to be a mature artist in about 1830. Until 1833 he lived with his parents in the Citadel in Copenhagen where he painted his first landscapes; then, until 1845, he lived at his parents' country home on Blegdammen near Lake Sortedam just outside the city. Whereas his early paintings were small and unpretentious, his compositions after 1834 became bigger and more monumental, and his studies and finished paintings often reveal different intentions. He moved away from Eckersberg's sober attitude in several of his pictures, and more Romantic qualities appeared. He spent 1838–40 in Italy, and his 1839 studies from Capri mark his freeing himself as a painter – something which, after his return, could be seen only in his studies of Lake Sortedam. The large compositions with Italian motifs are usually bland and uninspired. He exercised a certain influence on several younger painters, especially Lundbye, Skovgaard and Dreyer, but fell into virtual oblivion after his death.

KM

Johan Thomas Lundbye
(Kalundborg 1818–1848 Bedsted)

Lundbye received instruction at the Academy of Fine Arts in Copenhagen from 1832. He is one of the youngest painters of the Danish Golden Age, and characteristically he was a pupil not of C. W. Eckersberg, but of J. L. Lund, whose art was more influenced by Romanticism. At first he was also a pupil of the animal painter Christian Holm, and made a keen study of animal painting in seventeenth-century Dutch art. But landscape painting came to preoccupy Lundbye, and in this area it is obvious that the art of Christen Købke was of great significance to him. During a period of only about ten years from the end of the 1830s until his untimely death, Lundbye executed a large number of paintings and numerous drawings focusing on the Zealand landscape. He made intense studies of nature, but in his large-scale paintings he did not attempt to re-create the landscape with topographical accuracy. It was more important to him to express the essence of the Danish landscape and, not least, the interplay between the farming community and the countryside. Strongly influenced by the art historian Niels Laurits Høyen, Lundbye believed in the importance of examining the Danish cultural heritage and of deriving inspiration from specifically Danish qualities in landscape and manner of life. Despite opposition from Høyen, he nevertheless undertook a journey to Rome in 1845–46, although this did not provide the liberating experience it had done for so many other artists of the Golden Age. A strong patriot, Lundbye volunteered as a soldier in the war with Prussia in 1848–51, but was killed by a stray bullet before he went into battle.

SM

Ernst Meyer
(Altona 1797–1861 Rome)

Ernst (born Ahron) Meyer, a native of Holstein, went to Copenhagen in 1812, studying at the Academy of Fine Arts until 1819 as the pupil of Lorentzen; he appears also to have been influenced by Eckersberg. He studied in Munich in 1819–24 and was influenced by Peter Cornelius. In 1824 he settled in Rome, where he became a member of the Danish–German circle around Bertel Thorvaldsen. He specialized in portrayals of Italian street life, achieving great popularity with the Danish public and influencing several younger Danish painters with his Italian genre paintings. However, he was also responsible for architectural paintings that show the influence of Eckersberg's Roman views. During summer visits to Olevano he painted a number of landscapes; in these more personal pictures he often shows a keen sense of observation and spontaneity in his choice of motif and manner of painting. Apart from journeys to Germany, Denmark, Sweden and England in 1841–44 and to Germany, France and Switzerland in 1848–52, he lived in Rome until his death.

KM

Christian Morgenstern
(Hamburg 1805–1867 Munich)

As an apprentice from the age of eleven, Morgenstern learned backdrop and panorama painting. After 1824 he studied under Bendixen, who pointed the young artist to Dutch painting. He found the lessons "splendid, because the teacher adhered to the strictest study of nature". The art theoretician and patron Baron C. F. von Rumohr supported him and taught him to work in the open air. In 1826 he toured Norway, where he made many studies in this manner. At the Academy in Copenhagen he was influenced by Eckersberg and Dahl. He switched to the Academy in Munich in 1830, where he assumed control of a group of painters and became famous for his naturalistic portrayal of northern landscapes. Lichtwark called him the "Father of Munich Mood Landscapes" (*Stimmungslandschaften*), which he developed in the 1840s alongside Rottmann. He was devoted to the study of light and worked for a lively depiction of nature. He travelled extensively until the end of his life, in the Alps, Heligoland, Italy, France and Switzerland.

KvO

Ludwig August Most
(Stettin 1807–1883 Stettin)

From 1825 to 1827, interrupted by a stay in Stettin, and from 1829 to 1830 Most studied at the Berlin Academy together with his compatriot Heinrich Lengerich, a painter influenced by the Nazarenes. Berlin architectural paintings made a great impact on Most, and were reflected in several of his Pomeranian vedutas which he exhibited in Berlin in 1828. After 1830 he lived in Dresden where he concentrated on genre painting. In 1834 he returned to Stettin, where he was one of the founders of the Kunstverein and became the leading painter. He painted portraits and genre scenes, especially of Pomeranian peasant life, and the occasional cityscape.

HBS

Jørgen Roed
(Ringsted 1808–1888 Copenhagen)

Jørgen Roed participated in classes at the Academy of Fine Arts from October 1822. He was first a private pupil of the painter Hans Hansen, father of Constantin Hansen with whom he became close friends. After the death of Hans Hansen, he became a pupil of Eckersberg from 1826 until 1833. With his first teacher he had mainly copied Dutch painting from the seventeenth century, but with Eckersberg it was a matter of studying what he himself could see in nature. In the 1830s, Jørgen Roed was among those inspired by the art historian Niels Laurits Høyen to make paintings of medieval and Renaissance buildings to help create a greater awareness of the need for their preservation as part of the cultural heritage. From 1827 to 1841 Roed was in Italy, mostly in Rome where, like several of Eckersberg's other pupils, he painted views of the same Roman localities that his teacher had painted. After his return, Roed undertook increasing numbers of portraits; it was as a portraitist that he became well known and remained in demand from the 1840s for the rest of his long life. But he also painted a number of altarpieces, a skill he developed through an intense study of the art of Raphael; in 1850 and 1851 he was in Dresden to copy Raphael's Sistine Madonna. From 1862 to 1887 he was a professor in the Academy of Fine Arts.

SM

Martinus Rørbye
(Drammen 1803–1848 Copenhagen)

Rørbye was born of Danish parents in Norway, which at that time was part of Denmark. However, when Denmark was obliged to relinquish Norway in 1814, the family returned to Copenhagen. Rørbye entered the Academy of Fine Arts in 1829, becoming a private pupil of Eckersberg from 1825. He became closely associated with Eckersberg and was more or less connected with the Academy until the early 1830s. He undertook a journey around Denmark in 1833, becoming the first artist to visit the most northerly regions near Skagen which, at the end of the century, was to become a meeting place for a large number of artists. In May 1834, Rørbye went to Rome by way of Holland, Paris and Switzerland. In general, he travelled more widely than other contemporary Danish artists. Together with M. G. Bindesbøll, later the architect who designed Thorvaldsens Museum, he visited Turkey and Greece, and for the rest of his life this provided him with material for many paintings with motifs that were quite alien to a Danish public. Rørbye sought the picturesque and exotic in everyday life in the Near East and in Italy, in the same way as before his journey he had painted a number of pictures of everyday life in Copenhagen, reproducing both dress and architecture with great precision. He became a professor at the Academy in Copenhagen in 1844.

SM

Karl Friedrich Schinkel
(Neu Ruppin 1781–1841 Berlin)

An extremely talented and versatile artist, Schinkel was interested in influencing cultural developments in Prussia by all the means at his disposal. Painting was only one of the arts in which he was skilled. He was principally an architect, but his architecture should be seen as being pictorially in harmony with its surroundings. Living in Berlin from 1794, he became a student of the architect David Gilly and his highly gifted son Friedrich, who died prematurely in 1800 and whose unfinished private buildings Schinkel completed. A tour of Italy in 1803–5 took him as far as Sicily and schooled his visual perception of landscape. He returned via Paris. The Napoleonic Wars prevented the continuation of his architectural work for some years. In 1807 he concentrated on diorama paintings in which he particularly tried to show painted architecture in different light conditions to a wide audience. He gave this up in 1815 when he was given the opportunity to design stage sets. At the same time, he was becoming the leading architect in Prussia. His landscape paintings from 1807 to 1821 were executed initially in a strong Romantic, patriotic-didactic style, and then – especially in his cathedral paintings – as designs for the development of culture in which the prototypes of Greek antiquity and the German Middle Ages were evoked. As the result of a journey to Pomerania in 1821 he executed several paintings describing the immediate experience of nature. In 1828 he gave up working for the theatre and, while continuing as an architect, he turned to the depiction of figures in his paintings, which convey ideas through mythology and allegory. More than any other German artist of his time, Schinkel became a central figure in all the arts – his only equals were the great Renaissance masters.

HBS

Julius Schoppe
(Berlin 1795–1868 Berlin)

Schoppe was primarily a portraitist and history painter and only rarely exhibited his landscapes publicly; however, landscape often played an important role in the background of his figurative paintings. He began his initial artistic training in 1810 with the landscape draughtsman Samuel Rösel. In 1816 he was in Vienna, and in 1817 travelled to Rome with Carl Gropius, where he copied several works by Renaissance masters. In 1822 he returned to Berlin. Prior to his journey to Italy he had already been acquainted with Schinkel; the latter engaged him several times to paint murals in royal buildings, including the Berlin Castle, the Schinkel Pavilion across from the Charlottenburg Palace, and the Royal Palais Unter den Linden (now destroyed). In 1825 he became a member and in 1836 a professor of the Berlin Academy. He was most successful as a portrait painter.

HBS

Peter Christian Skovgaard
(Ringsted 1817–1875 Copenhagen)

P. C. Skovgaard first appeared in 1836 in a Charlottenborg exhibition with *Motif from Langebro*; he had been a student at the Academy of Fine Arts for five years, and would continue for nine more. In the Academy he was taught by J. L. Lund and also participated in some of the excursions that C. W. Eckersberg undertook with his pupils. Skovgaard was inspired by the older Dutch landscape art that he had seen in the Royal Gallery of Paintings in Copenhagen. From the early 1840s, Skovgaard was closely associated with J. T. Lundbye. In the summer of 1843, they went together to visit Skovgaard's family in Vejby near the north coast of Zealand, which resulted in a large number of sketches and paintings of the village and the surrounding area by both artists. Together with Lundbye, Christian Dankvart Dreyer and others, Skovgaard belonged to the group of young landscape artists inspired by the art historian N. L. Høyen and the national liberal movement in the country; they wished to bring out characteristically Danish elements in their pictures. And it was Høyen that Skovgaard spent time with in Italy in 1854–55. Another important source of inspiration for Skovgaard and Lundbye was the prominent theologian N. F. S. Grundtvig, who was keen to foster interest in Scandinavian mythology and legends and to promote poetry with a patriotic ring. Skovgaard had his real breakthrough in Charlottenborg between 1843 and 1845. While Lundbye was interested in the open countryside, Skovgaard's preferred motifs included the Danish forests. He painted his most important work, *Beech Forest in May*, at the mansion of Iselingen on Zealand shortly after returning from Italy. An interest in contemporary French art persuaded Skovgaard to travel with Høyen first to England to see the World Fair and then on to France in 1862. He became a professor in the Academy of Fine

Arts in 1860, and a member in 1864. He taught a number of students, including his own sons Joachim and Niels Skovgaard.

GW

Frederik Sødring
(Aalborg 1809–1862 Gentofte)

Sødring was one of the few Danish painters of the early nineteenth century who devoted themselves exclusively to landscape painting. He was born in northern Jutland, but spent most of his childhood in Norway. He entered the Academy of Fine Arts in Copenhagen in 1825, but did not make any close contact with Eckersberg. However, he was indirectly influenced by him through his fellow students, especially his friend Købke. This influence is particularly visible in his early paintings with Danish motifs. He developed an interest in Dahl's art even as a student. He travelled in southern and central Sweden in 1831–32 and went to Norway in both 1833 and 1834. On the latter visit he met Dahl and sailed together with him through the coastal archipelago. His panoramic Norwegian landscapes attest to a strong influence from the Norwegian painter. In 1836 Sødring went on his grand tour, but he progressed no further south than Munich and the surrounding mountains. During his stay in Germany he fell strongly under the influence of the contemporary landscape painters in Munich, especially Carl Rottmann, and he broke with the Eckersberg school's precise reproduction of light, introducing far more adventurous light effects into his landscapes. From then on he mainly painted German motifs, but returned to Norwegian themes in 1848.

KM

Adolph Vollmer
(Hamburg 1806–1875 Hamburg)

Vollmer began his studies under the panorama painter Suhr, but then switched to Rosenberg in Altona. In 1822, he met the patron Baron C. F. von Rumohr and studied open-air painting at his estate. Vollmer and Rumohr had a difference of opinion over the appropriate depiction of nature, with Vollmer giving more weight to a naturalistic reproduction of nature and repeated studies. After a number of visits to the estates of Rumohr's friends, Vollmer went to Hamburg from 1827 until 1831, and then for two years to the Academy in Copenhagen, where he was taught by Eckersberg. Afterwards, he went to Munich and toured the area of Lake Constance, the Tyrol, Italy, France and the Netherlands. He returned to Hamburg in 1839. He painted mostly small canvases and especially the landscape of Holstein and seascapes. He was prevented him from painting after 1866 by blindness.

KvO

Friedrich Wasmann
(Hamburg 1805–1886 Merano)

Wasmann began his studies under the Hamburg painter Soltau. In 1828, he went to the Academy in Dresden, where he continued his training under the Nazarene painter Naeke. There he drew principally on the collection of antique art. After one year he received a scholarship which allowed him to take up study at the Academy in Munich under Schlotthauer and Hess. He quickly made friends with a group of Hamburg artists. In 1830, poor health led him to Meran (Merano) in the Tyrol and then on to Rome. In Rome, he joined the Nazarenes and led a hedonistic life with Koch, Thorvaldsen, Overbeck and Erwin Speckter. But when Janssen arrived in Rome in 1833, Wasmann withdrew from his pleasure-filled life and developed a growing interest in religion, culminating in his conversion to Catholicism in 1835. He made another visit to Munich that year. Four years later, he travelled to Meran and then to Bozen (Bolzano), where he worked as a portraitist. In 1843, he went to Hamburg for the last time; his mother-in-law's objection to Catholicism, as well as the competition to his portraiture from the daguerreotype, made life difficult. He returned via Munich to Meran. Wasmann faded out of artistic memory until the Norwegian painter and collector Bernt Grönvold rediscovered him. He bought works from Wasmann's estate from an antique dealer, and in 1896 published the artist's biography. Grönvold's efforts brought about only a temporary revival of public interest in Wasmann's art. The *Jahrhundertausstellung* (Centennial Exposition) of 1906 in Berlin and an exhibition of his works in the Nationalgalerie in 1912 garnered lasting recognition for his work.

KvO

Wilhelm Bendz (1804–1832)

1

View of Nyhavn, c. 1822

Oil on canvas, 19.1 × 21.5 cm
Den Hirschsprungske Samling, Copenhagen,
catalogue 1982, no. 32

In May 1822 Wilhelm Bendz became a private student of
C. W. Eckersberg in the Academy of Fine Arts in Copenhagen.
As with a number of paintings done by Eckersberg's students
in the 1820s, Charlottenborg, where the Academy was located,
was not only the place where the students were trained but was
itself a world of possible subjects and a place from which they
could see the subjects in the world outside.

Here, Bendz depicts the view from the first floor in the
Academy across the Nyhavn canal towards the north, where a
few ships are moored, and across to the row of houses behind.
The houses rise to all conceivable heights, are of different
colours and are illuminated and shaded differently. It is as
though, forgetting himself, Bendz delights in the variety
which he so meticulously registers in this quite small painting.

The fact that all the details are allowed to live their own
lives and are not necessarily forced into a greater scheme of
composition gives the painting an attractive innocence, indeed
almost naivety, and it appears to be the expression of the young
artist's unprejudiced observation of what he chanced to see early
one morning in Nyhavn. And yet it is, of course, composed, with
the mast of the ship placed almost at the centre of the picture's
vertical axis. The various figures and groups of figures suggest
tiny narrative touches without being emphasized in the manner
of genre paintings. Bendz is still not entirely in control of his
artistic effects. Thus there is undoubtedly a disproportion
between the quite large figures and the dimensions of ships
and houses, which are far too small. One has a feeling of
looking into a doll's house. But Bendz was very young – only
eighteen years old – when he painted this view from the
protecting walls of the Academy looking out across the
Lilliputian city of Copenhagen.

SM

2

A Coach House, Partenkirchen, 1831

Oil on paper mounted on canvas, 33 × 26.5 cm
Signed and dated: "Partenkirch/WB. 18 28/9 31"
Statens Museum for Kunst, Copenhagen, inv. no. SMK 4081

Wilhelm Bendz arrived in Munich on 14 September 1831.
One of the places he had stayed en route was Dresden, where
he had often visited Johan Christian Dahl. Only two days after
arriving in Munich, he set out on a lengthy excursion on foot
in the mountains south of the city, together with Christian
Morgenstern. Among the places they visited was Partenkirchen,
and on 28 September Bendz signed this painting, whose subject
is so anonymous as to be almost abstract. Morgenstern painted
the same coach house from exactly the same spot (cat. no. 91)
and, although it is tempting to imagine that the two men
sat side by side painting on their tour, this was not the case.
Morgenstern had been in Partenkirchen the year before and
his painting of the coach house was sold in January 1831. But
he must undoubtedly have told Bendz about the painting and
the subject, and so Bendz produced his version of it without its
being obvious why just this same scene attracted both of them.
It is not the subject itself that is interesting but, at least in
Bendz's case, the way in which it is painted: the light, the
depiction of space and the mood.

Bendz's conception of the subject is very different from
Morgenstern's. Morgenstern has someone sitting by the table
with a beer mug and a pipe, and he meticulously depicts the
carving in the table legs, the cracks in the walls in the brightly
lit wall outside the gateway, the marks in the plaster of the
vaulting and so on. Bendz simplifies, abstracts, tightens up
the lines and focuses on light, space and size.

This painting is a late work from Bendz's short life. The
following year, only twenty-eight years old, he died of typhoid
fever in Vicenza. But it is fascinating to see how far he had
progressed as an artist in relation to the quite early picture
of part of Nyhavn seen from the window of the Academy
in Copenhagen (cat. no. 1). In that painting, small as it is,
the many details and Bendz's preoccupation with them give
it an almost naive charm and innocence. In the painting from
Partenkirchen he sees the motif as a whole. The depiction of

1

2

light has become Bendz's speciality, and here the light is of such importance that colours must give way. The oil paints are used in the same way as in an Indian ink drawing in shades of sepia, and an enormous variety of shades of brown and yellow fill out the scale between the dazzling whitish yellow light on the wall outside in the street in front of the coach house to the almost impenetrable darkness in the interior where the artist has stood.

Added to the depiction of light is the motif of the vertical divisions. The first opening in the gateway, with its pointed arch, is placed monumentally and symmetrically. The distance between the sides of the frame is divided by the side of the next opening in the gateway, and this again by the side of the gateway on the other side of the street – and then again by a wall or a wooden door and still further into space by more divisions. They seem to continue endlessly. The abstract run of the lines in the vertical divisions emerges as an independent motif, and it draws the viewer's gaze deep into the space of the picture.

Bendz wanted to make clear the importance of rules given by the perspective of line and colour, and in doing so he went far beyond a simple unprejudiced portrayal of what the eye can register and the brush reproduce in the way of individual observations without their necessarily being united into a pictorial whole. In the quiet, taut representation of the gateways in Partenkirchen, the real motif is the underlying skeletal foundation on which to construct visual space and reproduce the intensity of the light in relation to that space. Bendz has been called Eckersberg's obedient pupil, and that we can see here. Eckersberg was himself intensely preoccupied with the abstract and fundamental laws governing visual image.

SM

3

View towards Hoher Göll from Ramsau, 1832

Oil on paper mounted on canvas, 17.3 × 25 cm
Inscribed and dated bottom left: "Hohe Goel Ramsau 17.9.1832"
Private collection

Bendz painted landscapes only occasionally. His ambitions were in the field of figure painting. In Denmark, he made a small number of landscapes, all awkward in their technique and very traditional in their subjects. He does not appear to have been a keen participant in Eckersberg's excursions with his students to the area around Copenhagen. Against this background, it is surprising that during his stay in south Germany in 1831–32, he turned to landscape painting and made a number of oil studies in the open. On 21 September 1832, a few weeks after leaving Munich, he wrote in a letter to his fiancée: "Since leaving, we have had beautiful weather, for which reason I have not written for a long time, as we have made use of every moment to paint from nature. During that time I have painted eight studies, three with snow-covered mountains in the background; it is confoundedly cold in the mornings and evenings to sit painting out in the open, but it doesn't worry me."[1] His travelling companions were the genre painters Joseph Petzl and Thomas Fearnley. Fearnley was doubtless of special significance for Bendz's new interest in landscape painting.

This painting must be one of the three studies with snow-covered mountains in the background that the artist mentions in his letter. It was painted on 17 September 1832 – i.e., four days before the letter was written – in Ramsau, where the three painters stayed for several days eagerly painting. In this case Bendz has tried to capture the impression of the sunlit high mountain contrasting with the lower mountains in shadow.

3

When Bendz turned to painting in the mountains, he could hardly seek inspiration from the paintings of the Danish landscape he had seen before leaving home. On the other hand, Dahl's many Norwegian mountain landscapes, which had been exhibited in Copenhagen, were obvious models for him. But he chose not to follow in Dahl's footsteps. In contrast to the Norwegian painter, he never sought to depict a panoramic view across the mountain landscape before him, nor did he try to capture the character of the entire landscape. Bendz did not climb a mountainside for a broad view of the landscape. On the contrary, he painted his study on the spot where he happened to be on his walk, that is to say on the floor of the valley. It is a relatively sober record of what he could actually see from the place where he was sitting to paint. A year in Munich had not persuaded Bendz to depart from the fundamental principle he had been taught by Eckersberg.

KM

1. See Copenhagen 1996b, p. 225.

Carl Blechen (1798–1840)

4

Tower Ruin with a Dragon, c. 1827

Oil on canvas, 73 × 97.5 cm
Staatliche Museen zu Berlin,
Nationalgalerie, inv. no. NG 673
Rave no. 176

It is, perhaps, its unfinished condition that lends this painting its impression of lightness and spontaneity. It gives this incredible story its power of suggestion and surely reflects the world of theatre for which, from 1824 to 1827, Blechen worked as a stage painter. At that time he also took an interest in the romantic stories of chivalry that could be transformed into the grotesque, the reason why many contemporary critics considered Blechen a humorist.

5

The story spreads over most of the space in the picture and transforms it into a stage set. It is part of the production. There is a large dragon lurking on the massive ruins of a Romanesque circular tower that dominates the left side. The tip of the triangular pediment above the window points directly to the beast above it. It is looking at the rider who, on the right, is sketched with only a few lines and is galloping away enveloped in deep shadow. The spatial tension mirrors that of the story. How will the story end? The rider, coming from the right, is presumably moving with the morning light, which may be interpreted as an indication of victory. It is especially the clear blue sky with only a few cumulus clouds emerging from below that gives the picture a positive air. Later, Blechen frequently painted such immaculate skies, occasionally in an azure blue. Considering that the subject of St George the dragon-slayer, depicted here, was charged with patriotic pathos in the period of the Wars of Independence and thereafter, one cannot fail to see the irony implied by this scene. It can also be found in other works of this period. Formally, this irony is increased by the striking precision of the composition. The evil, which at the same time is the darkness, meets in the shadowy high ground, the dragon's hide-out and the window revealed below. In contrast to this is the ease with which the vivid preparatory pen sketch is executed and over which, as in watercolours, a thin transparent coating of colour is applied.

In 1829 when Blechen saw the exploded shot tower of the castle in Heidelberg, which he later painted, he must certainly have been reminded of this early work.

HBS

5

Boats and Lighthouse near Genoa, 1829

Oil on paper on cardboard, 17.7 × 20.9 cm
Stiftung Archiv der Akademie der Künste, Berlin,
inv. no. Akad. 464, Rave no. 1334

This study is one of the most famous in Blechen's oeuvre. It is not easy to decide whether it was painted from nature or later in his lodgings, but it is in any event a study for a painting.

The famous lighthouse of Genoa was already familiar to the artist. He saw it on his return journey from Italy in October 1829, inserted it from the reverse side in a stage design and also depicted it in a highly dramatic manner in a large-scale seascape. Here, the lighthouse is only a thin bright highlight dividing the picture surface and is nearly same size as the fishing boat's slanting mast in the front, which seems less compact and concrete than the sand around it.

6

The grandeur the lighthouse could have had is not apparent here. Blechen is far more inspired by a piece of insignificant landscape, an area that seems to disintegrate with its slope to the right thus revealing the drama of transition. It is a shapeless terrain continuously disturbed by the sea. It is not easy to determine where it begins as there is no definite border between the mainland and the continuously moving water. Only the dark blue stroke of paint fading to the right can be defined as the open sea and acts as a counterpart to the lighthouse. Similar to the mainland the sky moves upward from left to right. It seems possible to feel the direction of the wind. This small picture is less a composition than a mixture of the elements and colours. It is not structured but dissolves, and it becomes apparent that reality can only be captured moment-arily. This could be the reason for its sketch-like quality.

HBS

6

Wide Valley and Blue Mountains, 1829

Oil on reddish paper, 20.6 × 30.3 cm
Staatliche Museen zu Berlin, Kupferstichkabinett,
inv. no. SZ 271, Rave no. 1484
HAMBURG AND COPENHAGEN ONLY

From a vista on a raised site we experience the visual capacity of the human eye and it is this that arouses our enthusiasm. A seemingly never-ending expanse and countless details are presented and convey a feeling of the power of our senses. This elation gives the painter the strength to persevere and to document the abundance. Blechen transforms this feeling of exaltation into a forceful but carefully considered gesture as well as an intensified colour. Both are his response to the overwhelming reaction of his own spirit to the landscape.

He has only one view of the distance – a plane, in which here and there the band of a broad river and yellowish fields glisten with wooded areas and rows of trees inserted between, and the mountains behind these, all of this set in an azure-blue haze. The blue sky approaches turquoise and the cloud formations are executed in wet white paint and with broad strokes, so that their outlines result in highlighted borders.

The painting's effect is enhanced by the reddish paper which is still visible in the foreground and on the left where the mountains lie in the sun. On those patches of the paper where the brushstroke is light and little colour is used, small parts of the surface remain translucent. These create a swimming in the eye and are perceived as the abundant detail of cultivated land. Probably a region in Italy is depicted.

HBS

7

The Gulf of La Spezia, c. 1830

Oil on paper on cardboard, 22 × 32.5 cm
Stiftung Archiv der Akademie der Künste,
Berlin, inv. no. Akad. 219
Rave no. 1333

Blechen visited La Spezia on his return journey from Italy on 4/5 October 1829. In his strangely somewhat clumsily written account of the journey – done several years later – he mentions: "We went down to the inn, cleaned ourselves and then wandered around a bit, drew a little and when it was getting dark went home . . ." The following day they went on drawing for a while. In this account, however, there is no mention of an oil sketch; only two pencil drawings showing the outlines of the gulf with the Apuanian Alps in the background can be connected to this statement. This oil sketch was probably done later, perhaps in 1830, as a preparatory study for the large painting *The Gulf of La Spezia* (Schloss Charlottenburg, Berlin) with the intention of clarifying the distribution of colour masses. Other comparable studies of this painting exist.

As the evening atmosphere after sunset and the onset of dusk are significant components of the sketch and the painting, it could well be that Blechen's own experience of the landscape

on the evening of 4 October 1829 is reproduced here. The sensation of this picture is the deep blue sea, which gets lighter only on the left where it is touched by the vanishing light. What is churned up on the ground comes to rest in the blue of the sea. The pure element in the distance is the target and the object of longing. From above, the dirty-brown nocturnal clouds spread into the picture. To the left a wide sandy path leads to the plain and down to the coast, accompanied on the right by a dark line of bushes, while on the left there is a single patch of shrubs on a slope. Between the path and the sea Blechen distributed the viscous paint with vigorous, broad brushstrokes and touched the paper only lightly so that almost everywhere the base of the red surface shimmers through as a vibrant remnant of light. In other places, as in the mountains in the background, the paint is applied thickly. One senses the impulse of this creative artist who denies the melancholy of the dwindling day, which is yet so visible in the subsequently executed painting where melancholy culminates in the figure of the shepherd lying on the ground playing the shawm. In 1839, when the painting was exhibited in Berlin and Blechen was already gravely ill, a newspaper review commented: "This picture and perhaps its even more ingenious sketch . . . is apparently still in the possession of the wife of the unhappy artist." The high value put on it is also demonstrated by four contemporary copies.

HBS

8

The Bode Valley in the Harz, 1833

Oil on red-brown paper, 20.8 × 30 cm
Stiftung Archiv der Akademie der Künste,
Berlin, inv. no. Akad. 98
Rave no. 1822

From 12 to 22 September 1833 Blechen travelled in the Harz and made many studies. However, it is doubtful whether this fairly carefully executed oil study, which was apparently painted from nature (suggested by the fixing marks on the sheet), really dates from this trip and depicts the Bode Valley, as the trees are still a luscious green and the image does not resemble the wildness so typical of the real valley. Another element that is missing here and that Blechen expressed in other studies of the Harz is that of the demonic and of danger.

What must have motivated the artist to paint this study was the foreground with its sandy and stony path nestling between large blocks of rock which look like the ruins of an enormous building. The glistening sunlight creates a restless play of dark and light. Heat appears to be reflected and, in contrast, the wooded blue-green mountain slope to the left heralds coldness. Blechen's sensitivity for capturing the notion of temperature in his landscapes can be felt.

The movement leads from the front left, beginning with a small sapling on the slope which acts as a sign of the depth of space and the narrowness of the valley on the right. It is as if the hiker, at the sight of this view, recognized the harmony of this scene and captured it rapidly but precisely. The broad, energetic hatching strokes of the slightly greenish sky give it shape and solidity and at the same time fuse it with the other parts of the landscape. The white clouds seem to echo the large stone on the right and may have been added by the artist to tighten the composition.

HBS

9

Forest Landscape with Waterfall, c. 1833

Oil on paper, 31.1 × 35.5 cm
Signed bottom left (scratched): "Blechen f"
Stiftung Preussische Schlösser und Gärten Berlin-Brandenburg,
Potsdam, inv. no. GK I 30321

This landscape is drawn rather than painted. In the foreground, in the sky and also on the right the structure of the paper is evident and contributes to the vibrating movement that fills the picture. One seems to hear the sound of the water.

Perhaps this study-like painting was done from nature, because it is the atmosphere of a summer's day verging on the autumnal that is captured here with suggestive directness. The latent symmetry and with it nature's physiognomy contribute to this impression, a feature prevalent in some of Blechen's landscapes. Once one sees the two big round stones in the waterfall as eye sockets, the scene deserves a second glance. Below this Blechen has scratched his signature hastily and vigorously in the black colour of a stone, in a seemingly personal gesture.

The landscape does not provide any perspective. It cannot be penetrated and in many places the view ends in the dark. The water is rushing at us and gives the painting its direction from back to front. There is an isolated path and a bridge sketched rapidly in the middle of the picture. Distance can be experienced only in the yellow sky above the waterfall. Pure blue is visible only on the top right, where it lights up and accentuates the corner – often regarded as a crescendo in Blechen's work. The yellow of the sky, however, fuses with the autumn foliage which sparkles and illuminates this area of threatened nature. The painting might be connected with Blechen's trip to the Harz in 1833.

HBS

Hermann Carmiencke (1810–1867)

10

The Alster near Poppenbüttel in the Morning, 1833

Oil on paper mounted on cardboard, 26 × 35.5 cm
Signed and dated lower left: "H.C. 1833 19. Juni
Poppenbüttel. Morgend."
Hamburger Kunsthalle, inv. no. 1148

After returning from Dresden, the twenty-two-year-old artist trekked in the region near his home town of Hamburg, before setting off to the Academy in Copenhagen. He wandered through the valley of the Alster river, where it is still a mere brook and not yet a lake, as in Hamburg. Near the village of Poppenbüttel, he discovered a suitable site for painting

landscape, and although he follows all the traditional rules of *repoussoir* and extending depth, it still appears new and fresh.

Looking at his relaxed brushwork, we can see that Carmiencke was one of J. C. Dahl's students. Tiny brushstrokes, rendering the foliage in the foreground and in the middle, depict the effects of light above all. It is the light of a still early, hazy summer morning, of nature waking to life. The partially overcast sky occupies slightly more than half of the picture plane, and is mirrored in the water of the bay. The variety of greens of the fields, bushes and trees is mixed in only a few places with a reddish ochre. The light becomes clear through the juxtaposition of light and dark spots. There is neither direct sunlight nor its reflection. Carmiencke gives us a picture of nature at dawn.

Even though this study was certainly made for his own pleasure, the artist did inscribe it with his initials. Even more important are the date and place. He scratched both into the wash of wet paint with the brush handle, but he scribbled the time of day, "*Morgend*" (for *Morgen*, morning), and the day, "19", in pencil, giving the picture the character of an eye-witness account.

HRL

11

At Rochsburg Castle in Saxony, 1837

Oil on paper mounted on cardboard, 33 × 30 cm
Signed and dated upper right: "Carmiencke d. 26/6.37"
Hamburger Kunsthalle, inv. no. 5579

Steps lead to an archway, building the frame around the subject of this painting: the front of the St Ann Chapel at Rochsburg Castle located on the Mulde river, near Wechselburg, where Carmiencke taught drawing.

Time and its passing occupy Carmiencke. This is how the chapel looked on 26 June 1837. The painter records the day, even though he knows that a year later the chapel's appearance will not have changed. It is the condition of the building from the past that we see. With quick brushstrokes and extremely differentiated tone and colour, Carmiencke renders what he sees more patchy than linear. He depicts the old plaster, above all that already long ago peeled off on the buttresses; the rough stone, so weathered that its strong form has broken away; the traces of the water running down the tower; here and there sparse vegetation. The red sandstone – used in the window frames, the portals, and the long empty niches above – is a symbol of permanence, barely changed by the passage of time. The Late Gothic, tall, pointed arches of the chapel windows are divided in three by the tracery and closed by mullions, the bull's eye windows have been destroyed in several places, and we cannot see through most of the remaining ones. The loose painting is suggestive, not descriptive.

A peculiarity of this study is that, in spite of the architectonic space, the painter is not interested in the gradation of depth; the space between the top step and the tower cannot be measured. Only the sharp diagonal of the sunbeam and the small piece of mortar illuminated between the pillar and archway give the picture a sense of depth.

HRL

11

Carl Gustav Carus (1789–1869)

12

The Studio Window, 1823/24

Oil on canvas, 28.8 × 20.9 cm
Signed lower left: "C Carus"
Museum für Kunst und Kulturgeschichte, Lübeck,
inv. no. GK 538/1926/231
Prause no. 77

Did any painter before Carus see such a thing and turn it into
a picture? We see nothing more than a small part of his studio,
but yet everything is there: an easel propping up a small
painting, bright daylight shining through the window, and

even the provisional screen over the lower portion of the
window which should direct the light. The screen is nothing
more than a stretched canvas placed over the mullion and
transom of the window. A paintbrush and jar of paint sit on the
windowsill, with two small sliding drawers fastened underneath.
A dark thin rope hangs on the side for raising and lowering the
blinds mounted above the window.

Everything is soberly noted and exactly reproduced, down
to the many nails above the small picture on the easel. Carus
depicts with special care the play of light in the right corner
of the deep window niche, closed off with a basket-handle.
Despite this exactness, there is a tinge of the mysterious, and
we perceive something almost romantic. Not long after this
painting, Carus painted the studio bathed in moonlight (above).
The full moon shines through the blinds and the romantic
atmosphere is more explicit and dominant.

In 1811, Kersting painted his friend Caspar David Friedrich
in his studio (left). The niche of the window resembles the
treatment here, as does the bright light of the blue sky with
the puffy white clouds. When comparing the two pictures, the
absence of the artist in that by Carus is startling.

HRL

Fig. 23. Georg Friedrich Kersting,
Caspar David Friedrich in His Studio,
1811. Hamburger Kunsthalle

13

Boat Trip on the Elbe, 1827

Oil on canvas, 29 × 21 c
Signed and dated lower left: "Carus 1827"
Kunstmuseum im Ehrenhof, Düsseldorf, inv. no. 130
Prause no. 49

From out of the dark of a box-like structure, the view materializes; a pole supports its pediments. It is like looking through a window with pentagonal casements. The structure belongs to a boat, which is being rowed up the Elbe to the centre of Dresden. We see the rower from behind, wearing a billowing white shirt and a light vest; the sunlight accentuates his head and left shoulder. On a bench under a canopy sits a well-dressed young girl with a straw hat. She looks towards Dresden, wrapped in a hazy morning light, and sees the magnificent dome of the Frauenkirche. The two towers on the right side belong to the castle and Hofkirche. The first four of the Augustus Bridge's seventeen arches are just visible.

The perspectival construction of the boat and the roof leads our gaze into the distance, from dark into light. The areas in shadow have been painted freely and transparently, while the lighter areas are more opaque. The blue, partially cloudy sky has been separated distinctly, and the shadowed and illuminated areas in the rest of the picture cross artistically. The viewer takes part in a journey at the beginning of the day.

One would like to call the character of this small picture romantic, meaning full of atmosphere. One does not leave the world of the known and the sheltered, the path does not lead into the unknown. But Carus is both an exact observer and depictor. He is more concerned with light than with the boat and the people, and in particular he is struck by its relation to shadow. This carefully composed painting is essentially determined by the prior awareness of how light determines the appearance of colour.

HRL

14

Bushes near Pillnitz, c. 1830

Oil on paper mounted on cardboard, 23.3 × 29.8 cm
Hamburger Kunsthalle, inv. no. 5557

Maybe it was a wild garden that inspired the painter and natural scientist Carus to prepare paint, grab his brush and head outdoors. Only paint, not ink or pencil, could help him record the sights in the area around his country house in Pillnitz, a small town near Dresden. Only after careful observation does the variety of plants become clear. First we see the twigs and branches on the right edge and the tree-top in front of the grey sky, only then do we notice a bush in the centre and the small tree on the water and field to the side. It could be hops that wrap around the bush on the left and right, and separate the foreground from the background in a large curve. The main branch of a tree that is no longer visible lies to the right. Blue blossoms stretch to the light. Two frogs sit on a tree stump.

Carus was preoccupied with systematically capturing a piece of vegetation close-up. It is a system that the eye discovers while viewing, a system that is defined by light rather than a planned composition. Sunlight hits the variety of plants, sometimes sharp, sometimes diffuse: leaves, blossoms, branches, twines, stalks and the meadow. And there are the areas of darkness, which no light reaches. Carus recognizes this order, this system: the opposition of light and dark, sudden change and gradual transition. Light connects to the colours, creates light and dark greens, cool and warm. What Carus perceives is the change in colour caused by changes in intensity of light, and this he records with quick brushstrokes. He is not satisfied with merely cataloguing nature, instead he tries in painting to distil the eternal from the transience of light.

Carus practised painting nature studies occasionally after Dahl's arrival in Dresden in 1818. He created several studies in oil during his second trip to Italy in 1828. Afterwards, he painted outside, especially during the summers he spent in Pillnitz. We must view this recently discovered study in this context.

HRL

Johan Christian Dahl (1788–1857)

15

View near Præstø, 1816

Oil on canvas, 57.5 × 71 cm
Nasjonalgalleriet, Oslo, inv. no. NG.M. 710

Seeing Dahl's painting of a view near Præstø in southern Zealand with Danish art of the first half of the nineteenth century in mind, one thinks immediately of the close similarities to Johan Thomas Lundbye's landscapes over twenty years later (see cat. nos. 85–87), especially in regard to the detailed depiction of the plants in the foreground and the wide view behind, continuing into infinity. And the lone tree, which is given such a dominant position in the composition that it calls for a symbolic interpretation in addition to being a pure depiction of landscape, brings to mind the paintings of Caspar David Friedrich. It is also impossible not to be reminded of Dutch landscapes from the seventeenth century, where the landscape also forms the background for the painting of an animal, for instance in Paulus Potter's pictures.

All three associations are surely correct. Dahl came to Copenhagen from Bergen in Norway in July 1811 and entered the Academy of Fine Arts. Norway was still part of the twin monarchy of Denmark–Norway, and Copenhagen was its capital. In Copenhagen, Dahl was able to study the seventeenth-century Dutch masters, who were represented in both the royal and private collections; at the same time as he was painting *View near Præstø*, he made a full-scale copy of Jan Both's *Italian Landscape* in the Royal Gallery of Paintings in Copenhagen (now Statens Museum for Kunst), which has striking parallels with his own composition.[1] At the same time, he came with memories from Norway of landscapes that were far grander and more dramatic than that of Zealand, and this must surely have been of significance for his seeing the Danish landscape as more dramatic and romantic than other artists did at this early time in the Danish Golden Age. Only later, in the 1830s, when landscapes had to conform to a growing sense of Danish national identity, as was the case with Johan Thomas Lundbye, did this way of seeing things also become a creed for younger artists, and Dahl was an important source of inspiration to them.

Dahl left Copenhagen in 1818 to embark on a prolonged journey abroad. It was his intention to return after finishing his studies in Germany and Italy; however, he settled for good in Dresden. He undertook several journeys to Denmark and Norway, however, and maintained his connection with artistic life in Copenhagen, partly by showing regularly in the art exhibitions at Charlottenborg.

His final decision to become a landscape painter was taken during his time in Denmark, and he favoured views of southern Zealand most. In the summer of 1816, together with the eminent Danish museum curator Christian Jürgensen Thomsen (the first scholar to divide pre-history into the Stone, Bronze and Iron Ages), he studied the Danish pre-historic stone dolmens of Zealand. He was influenced by Thomsen's desire to preserve the original Danish countryside in art at a time when it was changing on account of more intensive cultivation of the land.

In the painting depicting the area around Præstø – then, as now, a small town – it is remarkable to note with what minute accuracy Dahl was able to represent nature, down to the individual blade of grass, while at the same time the picture extends into infinity. Unusual, too, is the way in which the oak tree in the foreground is cut. It is as though the painting has at least two clearly distinct parts: the limited, detailed portrayal of the tiny world in the foreground, where the whole variety of nature is revealed, and the broad view with the vast sky above. It is impossible not to read some symbolism into this painting, where plants are sprouting and growing afresh both from the stone walls of the ancient past and from the old, knotted and decaying oak tree, testifying to the vitality of the present.

SM

1. Marit Lange, in *"Nature's Way": Romantic Landscapes from Norway*, exh. cat., The Whitworth Art Gallery and Fitzwilliam Museum, Cambridge, 1993, p. 29.

16

Study of Clouds at Full Moon, 1822

Oil on paper mounted on wood, 15.8 × 18.6 cm
Signed and dated bottom left: "1822 JDahl"
Fine Arts Museums of San Francisco,
Magnin Income Fund, acc. no. 1992.128
OTTAWA ONLY

Dahl painted his first studies of clouds in 1820 during his
stay in Italy and continued to pursue this kind of study after
returning to Dresden in July 1821. During the following
years he painted a large number of cloud formations of every
conceivable kind in differing light conditions. In contrast to the
Danish painters, he had a predilection for painting the sky at
sunset or by night. In this study, he has been looking at the sky
one evening when a full moon is partly hidden by a light
covering of cloud. A rocky area with some spruce trees in the

foreground and a ridge in the distance form the framework
around the scene and create depth in the picture.

This painting is quite an unorthodox composition insofar as
both the rocks in the foreground and the moon are in the lower
left half of the picture. Despite this, Dahl manages to create a
balance thanks to the cloud formations. The group of rocks with
fir trees is clearly reminiscent of Friedrich's *View of the Elbe
Valley* from c. 1807 (cat. no. 37), but it is entirely devoid of the
religious symbolism of his friend's picture. A ring can be seen
around the moon, a halo created as the light from the moon is
refracted by the fine droplets of water in the atmosphere – an
unusual phenomenon which nevertheless can be observed in
the sky with some frequency. Dahl's interest in the special effect
of the moonlight must be seen as an extension of his, and his
colleagues', interest in meteorological phenomena. On account
of the uneven cloud cover, however, the circle is broken, and the
halo is almost spiral in shape. While in a corresponding picture,
both Friedrich and Eckersberg would in all probability have

17

attempted to paint a perfect, unbroken circle around the moon – and have waited until the right moment occurred – Dahl has clearly been fascinated by the circle's irregular shape. Here we undoubtedly see an essential difference between Dahl's artistic endeavours and those of his two friends. He was far more open in his studies to the more fortuitous and irregular aspects of nature.

The study is one of Dahl's lesser-known works, and its whereabouts were unknown for a long time. It is possibly identical with a study described as "Moonlight study, a ring of spruce trees to the left in the foreground. Dark sky. Signed 1822 (?) JDahl."[1]

KM

1. See Bang 1987, II, p. 142, cat. no. 398.

17

View of Pillnitz Castle, 1823

Oil on canvas (lined), 70 × 45.5 cm
Signed lower left: "JC Dahl" (initial capitals linked)
Museum Folkwang, Essen, inv. no. 35
Bang no. 420
HAMBURG ONLY

This work radiates magic, since the view from the open window looks so bewildering as to be nothing but sorcery. The backlit room, which is almost dark, appears completely tangible, like *trompe-l'œil*. The view, however, is pushed into the distance and shrunk like a small toy, so that it looks like an apparition, but it is completely sharp and clear.

Strong sunlight from the side accentuates Pillnitz Castle in the distance. The summer residence of the elector August the Strong, located not far from Dresden, was built in 1720–21 by Daniel Pöppelmann. Behind the castle and its park, the Borsberg rises to the left; to the right our view wanders to the bizarre cliffs of Saxon Switzerland. Overhead the almost cloudless sky is bathed in evening light, which has begun with a silvery mist and then slowly passes from violet, then orange to yellow, and finally to blue. The sky is actually the focus of the picture. In the upper part of the window, behind the closed casements, only sky is visible; in the lower part it takes up nearly two-thirds of the picture area.

Our view of the castle moves slowly into the distance, following the path at first, passing by the bush to the Elbe, where we can make out a canoe with a tall construction and several boats being towed. Our eye embarks on this slow movement only after it has long since noticed the castle.

In the panes on the sides of the window, the sky and the land are reflected, joining the room and the view. The window niche, with a basket-handle, is illuminated by the light streaming in. The room, however, lies in darkness. The walls are painted black, which is clearly recognizable under the windowsill, while the side walls of the niche are painted to appear marbled.

The observer assumes that this is the view of Pillnitz Castle as seen from the artist's studio, but it was in fact in Dresden. Dahl transferred his studio into the realm of imagination, in order to create the sensation of the view from his window: released from exact representation in nature, the rational, not fathomable (one might even call it romantic), becomes reality.

HRL

18

View across Green Fields with Church Tower near Meissen, 1828

Oil on paper mounted on canvas, 23 × 28.5 cm
Signed and dated bottom right: "Meissen d. 24 Maÿ 1828. JDahl"
Nasjonalgalleriet, Oslo, inv. no. N.G.M.01681

During a visit to his father-in-law in Meissen at the end of May 1828, Dahl found the opportunity to paint four oil studies in the open air (all dated between 23 and 29 May; the earliest belongs to the Nationalmuseum, Stockholm, the others to Nasjonalgalleriet, Oslo; see Oslo 1988, cat. nos. 110–13). The four paintings differ greatly from each other and demonstrate the range of Dahl's landscape studies. He worked both with open and enclosed landscapes, in both daylight and by night, with linear perspective and aerial perspective. The pictures vary in size and were clearly not intended to serve any common purpose.

The most surprising and original of the four is this study. It presents a wide view across an undulating countryside, but the painter has positioned himself in such a way that the rise in the foreground hides the church – apart from the spire rising up unexpectedly. The painter has clearly been fascinated by the almost unnatural effect of the isolated tower in the midst

18

of the landscape, and the church has completely lost its traditional symbolic significance. The idea for the picture presumably arose spontaneously when the painter was looking out across the landscape and caught sight of the church tower between the hills. Meanwhile, it has been suggested that Dahl might have been inspired by Friedrich's *Hill with Ploughed Field near Dresden* from c. 1824 (Hamburger Kunsthalle).[1] There are admittedly some visual parallels, but Friedrich nevertheless allowed the city's towers and dome silhouetted behind the hill to rise up so high that they give a clear impression of the buildings. The symbolic meaning of the churches here is an essential part of the picture's idea, and the composition seems to be have been worked out to the last detail. In comparison with this, Dahl's lone spire gives the feeling that the painter has made use of a chance opportunity.

Dahl chose to look out with the light against him, the sun just above the edge of the picture. He even avoided shadows in the picture, so that the intensity of the light is created purely on the basis of the colours. As there are no lines leading into the depth of the picture, the effect of perspective is achieved exclusively by means of aerial perspective deriving from the gradual transitions between the shades of colour in the light haze over the landscape.

KM

1. See Torsten Gunnarsson, *Friluftsmåleri före friluftsmåleriet. Oljestudien i nordiskt landskapsmåleri 1800–1850*, Acta Universitatis Upsaliensis. Ars Suetica 12, Uppsala, 1989 (English summary, "Open-Air Sketching in Scandinavia 1800–1850"), p. 197.

19

Study of Clouds, 1830/35

Oil on paper, 15.8 × 25.2 cm
Kunsthalle Bremen, Kupferstichkabinett, inv. no. 65/49

Here Dahl chose a small detail from the mass of clouds in the sky, all the same but always different. Nevertheless, he gave this detail a closed shape, by alluding to a mountain peak with a few brushstrokes in clear blue, creating a sort of base, and by letting the cluster of clouds thin out to the right side. Two forms are clearly emphasized in the variety of clouds, which Luke Howard certainly would have described as cumulus; Dahl would have read Goethe's essay of 1820, "Wolkengestalt nach Howard [Cloud forms according to Howard]". The lower cumulus is illuminated with sunshine at the top, where the clouds converge. From the perspective of the viewer, the cumulus above is dark, and is illuminated only on the right edges, where it protrudes pointedly.

When Dahl painted this study, he had only a few colours on his palette, perhaps blue, white, black and yellow. The connection between white and pale violet is decisive. Dahl painted a picture without strong contrasts, as if that was what was special in this cloud formation: it is completely different from his *Cloud Study over the Elbe* with poplars of 1832 (cat. no. 20), which is totally structured by extreme contrasts. He painted quickly, in order to capture the changing clouds in their shape, in several places with a very fine brush, mostly in horizontal or slanting strokes, using the turning movement of the bristles.

In Marie Lødrup Bang's catalogue raisonné (1987), she lists more than fifty undated cloud studies (to which we can add this one, a study from the print collection in Bremen which apparently escaped her attention). The earliest known cloud study by Dahl is of clouds only, without landscape, and is dated 1820. From his early years in Dresden such studies are rare, but after 1829 they become more frequent. This picture comes very close to studies from 1831, 1832 and 1834 (Bang nos. 678, 710, 747) in Dahl's preoccupation with the appearance of mountains of clouds. This speaks in favour of dating this work to that period. Dahl painted his last dated study of clouds in 1847.

HRL

20

Cloud Study over the Elbe, 1832

Oil on board, 21.5 × 26 cm
Nasjonalgalleriet, Oslo, inv. no. N.G.M. 01530

Dahl, born in Norway, spent the period 1811–18 in Denmark, and then settled in Dresden for the rest of his life. Here he made a large number of varied studies of the city and the surrounding area. They consisted both of city views and evocative romantic landscapes. The Elbe, which runs through Dresden, was a favoured subject, and he often portrayed it from different angles. In this study of clouds over the Elbe in the light of evening, Dahl might have been standing on or near Brühl's Terrace with his back to the city looking out across the river, as the poplars on the left of the picture correspond to those seen in Brühl's *Terrace by Moonlight* painted two years earlier.[1]

In this pastoral painting, the Elbe is indicated only as a lighter horizontal line breaking the dark foreground. Above it, a golden glow from the sun forms the transition to the great, greyish blue cloud formations that give the scene a dramatic dimension. The poplars, depicted as long black poles to the left, help to underline the drama. Dahl's interest in clouds can be traced back to his years in Denmark, but it was reinforced in Dresden, where from the house he purchased in 1823 he had a view of the Elbe and a wide area of sky. In addition to the prominent space often given to clouds and sky in many of Dahl's pictures, he also painted independent studies of clouds, which at times were almost abstract in character. Clouds are an element often emphasized in Romantic landscapes and they were eagerly discussed in Dresden at this time.

GW

1. See Bang 1987, II, cat. no. 657.

21

Two Copenhagen Steeples
in the Evening Light, 1837

Oil on paper mounted on canvas, 11.5 × 15.2 cm
Hamburger Kunsthalle, inv. no. 1061
Bang No. 1233

From Copenhagen one sees only two steeples and a rooftop, next
to the pointed spire of St Peter's, the neoclassical Frauenkirche,
completed in 1829. Dahl's attention centred on the change of
colour of the thin clouds in the fading evening light between
the reddish yellow below and the light blue above. The almost
orange clouds are coloured by the light of the setting sun, while
those in shadow are grey. Dahl applied the colour, which he
mixed on the palette, in differing intensities, which was enough
to change tone. In many places, he applied the grey paint
thinly over the orange; and in one place, on the left, some blue
brushstrokes have been put on the grey.

The clouds float gently upwards. Although paint gives them
a concrete shape, they still appear to be in motion. This is the
result of Dahl's sketch-like style of painting, which placed them
on the light background. In noting the shape of the two towers,
Dahl used the same technique inside the closed form.

The selection of this view might have been determined by
the contrast between concrete and continually changing colours,
which are dark and light, cold and warm. The manifold
character of both buildings – one pointed, thin, dark; the other
short, stout and lit due to the bluish and reddish reflections
of light – must have inspired him, too. This study can be dated
to 1837, the only time during the 1830s that Dahl visited
Copenhagen for a longer stay.

HRL

Ludwig Deppe (active c. 1820)

22

Houses on the Mühlengraben in Berlin, c. 1820

Oil on canvas, 45.5 × 56 cm
Signed bottom left: "Ludw. De . . ."
Stiftung Preussische Schlösser und Gärten
Berlin-Brandenburg, Potsdam, inv. no. GK I 7891

When this painting was shown at the exhibition of the Berlin Academy in 1820 a reviewer criticized its very accuracy: "no one can be blamed if he were to wish that the painter should have turned his eye to a more pleasurable scene, rather than depicting, with precision, the crooked beams of the back of this house, the passages in which the washing is hanging, and other details." Indeed, it was quite unusual for this city, which was beginning to prosper after the Wars of Independence and was proud of its new architectural projects, to depict the back of a row of houses, generally not shown. It has been discovered to be the house of a merchant's widow named Deppe, probably the artist's mother, who lived in a house at 2 Brüderstrasse, and it is from this courtyard that the scene could have been painted. The artist, known only as the "Private Secretary of Prince August of Prussia", probably chose this view because he could paint the scene in detail from his window without being disturbed.

He has dispensed with people. Signs of life are visible only in the traces it has left on inanimate objects, such as the hanging washing and the vegetable refuse strewn at the front of the picture. The dilapidated buildings, however, have artistic appeal, such as in the grey colour of the weathered wood. A calm reminiscent of a still life dominates this picture. Surprisingly, it forgoes the atmospheric glorification of simple living conditions and dilapidation, and impresses with a poetic sobriety. This is especially apparent in the crystal-clear blue sky, whose pure, evenly painted hue contrasts with the multiple colour-tones of the houses.

HBS

Christian Dankvart Dreyer (1816–1852)

23

Foreground Study with Docks, 1840s (?)

Oil on board, 20 × 29.5 cm
Statens Museum for Kunst, Copenhagen, inv. no. 6780

Dankvart Dreyer has here made a close study of docks. In this picture, probably representing the edge of a ditch, the plant is surrounded by others, and its elongated leaves fall out to the sides. The picture is probably a sketch for a larger composition that may never have been completed. It cannot be ascertained where it was painted, as docks are found in many parts of Denmark. This is no coincidence: Dankvart Dreyer, like other artists including Lundbye and Skovgaard, belonged to the group of young landscape painters who were fired by nationalistic romantic ideals and sought to portray things typically Danish in their pictures. Dankvart Dreyer painted in many different parts of the country and did not limit himself simply to Zealand, the region preferred by most landscape artists. He was thus the first painter to go to Jutland to commit to canvas his impressions of this part of the country.

GW

C. W. Eckersberg (1783–1857)

24

Landscape with a Stile, Møn, 1810

Oil on canvas, 58 × 74 cm
Statens Museum for Kunst, Copenhagen, inv. no. SMK7694

In 1809, Eckersberg received a commission for a series of landscapes on the island of Møn from Christopher von Bülow, owner of the mansion of Nordfeld on the island. His subjects ranged from views of the mansion's garden to scenes from the surrounding landscape looking towards the most striking sight on the island and the great chalk cliffs overlooking the Baltic. During a visit in July, Eckersberg drew a number of studies for the paintings which he made the following winter. The paintings were thus all done in his studio on the basis of drawings and memory, and this is clearly reflected in the finished pictures. There is a noticeable disparity between the observed subject and the form it finally took in the paintings, and the sharpness of detail and the clarity of light later characteristic of his art are lacking. In an artistic sense, we notice especially the influence of Jens Juel, whom Eckersberg did not manage to meet before Juel's death in 1802, but whose paintings he had seen in Copenhagen.

One painting is clearly distinguishable from the rest, and that is the landscape in the light of the setting sun. The basis for this picture was a drawing made on the spot in July 1809 (Statens Museum for Kunst).[1] The artist adhered closely to the composition of the drawing, but the most important element in the painting, the dying tree, was clearly added after the drawing was largely finished – a not unimportant adjustment to the composition. So the tree was not observed on the spot together with the rest of the scene. The shadows in the drawing show that it was done in broad daylight, which means that the sunset sky in the painting was also created in the studio, though doubtless on the basis of observations made in the countryside.

Both the tree and the composition are indebted to Juel's painting *Landscape by Lake Geneva*, which Eckersberg had seen at the home of the copperplate engraver J. F. Clemens in Copenhagen. This picture was obviously also a source of inspiration for Caspar David Friedrich.[2] Eckersberg's painting is one of his few youthful works showing a patent similarity to the German painter, and it suggests the completely different direction that Eckersberg's art could have taken if he had gone to Dresden instead of Paris in 1810.

Altogether, Eckersberg produced twelve paintings for von Bülow, most of them still in private collections, apart from this one and another in the Statens Museum for Kunst and one in the David Collection in Copenhagen. In addition, he made a couple of other paintings on Møn, which are variants of the pictures painted for von Bülow.

KM

1. See Copenhagen 1983b, cat. no. 28.
2. See Copenhagen 1991, pp. 23 ff., 122, cat. no. 56.

25

St Peter's Square, 1813–16

Oil on canvas, 31.4 × 26.8 cm
Thorvaldsens Museum, Copenhagen, inv. no. B 214

Eckersberg has depicted St Peter's Square in Rome from an unusual angle, from the space between two columns in Bernini's colonnade. From here, he could see both the obelisk and the two fountains, while St Peter's Cathedral is out of view on the right. The enormous size of the square is rendered optically by the difference between the huge columns in the foreground and sections of the colonnade closing the picture at the back. The figures in the scene, including the woman seated with her back to us and holding a child in her arms, the man in the centre of the square and the two women quietly moving towards the centre of the picture, are decorative figures helping to indicate depth.

The picture itself is so meticulously painted that it is possible to distinguish even small details in the stones and columns in the foreground. As is characteristic of many of Eckersberg's other pictures of Rome, a relatively large area of the foreground is open, creating a sense of space in the part of the composition unfolding in the square itself. This principle, together with the painting's mixture of linear and aerial perspective, might well have been inspired by Pierre-Henri de Valenciennes' book *Eléments de perspective pratique . . .* (1799–1800), which was particularly popular among landscape artists at this time. Eckersberg could have come across the book

24

in Paris or seen it in Rome, where Thorvaldsen, in whose house he lived, had owned a German edition since 1803.[1]

Eckersberg made three identical paintings of this scene. One example, which he himself owned, is now in the David Collection in Copenhagen. The second, which originally belonged to Eckersberg's patron Johan Bülow, is now in the Ordrupgaard Collection just outside Copenhagen. This is the third, which Thorvaldsen acquired in Rome. Eckersberg painted these views for his own amusement during his stay in Rome in 1813–16, in the intervals between the more ambitious historical paintings he was most concerned with at the time. On 9 May 1814, he noted in his diary: "A paint box to carry with a rinsing trough – and fresh frame for a camp stool and two small stretchers."[2] Purchasing equipment to work in the open was unusual at the time. He probably worked according to the following method. The composition was sketched facing the scene. At home, the study was transferred to canvas and the most important colours applied. When the paint was dry, the picture was finished in the open, where it was possible to correct shapes and colours while directly facing the scene.[3]

As a result of his keen observations of nature, Eckersberg's views of Rome are almost photographic reproductions of what he saw, but at the same time the impression they give is one of amazing freshness and immediacy. Paintings based on on-the-spot studies were something new and epoch-making in Danish art at the time. The value of careful firsthand study was something Eckersberg instilled in his pupils after being appointed professor at the Academy in Copenhagen in 1818. The consequences were far-reaching for generations of Danish painters.

GW

1. Dyveke Helsted, "De romerske prospekter", *Eckersberg i Rom*, Copenhagen, 1983, p. 56 and n. 12.
2. "Eckersbergs dagbog 1813–1816", ibid., p. 18.
3. Hans Edvard Nørregård-Nielsen, *Meddelelser fra Ny Carlsberg Glyptotek*, 1982, pp. 15–31.

25

26

View of the Garden of the Villa Borghese, 1814

Oil on canvas, 28 × 32.5 cm
Statens Museum for Kunst, Copenhagen, inv. no. 1310

The Villa Borghese in Rome was a favourite destination for
Danish artists, painters and authors visiting Rome in the
nineteenth century. It was also common for them to live near
the district around the Spanish Steps. During the last decades
of the eighteenth century, the strictly symmetrically laid-out
garden dating from the beginning of the seventeenth century
had been transformed into a romantic garden modelled on the
English landscape style. Buildings, sarcophagi and obelisks
inspired by Classical art were now placed suitably around
the park.

The aqueduct carrying water from Acqua Felice across
the bridge and on to the lakes and many fountains in the park
was an example of a building inspired by antiquity. The right-
angled building complex seen in Eckersberg's picture consisted
of a wall running parallel to the road, decorated with a relief
surrounded by sculptures and pilasters and in addition a bridge
borne on fluted Doric columns. The aqueduct, which was
connected to the Casino de Muro Torto, had probably looked
like this since a thorough renovation in 1776–78.[1] The bridge
across the road was decorated with the inscription: "NE QVEM
MITISS(IMUS) AMNIS IMPEDIAT [So that the constant stream shall
not hinder anyone]". It was destroyed during a bombardment
of the garden of the Villa Borghese in 1849; the remainder,
the wall on the left, still stands, not far from the Piazzale delle
Canestre. Eckersberg also made a drawing of the aqueduct,
though this does not include as many details as the painting;

27

it is squared, which means that it was a working drawing probably done immediately before the painting and used to transfer the scene to canvas.

The strong Roman light characteristic of Eckersberg's views of Rome from 1813–16 is seen again here. The distinction between the sun-drenched right side of the picture and the shaded left is marked by a striking diagonal forming part of the network of perspective lines, all with a common vanishing point behind the column on the left. However, the light has not deprived the trees of their colour and luxuriance. On the contrary, the building is framed in pure green branches and flowering bushes.

There has been some discussion of the time of year at which this was painted. For many years it was thought to be May, on account of the identification in 1918 of the flower above the gate as a Paulownia.[2] This has been refuted, partly because the Paulownia flowers before or at the same time as the leaves come out, and partly because its flowers are deep blue and not yellow as in the picture. The flower is probably a Catalpa speciosa, which flowers in Rome in July and August,[3] suggesting that the painting was most likely done a couple of months later than at first believed.

GW

1. Bjarne Jørnæs, *Eckersberg in Rome*, Copenhagen, 1983, p. 100.
2. M. Galschiøt, "Eckersbergs Romeraar", *Kunstmuseeets Aarsskrift*, 1919, p. 49.
3. Erik Fischer, *Tegninger af C. W. Eckersberg*, Copenhagen, 1983, p. 168.

27

Building in the Roman Campagna, 1815

Oil on canvas, 27.5 × 31.5 cm
Statens Museum for Kunst, Copenhagen, inv. no. 720

Eckersberg referred to this picture of a building in the Roman Campagna in a diary entry of 25 March 1815: "Painted a small factory outside Ponte Molle by the Tiber."[1] This idiosyncratic construction consisting of a circular tower and adjacent rectangular buildings on various levels was not a factory in the modern sense: Eckersberg was using it in the sense of building. To judge by the woman shaking something or other over the balcony on the left of the picture, it was used as residential housing.

In his sketchbook (now in the Royal Norwegian Society of Science and Letters, Trondheim), Thorvaldsen made a drawing of the same small tower-adorned building on the slope. It is seen here at a rather greater distance and is moved slightly further towards the left so that the scene is framed at the back by the mountains. At the same time, Thorvaldsen's drawing of the building provides us with further information, as he has noted the following on it: "Cylindrical tower with buildings alongside, in the foreground river and road. In the background mountains. Tor di Quinto Lazzaroni and the Tiber." The Tor di Quinto Lazzaroni can be identified as the present-day Viale Tor di Quinto no. 58.[2]

It is scarcely a coincidence that Eckersberg has determined the position of the building as "outside Ponte Molle", that is to say the bridge over the Tiber crossing the Via Flaminia a little to the north of Rome. This place had a quite special significance for northern European artists: it was here that they were received by their colleagues on arriving in Rome, and were given what they called the Order of Bojacco as a welcoming gift. When they left Rome again to travel north, artists would often be accompanied as far as Ponte Molle.

GW

1. *Meddelelser fra Thorvaldsens Museum*, Copenhagen, 1973, p. 30.
2. Dyveke Helsted, *Meddelelser fra Thorvaldsens Museum*, 1965, p. 38.

28

View towards Nyholm, with a Crane and Warships, 1826

Oil on canvas, 19.6 × 32.4 cm
Signed and dated bottom left: "E. 1826"
Den Hirschsprungske Samling, Copenhagen, catalogue 1982, no. 103

Eckersberg found the motif for this painting only a few hundred metres away from the Academy, at Charlottenborg, where he lived and worked. From Larsen's Yard in Copenhagen, he has looked out across the docks towards Nyholm, where a number of warships are lying at anchor without sails. On the overgrown space behind the Amalienborg Palaces, we see some abandoned anchors, planks and mounds of earth. There is nothing spectacular or striking about the subject, and Eckersberg is following the advice he always gave to his

28

students that they should paint anything they came across. The exhortations he made in his teaching are probably the same as those he sent in 1821 to his son Erling, who had embarked on a grand tour: the solicitous father reminded his son that he had promised "to draw something from nature, no matter what — farms, churches, castles, trees or plants or animals, in brief, whatever there is."[1]

This unostentatious picture reflects one essential aspect of Eckersberg's art — the small study reproducing the selected subject without any particular compositional arrangement or change in detail. In contrast to this were the large-scale paintings, in which he more or less reconstructed the subjects as they would have looked under ideal conditions. In the first type, the actual motifs seem only to have played a limited role for him, whereas in the latter they were of crucial importance.

A study like this doubtless reflects the fact that Eckersberg had developed his method of working after returning from his travels abroad in 1816. In his city views of Rome he had introduced Danish *plein air* painting in his oil studies, though only in the sense that after the preliminary drawing he continued working mostly in his studio; he would then finally finish the picture on the spot, enabling him to paint the details on the basis of fresh impressions of the light and weather conditions. On the other hand, this picture could very well have been painted outdoors from start to finish. Although it is a study from nature, the picture is — true to Eckersberg's style — meticulously done. Roughly painted oil sketches done with a light, flowing use of the brush are scarcely otherwise known in Danish art.

Some years later, in 1838, Eckersberg again turned to Larsen's Yard in order to work. This time he chose to draw, making the abandoned anchors his principal subject (Statens Museum for Kunst)[2] — the composition is tightly knit and is characterized by a strict geometrical construction.

KM

1. Quoted in Emil Hannover, *C. W. Eckersberg*, Copenhagen, 1898.
2. See Erik Fischer in Copenhagen 1983b, cat. no. 137.

29

Study of Clouds over the Sea, 1826 (?)

Oil on canvas, 19.8 × 30.8 cm
Statens Museum for Kunst, Copenhagen, inv. no. SMK6433

After returning from Rome in 1816, Eckersberg had only very limited contact with foreign art. He no longer sought artistic inspiration outside Denmark. But he was nevertheless in contact with contemporary German painting to a certain extent thanks to his friendship with the Norwegian artist J. C. Dahl, who regularly spent time in Copenhagen on his way from Dresden to Norway. It might have been Dahl who in 1826 motivated Eckersberg to take a greater interest in weather conditions than he had done hitherto. Eckersberg started keeping a special meteorological diary, and he made several drawn and painted studies of cloud formations. The two painters had met on various occasions during Dahl's visit to Copenhagen in the spring. From the Norwegian painter he undoubtedly heard of the eagerness with which artists and art theorists in Dresden were applying themselves to the atmosphere, clouds and skies. Eckersberg also studied the recently published treatise by the scientist J. F. Schouw, *Skildring af Vejrligets Tilstand i Danmark* [A Study of the Weather Conditions in Denmark] (written as a submission for a prize competition in 1823, published 1826); it followed the classification of clouds developed by Luke Howard (and Goethe). In his study *Linearperspektiven* [Linear Perspectives] of 1841, Eckersberg directly referred to Schouw's work. Eckersberg consistently kept a meteorological diary from 30 June 1826 to 6 March 1851.

Eckersberg's first studies of clouds – two drawings – are dated 13 August 1826 (Statens Museum for Kunst), and according to his diary he then painted some "sketches of air and clouds" on 1, 3, 4 and 7 September that year. This study might have been made at that time. It shows some cloud formations over the sea and might have been intended as a study for a seascape. It lacks the dramatic devices found in cloud studies by Constable, Dahl and Købke, but is thoroughly worked out (except for the sea) and endowed with a classical balance.

KM

30

The Russian Ship of the Line "Asow" and a Frigate at Anchor in the Elsinore Roads, 1828

Oil on canvas, 63 × 51 cm
Signed and dated bottom right: "E.1828"
Statens Museum for Kunst, Copenhagen, inv. no. SMK608

When Eckersberg returned home from Rome in 1816, he made a brief stop in Dresden and visited Caspar David Friedrich. In all probability he had the opportunity to see one of Friedrich's most recent works, *View of a Harbour* (Potsdam). At that time the Dane had not painted seascapes for several years, but when, twelve years later, he set about painting a Russian man-of-war, Friedrich's picture might well have served as a source of inspiration to him in the actual choice of subject and the monumental depiction of the ships.

Eckersberg has produced an accurate portrayal of a Russian ship of the line, anchored close to a frigate in the sound off Elsinore. Taking great care, he has given an account of all the details in the ships and ensured that they have the right proportions in relation to each other. He has also captured the weather in details – from the rain clouds gathering over Sweden on the right, to the small patches of foam capping the waves. We are given the impression that the painting is the work of someone who has experienced the scene at close quarters on the day in question. But this was not the case. The picture shows not one specific episode, but has been pieced together from observations Eckersberg made on three different occasions, even in different places.

Eckersberg certainly saw some Russian ships off Elsinore one day in 1826, but at a great distance. Not until the following year did he have the opportunity to study Russian ships of the line at close quarters, and that was not at Elsinore, but in the Copenhagen roads. He even had the opportunity of going aboard one of them, the admiral's ship *Azob* (which he called "Asow"). However, it was not until the summer of 1828 that he started on this painting, after a Russian naval visit.[1] He went about things thoroughly: he borrowed constructional drawings of ships of the line in the naval dockyard in Copenhagen so as to be sure that his picture was correct, and he carefully worked out how the ships would float in the water. He also made use of his meteorological diary, where he kept daily records of the weather. First he made a detailed constructional drawing, and finally he set about the painting itself. It took him four months to finish it. Eckersberg did not depict what he had actually seen,

but what he would have seen if he had been out in the sound observing the ships concerned.

This painting is one of many seascapes Eckersberg made after he seriously set about marine painting in 1821, when he made a nocturnal scene near the island of Saltholm (Nivaagaard Collection), presumably under the influence of a moonlit coast done by Friedrich (location unknown), which the Danish Prince Christian Frederik (later Christian VIII) then owned and allowed to be exhibited that year.[2] Marine painting gradually came to replace landscapes for him and, in his later years, the 1830s and 1840s, this type of picture was what he preferred to any other.

KM

1. See Erik Fischer in Copenhagen 1983b, p. 183 ff.
2. See Kasper Monrad in Copenhagen 1991, pp. 81 ff., 150 ff.

A View towards the Swedish Coast from the Ramparts of Kronborg Castle, 1829

Oil on canvas, 47 × 66 cm
Statens Museum for Kunst, Copenhagen, inv. no. 3241

When he painted this picture, Eckersberg was standing on the ramparts close to Kronborg Castle in Elsinore looking across towards the Swedish coast. Here, where the sound narrows, Denmark and Sweden are quite close to each other. From his viewpoint, Eckersberg could see life unfolding at the foot of the mighty Renaissance castle, both in the figures of two maids, one of whom is shaking out some clothes, and a large number of uniformed military figures keeping guard on this fortress whose strategical importance is also emphasized by the Danish flag. In addition, Eckersberg had an eye on the sea, where a large naval vessel is surrounded by several smaller ships.

We can follow Eckersberg's work on this picture quite closely, as he writes in his diary on 29 September 1826: "Began painting the flag station at Kronborg." The next reference to the picture is on 18 December 1828, when he writes: "Started putting the finishing touches to the painting of the view of Kronborg and the flag station which I began a couple of years ago." And finally, on 14 January 1829, he notes: "Finished a painting of the view from the ramparts of Kronborg across the flag station, the sound and the Swedish coast."[1]

Eckersberg was very interested in ships throughout most of his life. Consequently, alongside his portraits, landscapes and other paintings, he did a relatively large number of marine

30

31

paintings. His first attempt at the genre was a watercolour from
1804, which was used as the basis for a print in N. Truslaw's
book *En samling af skibe i næsten alle mulige stillinger i Søen* [A
Collection of Ships in almost every Conceivable Position at Sea].
Dutch seascapes provided the pattern for Eckersberg's pictures.
He also made a keen study of the actual ships and derived
inspiration from various prints of naval vessels.[2]

GW

1. Emil Hannover, *C. W. Eckersberg*, Copenhagen, 1898, no.
   409.
2. Henrik Bramsen, *Om C. W. Eckersberg og hans Mariner*,
   Copenhagen, 1972, pp. 8–9.

32

Renbjærg Tileworks near Flensborg Fjord, 1830

Oil on canvas, 22.5 × 32.5 cm
Statens Museum for Kunst, Copenhagen, inv. no. 1350

Eckersberg painted only a small number of true landscapes,
and most of them date from his early years, before he became a
professor at the Academy in Copenhagen in 1818. In about 1828,
he began to take an interest in the sea and in large schooners,
which he carefully analysed with brush and canvas in a large
number of seascapes. This is one of the few landscapes he
painted in later life, in which he combined his studies of
landscape and sea.

   The tileworks can be seen from a distance, surrounded by
fields on one side and the fjord on the other. They were on the
eastern part of the Broager peninsula, about three kilometres
south-east of Gråsten and thus very close to what was then the

32

border with Germany. Eckersberg painted the picture on one of his very few visits to the region where he grew up; according to his biographer Emil Hannover, he visited a brother in Nybøl, his elderly mother in Blans and good friends in Flensborg and the surrounding area.[1]

Eckersberg painted the picture of Renbjærg Tileworks standing in front of it, as can be seen from his diary entry for 31 May 1830: "Spent this day very pleasantly at Renneberg. During the morning painted a view of the tileworks. There was something of a south-westerly gale . . . which produced a few showers." On the following day, 1 June 1830, he notes briefly: "Worked a little more on the sketch begun yesterday." And finally, on 2 June, he says: "Worked on and finished the little presentation of Renneberg Tileworks."[2] Although painted in the open, according to Emil Hannover, the picture was finished in three days at home.[3]

The tileworks are viewed from an aerial perspective at a distance estimated at 500 metres.[4] A large area of foreground provides space for the middle distance with the tileworks'

cluster of roofs, which are almost cubic in shape, calling to mind early cubism after the turn of the following century. Finally, a thin strip of land finishes off the low horizon in the background.

Eckersberg's use of complementary colours – the red roofs of the tileworks against the grass-covered landscape and the blue of the sea against the yellow shade of the sand dunes – clearly separates the elements making up the landscape. The red roofs of the tileworks surrounded by foaming waves in the left half of the picture also provide a balance both in composition and colour to the relatively uniform green right half.

GW

1. Emil Hannover, *C. W. Eckersberg*, Copenhagen, 1898, p. 273.
2. Niels Winkel, *Naturstudiet i C. W. Eckersbergs marinemaleri*, Copenhagen, 1976, p. 125.
3. Emil Hannover, op. cit., p. 273.
4. Niels Winkel, op. cit., pp. 125–27.

33

The Starboard Battery and Deck
on the Corvette "Najaden", 1833

Oil on canvas, 22.5 × 22.5 cm
Originally signed and dated bottom right: "E 1833"
Statens Museum for Kunst, Copenhagen, inv. no. 2060

In July 1833, Eckersberg sailed in Danish waters on board the
corvette *Najaden*, and during this expedition he began this
painting of a section of the ship's deck. Not until a few weeks
later, 15 August, did he again turn to the picture, working on
it every day for the following week until he finished it on
22 August, as is seen from his diary: "Worked on and finished
a small painting, begun on board, portraying the corvette
Najaden's starboard and deck." The painting is quite small
(perhaps because Eckersberg needed to keep it in his painter's
box while on board the ship). But the diary entries document
that at no time was it intended as a study. The meticulous work,
which went on for several days, meant that each layer of paint
was able to dry before the next was applied.

This painting can be grouped with Eckersberg's large
number of seascapes; however, the area covered is unusually
limited. To a superficial view there are striking parallels
between this and Friedrich's *On the Sailboat* (cat. no. 41): both
works show a section of a ship's deck, and both allow the mast,
the sails and the rigging to play a central role in the overall
picture. This said, the differences are more striking: to Friedrich
the ship represents the framework around the actual theme of a

journey towards the distant city (which might symbolize the
newlywed couple's life together or perhaps eternal life in the
hereafter). But for Eckersberg, the ship itself is the central
feature. It doubtless also had a symbolic significance for the
Danish painter, but for him it was an expression of a superior,
divine order. All the details serve a purpose and a related overall
scheme. Eckersberg was also intensely fascinated by the visual
interplay of so many lines created by the straight lines of the
ropes and masts and the taut curves of the sails – an apparent
chaos, which is nevertheless clearly structured and has a
meaning.

There are scarcely any other paintings by Eckersberg
in which the geometrical construction is so precise and so
consistently executed. On the other hand, the picture points the
way forward to some drawings he made a few years later, with
a similar abstract effect; this is most striking in one of his best
known drawings, *Ships' Anchors at Larsen's Yard in Copenhagen*
from 1838 (Statens Museum for Kunst).[1]

KM

1. See Copenhagen 1983b, cat. no. 137.

Friedrich August Elsasser (1810–1845)

34

Forest Landscape with Glade, c. 1835

Oil on canvas, 24 × 33 cm
Staatliche Museen zu Berlin, Kupferstichkabinett,
inv. no. SZ 432

Without the inner excitement apparent in the studies by Blechen, this small landscape by Elsasser would be unimaginable. It is probably a preparatory study for an unknown painting in which the artist wanted to discover more about the composition of colour; however, the artistic intention is overwhelmed by the forceful gesture of the brushstroke, which gives us little information about the objects depicted.

There is a seemingly stagnant, shallow lake in the foreground with stones and branches in it; on the right stand two dead birch trunks whose white bark dazzles in parts and towers in front of a group of trees on the other side of the lake, but is outshone by the white of the clouds in the sky. At the centre is a brightly lit meadow, coloured a poisonous yellow-green and avoiding any notion of the idyllic. Additional, in part autumnal-coloured, trees and a long, bare trunk rising in front of the background of a sloping conical stone enclose this meadow. Differing grades of colour tones emphasize the spatial levels. There are, however, other spots of colour which do not indicate specific objects. The enigma, which is set in this painting with great precision, disquiets.

Landscapes, which we are used to experiencing as the exterior world, are encountered here as the fantastic inner life of the artist's soul. These effective dramatics can be interpreted exotically — a small tree with a straight trunk and a fan-shaped crown resembles a palm — but they can also be regarded as a stage set.

HBS

Thomas Fearnley (1802–1842)

35

Study of Cliffs on Capri, 1833

Oil on paper mounted on canvas, 36.5 × 52 cm
Signed and dated bottom right: "Capri 11 t sept. 33. TF"
Nasjonalgalleriet, Oslo, inv. no. NG.M.3588

During his stay in Italy, Fearnley went to Capri in September 1833, where he painted a couple of rather unusual oil studies, one a view across the Marina Piccola on the south side of the island and the other this close-up picture of some coastal cliffs. The two paintings, more or less the same size, are amazingly large considering that they were probably done in the open; the artist would not have been able to fix them to the lid of his painter's box while working in the way painters were accustomed to do (and as is seen in *The Painter and the Boy*, cat. no. 36). The two studies might well have been an experiment, in that Fearnley wanted to try out the *plein air* study in large format. They also differ from Fearnley's other studies from Italy, as they are devoid of any atmosphere-creating artistic effects in the shape of flickering sunlight, heat haze or low clouds. On the contrary, this picture in particular is characterized by a very sober approach and keen observation. The close-up view of the cliffs is atypical of the painter's studies of nature, and there are clear parallels to studies by several of the Danish painters.

Fearnley derived inspiration from the Danish painters only to a limited extent, but on the other hand he himself influenced some of his Danish colleagues.[1] With his studies from Capri, the Norwegian artist might very well have had a certain influence on Købke. Both the viewpoint and the way in which the motif is cut off, as well as the manner of painting, are surprisingly close to one of the studies Købke painted in Capri in 1839, *View of Cliffs from Marina Piccola on Capri* (Museum of Fine Arts, Boston).[2] Before leaving for Italy, Købke had prepared himself for painting near the Marina Piccola partly by copying a couple of studies that Fritz Petzholdt had painted there. It is, however, not clear whether he could also have seen Fearnley's Italian studies, as it was not until 1841 and 1842 that some of these were exhibited at Charlottenborg in Copenhagen. One possibility is that the Copenhagen Art Association might have presented a small number of them in one of the small exhibitions of artists' new works, which were regularly put on in the Association's premises.

KM

1. See Sigurd Willoch, "Thomas Fearnley og de danske malere i Italia", *Kunst og Kultur*, vol. 64 (1981), pp. 249–57.
2. See Copenhagen 1996a, cat. no. 152.

36

The Painter and the Boy, 1834

Oil on paper mounted on canvas, 26.5 × 37 cm
Nasjonalgalleriet, Oslo, inv. no. NG.M.1750
COPENHAGEN ONLY

In contrast to so many other European painters, Fearnley
did not experience a true sense of liberation as an artist during
his stay in Italy – he had already progressed far in his artistic
development, and he had already acquired a vibrant style of
painting in his oil studies. At the beginning of February 1835
he wrote to J. C. Dahl: "This journey to Italy has been of great
benefit to me, for although I am actually painting basing myself
on the same principle as in Germany and in part on the same
subjects, without having comprehended what can be called the
real Italian quality . . . I think that all this painting from nature
that I have had the opportunity to do has strengthened my
reasoning as regards the truth in what is the same everywhere:
such as light, shade, reflections, etc. As a result, I have produced
quite a collection of studies, most of them thoroughly worked
out."[1]

It was the intense sunlight that came to play a major role for
him. He now more consistently exploited light in its interplay
with shaded areas, and he liked to conjure up the bluish heat
haze in the distance. But he was also interested in the strong
sunlight itself and often painted facing the light. The most
famous instance is this picture of an artist, watched by a boy,
painting on the shore near Sorrento, with an oil study fixed to
the lid of his painter's box. The work has the lightness of a

plein air study in its brushstrokes and composition, as well as
the quality of a momentary impression. The picture has been
given a delicate and untraditional balance with the painter in
the left foreground forming a counterbalance to the buildings
on the opposite side. A closer technical examination shows that
it was painted over a period of several days, and that each
individual layer of paint was allowed to dry before the next was
applied. Most striking is the fact that one of the main figures,
the boy, was added as a late inspiration after the scenery had
been painted (the waves on the water's edge can just be
distinguished through his legs). In other words, it was only at
a late stage that the picture acquired its main theme.

In several of his studies, Fearnley depicts a man standing
with his back to the viewer, often dressed in an artist's smock,
as a kind of alter ego of himself. Fruitless attempts have been
made to discover who this particular painter was. It could not
be Fearnley himself, since he was quite corpulent. In his Italian
studies Fearnley was less dependent on the many varied
influences from earlier in his career. Only the inspiration
from one of Dahl's oil studies makes itself felt here.

KM

1. Quoted in Védastine Aubert, "Breve fra Thomas Fearnley
   til J. C. C. Dahl", *Kunst og Kultur*, vol. 12 (1925), p. 13.

Caspar David Friedrich (1774–1840)

37

View of the Elbe Valley, c. 1807

Oil on canvas, 61.5 × 80 cm
Staatliche Kunstsammlungen, Gemäldegalerie Neue Meister,
Dresden, inv. no. 2197 F, Börsch-Supan and Jähnig no. 163
COPENHAGEN ONLY

Friedrich decisively separates foreground from background.
Four spruces grow on a rocky mountain peak, a single spruce
and a bush at the top, in the distance a river winds through
the mountains. At most, the middle ground is a forest, which
is visible in the left corner.

In the foreground, everything is clearly drawn. Each branch
of the spruce, each flower is precisely recognizable, but it is the
context that is decisive. Friedrich seizes the shape of the trees –
plants in general, really – and the cliffs, treats each as a single
object, and then joins them together. They do not appear as
mere objects in an academic composition, but as part of divine
creation. It is light that creates this context, which although
separating the illuminated from the shaded, is also in the
shadows as well. His brushstroke is most clearly recognizable
where the cliffs are struck by direct sunlight. It is free and loose.

The mountainous region in the far distance sinks into the
valley where the Elbe river flows. Jähnig suspects that this is
a Bohemian landscape. The air hangs misty over the mountains
and the valley. However, we can still clearly recognize fields,
meadows, woods, single trees and even a fence. The painting is
just as exact as loose. Blue and white clouds float across the sky,
which above the far-off mountains shifts slowly from yellow into
light blue.

Friedrich did make open-air studies, but (with a few
exceptions) only in pencil. In painting such a picture, he
referred back to drawings, which he often dated exactly; this
allows us to attribute the withered spruce to a drawing from
20 May 1799, the cliffs to a study from 9 July 1800, and the
highest tree to 3 May 1804. On the other hand, Friedrich
painted atmospheric effects from memory; he must have had
extraordinary visual recall, since his outstanding ability to
differentiate colours in reproducing tangible air, mist, fog and
clouds barely departs from what can be perceived in nature.

Significant is not only Friedrich's clear division of the
distant and the near, but also the growth of the spruces. The
four trees in the group stand secure and reach for the sky, while
the single spruces growing next to the ravine tilt precariously.
We can understand Börsch-Supan's interpretation in this way
– that the artist juxtaposed present and future, faith in life and
hope of paradise.

HRL

38

Morning Mist in the Mountains, 1808

Oil on canvas, 71 × 104 cm
Thüringer Landesmuseum Heidecksburg, Rudolstadt,
inv. no. 529, Börsch-Supan and Jähnig no. 166
COPENHAGEN ONLY

Clouds of mist wrap around a towering mountain so that its
contours are not always discernible. The last wisps of mist do
not reach the mountain-top, leaving only the peak with its
naked cliffs clearly visible. Spruces and, farther up, pines peek
out above the mist. Friedrich situates the tallest pine directly
next to the central axis, growing skyward like an arrow. The
other upward movements are formed by slants on the contour
of the left side rising to the peak. The mountain appears to
stand alone, other peaks cannot be seen, and to the left, one
can just make out a valley.

The mist passes into the whitish-grey blanket of clouds.
Only in a few spots does the pale blue of the sky shine through,
mostly over the highest cliffs. In front of the clear sky is a
cross, which was placed on the highest spot. Only at closer
examination do we notice it. The summit is bathed in bright
sunlight, which becomes weaker at the bottom and also at the
sides. It appears as if the light comes from the summit itself.

Initially the painting may look pale to the viewer since,
except for the dark green of the spruces, powerful colours are
absent. It becomes increasingly clear, however, that colours
containing light, indeed light-filled colours, dominate. The
real theme of the painting is light, which comes from above
and fills the world.

37

38

In this painting, one of the world's great works of art, awe has become an image.[1] In its sublimity, nature appears filled with a divine spirit. Friedrich, a devout Christian, also alludes to Christ, "who opened heaven to man", as Börsch-Supan has put it, using the sign of the cross. In the same year, Friedrich painted *The Cross in the Mountains* (Gemäldegalerie Dresden), depicting a cross planted on a mountain peak in the evening light, which was even planned as an altarpiece for a chapel (thus it is known as the Tetschen Altar); here, the message of Christian faith is a barely noticeable part of a picture of divine omnipotence.

Moreover, as Börsch-Supan has observed, "There is no reference to a real location for the viewer. Only a bird in flight could actually see the mountain in this way. The picture thereby becomes a vision, in spite of its exact observation of nature."[2]

Claude Keisch's view that the picture seems released from the ground and the elements appear to sway, while only the geometrical constructions keep a firm hold, leads to a final conclusion: "From that comes the effect of inaccessibility and loneliness."[3] To agree with this assessment is not to contradict what has already been said, for it is the inaccessible sublime that shows man his loneliness – if he recognizes the cross.

HRL

1. J. Carter Brown, *Rings. Five Passions in World Art*, exh. cat., High Museum of Art, Atlanta, Georgia, in conjunction with the 1996 Summer Olympic Games, Harry N. Abrams, New York, 1996, p. 156.
2. Helmut Börsch-Supan, *Caspar David Friedrich*, Munich, 1990, p. 78.
3. *La Peinture allemande à l'époque du Romantisme*, Orangerie des Tuileries, Paris, 1976/77, p. 46.

39

Evening, 1817

Oil on canvas, 22 × 30 cm
Private collection
Börsch-Supan and Jähnig no. 236
OTTAWA ONLY

A boat has sailed into a round bay and set course to a massive anchor on shore. Both white sails, which have just been pulled in, are illuminated by the light of the setting sun. The boat also emphasizes the bordering foreshore. Thin clouds, yellowish with a bit of red, float at an angle to the top across the grey sky. The

39

picture appears almost colourless – one searches in vain for blue in the lake; the water, with its gently wind-tossed waves, appears brown, grey and a bit green, and only in the foreground does the sparsely vegetated beach lie in shadow. But appearances are deceiving. It is the reduction of contrast of the colour in the sky, sea and land that causes this mistake and allows the differences of colour to be overlooked. As if painted in one brushstroke, a thin, grey, but silvery stripe, separating and joining the water and clouds at the same time, runs along the horizon. The light set in the hazy tenderness is a sign, reflected in both the sails and the two foreshores, signalling the safe entry into the secluded bay. The strokes of the thin painting and the tightly pulled rigging are a significant sign of the turn above.

The ship's anchor, determined by exact contour, is a recognizable symbol, an old Christian sign of hope in faith. Finally, the contours of the foreshore are clearly emphasized. It must remain an open question whether the three poles stuck in the ground, used by fishermen for drying nets, mean something, and how to read the two men in the boat with their lifted oars; they seem to be wearing two-cornered hats, and a white sash over the left shoulder of one of the men is visible – are they naval officers? One thing is certain: Friedrich is not telling a

story here. Can one assume that the two men in the twilight want to end their life's journey?

This picture is part of a cycle of works depicting times of day. However, the painter did not intend, as in earlier cycles, both the seasons of the year and of life. Each of the four small pictures stands on its own.

Friedrich applies the paint thinly, so that it often appears like watercolour. The parallel brushwork does not appear everywhere. Only the two sails have been painted in impasto, in addition to the wake and the highest bands of clouds – yet another allusion to the hereafter.

HRL

40

Coastal Landscape in Evening Light, c. 1817

Oil on canvas, 22 × 31 cm
Museum für Kunst und Kulturgeschichte, Lübeck,
inv. no. 1950/5
Börsch-Supan and Jähnig no. 242
HAMBURG AND COPENHAGEN ONLY

40

In the evening light our view passes over a shallow cove leading to the Baltic Sea, while a sailboat moves along the coast. The sun has already set. Beyond the horizon, the sky is a deep violet-red, and lightens from orange to yellow and finally to blue, while the sun lights the veil of clouds orange. However, short, grey bands of clouds are interspersed in the evening sky, and the dusk descends from above.

To the left on the shore there are two long buildings with thatched roofs, a house and a shack, often found in Pomerania, while on the right a long line has been suspended. Another tube-shaped net, a wicker fish trap, hangs along the cove, and nets hide much of the colourful reflection of the sunlight in the shallow water. Just next to it, a small boat has landed, with two fishermen still at work. The large and small polished round stones in the nearby water are much more noticeable than the anchor or the meadow in the dark. Only the water of the sea and the cove and the narrow side of the buildings are still lit; everything else appears lit from behind, while the neatly spread-out rows of hay reflect the glow of the sunset.

Friedrich painted this small picture with a fine brush, in quick, parallel running lines. It has been systematically painted, without pauses or modulations. The pencil studies he used for

the picture, for the sailboat, the houses, the fishing boat, the anchor and the nets are all from 1815, thus done at most two years before this painting.

Closeness and distance are important themes in this picture. The foreground is filled with signs of human activity, while in the distance on the shimmering silver sea are only an apparition-like sailboat lit from behind and a second boat along the coast, which can just be made out. Despite the darkness, everything is still corporeal in the foreground, while in the light in the distance appears an otherworldly promised land.

HRL

41

On the Sailboat, 1818/19

Oil on canvas, 71 × 65 cm
The State Hermitage Museum, St Petersburg, inv. no. 9773
Börsch-Supan and Jähnig no. 256
OTTAWA AND COPENHAGEN ONLY

On the bow of a sailboat, a young couple look together towards their destination, a large city with many churches and towers.

41

The viewer is also on the sailboat, near the mast, which splits the picture into two unequal halves. To the right is a piece of the main sail, appearing green in the shadow, and a piece of the foresail with all of its rigging can be seen a short distance from the ship's galley. On the left side, however, outside the main focus of the picture, one can see many parts of the boat: the tightly pulled ropes that hold the mast, pegged on the board, the sheets of the two transparent foresails, whose lower corners are fastened to the bowsprit, a boom and the dark opening to the small cabin in the prow. Every detail has been noted with such precision that the boat can be identified as a fishing boat, just like those in service on the Baltic Sea at the time.

We also see the sky, over the lightly tossed sea, which appears brownish in the distance, and which wraps the city in a greyish violet haze, which slowly becomes lighter and soon is increasingly covered by grey clouds. The bright sky is reduced to a band by the heavy clouds. We cannot determine the time of day with certainty. Though we might like to think of the couple at sunrise, sunset seems more likely, when we take into account that sea voyages tend to end in the evening and not in the morning.

We see the man from behind, in a long, dark green coat, his long, curly blond hair falling over his shoulders, a draping hat on his head. The woman can be seen in half-profile. Her hair is up and she wears a reddish brown dress with lace collars. They sit next to each other, holding hands, and are lost in the view of the distant city. The warm light of the setting sun illuminates the woman and both of their clasped hands; a little light still plays on his hair. The two figures are turned to each other and directed to the same goal. In complementing each other – through green and red, narrow and wide, light and dark – they create a unity.

The row of churches and other buildings along the horizon are not meant to depict a particular city. Many of the buildings are reminiscent of those in Friedrich's birthplace of Greifswald, in Dresden where he had lived, and in the port city of Stralsund on the Baltic, while some clearly belong to the realm of fantasy.

The young couple are an idealized depiction of the newlywed artist and his wife Christiane Caroline Bommer. They had married on 21 January 1818 and travelled on their honeymoon to the Baltic Sea, by way of Wolgast (the home town of Friedrich's friend Philipp Otto Runge), Stralsund, Rügen and Greifswald. Their honeymoon was certainly the occasion for this painting, which is unique in Friedrich's oeuvre. The choice of the extreme close-up, which leads to a very limited pictorial excerpt, can be found in a composition study without figures (Nasjonalgalleriet, Oslo), one of the few that

exists: the watercolour drawing is even more limited in its depiction. The artist, who might have sat up on the fish-hold, certainly did not record more than what we see here; he quickly realized that cutting back the close-up and limiting the field of vision to the top and right would lead to an expansion of the view in distance. The future, to which the couple sail on their life's journey, spreads out under the light of the sky; this appears before their eyes,

not the heavy clouds above. As Börsch-Supan has stated, they are "lost in observation of the vision of the hereafter."

Grand Duke Nicholas, the future czar, visited Friedrich in his studio in 1820 and bought a picture. It has recently been revealed that a year later, in August 1821, Vassily Jukovsky, Russian instructor to the Empress and tutor to the crown prince, bought three paintings from Friedrich at Georg Andreas Reimer's for the Grand Duke's wife Alexandra Fedorovna, Princess of Prussia by birth. It is likely that this picture was one of the three. Until 1945, when it was moved to the Hermitage, it was in the "Cottage" in Peterhof, Petrodvorec, where it hung over the salon door leading to the Baltic Sea.

HRL

42

Ship on the Elbe in the Early Morning Fog, c. 1821

Oil on canvas, 22.5 × 30.8 cm
Wallraf-Richartz-Museum, Cologne, inv. no. 2667
Börsch-Supan and Jähnig no. 283
OTTAWA ONLY

Friedrich distinguished between the foreground, which is almost tangible in an impenetrable and transparent green, and the distance, which furls out of the fog, in white and violet.

It is easy for the viewer to become preoccupied with the sloping landscape's three bushes in a meadow of flowers, and to see two kinds of flower in constant change from white to red as well as a mass of grasses, although the foreground lies in shadow. The bushes and the edge of the hill appear in the light. One imagines that the hill sinks slowly on the other side of the riverbank, the highest blossoms in front.

The viewer will quickly direct his gaze to the flat freighter, which is propelled by the current of the Elbe, without a sail. The mist rising from the water joins the river and the mountains into a blurred unity and completely obscures the other bank. Two gently sloping hills covered with rows of trees can be made out, with a high mountain range in the distance. The rising mist, like clouds of smoke, blurs the haze of the sky,

42

which is otherwise pale in barely noticeable bands of blue and yellow. Should the viewer's gaze pause at the ship, he might be tempted to count its lines; he sees one man with long oars and two men on the bow, one with a long pole, the other bent over a load. Despite their small size, the figures will probably be noticed.

The composition of this small picture also draws attention to the boat in the contours of an equilateral triangle. The tilting bushes that appear in the fog set the imagination free: they are like stage curtains. The balance of movement – in front, the countryside rises to the right; at the back, the hill slopes to the right – also leads to concentration on the boat. It seems to move it to the right in the picture, propelling it as it has just passed by the imaginary centre axis.

Despite being a carefully planned composition, this little picture has the freshness of a nature study. This comes from the precision of recording things with brushwork free of contrivance. We can see that Friedrich must have painted very quickly. This picture is more than first meets the eye. Friedrich transmits his message subtly. The mast of the boat points upward into the sky, and the meaning of the boat, which is pushed along by the current, is also possible to ascertain.

HRL

43

Raven Tree, c. 1822

Oil on canvas, 54 × 71 cm
Inscribed (back of frame): "Hünengrab"
Musée du Louvre, Paris, inv. no. R.F. 1975–20
Börsch-Supan and Jähnig no. 289
OTTAWA ONLY

As the inscription on the back of the picture indicates, the hill overlapping with the horizon is a dolmen (*Hünengrab*). This awakens memories of the time when the island of Rügen was still pagan, since in the background we can see the unmistakable chalk cliffs of Arcona, a subject Friedrich painted repeatedly (the gaze that looks for the deep metaphorically focuses here). The sea radiates in pure blue.

It is a winter or spring evening; there are only a few dead leaves on the oak. A flock of ravens flies towards the tree, where two other birds already perch. Their black silhouettes seem to belong to the branches. Friedrich drew this oak on 3 May 1809 in Neubrandenburg. He added several branches on the left and stretched others in the bizarre melody of its growth, giving the

43

tree the contours of a rhombus, which at the same time covers the picture in tangles – the branches are spread out only on the picture plane. It is as if they fight with the calm, sinking bands of colourful clouds. The wild dramatics in the variety of forms in the foreground are intensified by the stump of another oak tree and a hacked and dying trunk lying on the ground. That the foreground belongs to the world of the dead is clearly felt. All the more consoling is the beauty of the evening sky.

We know of two later vertical format paintings by Friedrich, in which a single oak dominates as the main object of the picture. In contrast to these pictures, the peculiarity of this landscape becomes clear. If these damaged trees remain standing in resignation like lost souls, then the oak, with its many flailing arms, is like a fighter in despair.

HBS

44

Rural Plains, c. 1823

Oil on canvas, 27.4 × 41.1 cm
Stiftung Preussische Schlösser und Gärten
Berlin-Brandenburg, Potsdam, inv. no. GK I 30093
Börsch-Supan and Jähnig no. 302
HAMBURG AND COPENHAGEN ONLY

45

Landscape with Windmills, c. 1823

Oil on canvas, 27.7 × 41.1 cm
Stiftung Preussische Schlösser und Gärten
Berlin-Brandenburg, Potsdam, inv. no. GK I 30094
Börsch-Supan and Jähnig no. 303
HAMBURG AND COPENHAGEN ONLY

44

45

In the first half of the 1820s, Friedrich painted a number of landscapes, which at first glance appear to be carefully reproduced scenes, unaltered by composition or artistic enhancement. One would like to deny them all significance and accept them as modest records of reality. However, it was Friedrich's intention to get behind appearances to reveal deeper truths.

Friedrich pursues these possibilities of the seemingly correct view to the furthest in this pair of pictures, which he exhibited in 1823 at the Dresden Academy. Their exhibition prompted a critic to charge: "The small flat landscapes with windmills prove how poorly it suits Friedrich, when he tries to be prosaic." He did not want to be prosaic, but he wanted to bring nature alive for those who watch, feel and contemplate it. As in all of his pairs and cycles of pictures, Friedrich shows a line of development here as well.

The first picture is a cheerful summer landscape, where the sun lights things up brightly; only the high, darkly coloured clouds herald the coming of the night. The magic of the present is so strong that one could easily overlook references to the ephemeral. The friendly village invites one to seek shelter for the night. Two women bale hay. To the right, a windmill stands in front of a cornfield in the distance.

This theme carries over to the other picture, a morning landscape differing little in its pleasant atmosphere. With the city of Greifswald behind him, the view spreads out to the north over the small river Ryck, which Friedrich drew in 1801 or 1802. This study of nature is the basis for the painting. Through the boats with the fishermen and the women bleaching the canvas, Friedrich made a surprising and meaningful addition. In order to reach the other bank, one must cross the river. The gate is open behind the dock and leads one's gaze to a pyramid covering a fountain, whose form reminds one of a gravestone. The morning light falls on the foreshortened wall of the small house in the centre, which appears like an illuminated beacon pointing skywards. It also hints at the meaning of washing and bleaching. It is the power of the sun that bleaches the linen. It is no coincidence that the stretched-out pieces of linen point to the church spire in the background. The windmills can also be understood in this context. They are dependent on the wind, a heavenly power, beyond man's control.

What appears at first glance as a meaningless landscape reveals itself to be full of eschatological meaning below the surface. The riverbank opposite is a parable for the hereafter in its religious sense, its reality underscored by the powers of conviction of the reality on this side of the river.

HBS

46
Rocky Reef on the Beach, c. 1824

Oil on canvas, 22 × 31 cm
Staatliche Kunsthalle, Karlsruhe, inv. no. 2261
Börsch-Supan and Jähnig no. 315
HAMBURG AND COPENHAGEN ONLY

This picture belongs to a group, dated around 1824, of evening seascapes with barren mountain formations, and conjures images of regions far to the north. All of these works are views of the distant landscape seen from above. It is not known which studies Friedrich used. He apparently did not even see these mountains himself: although he had planned a trip to Iceland in 1811, he did not actually go. Despite his interest in Scandinavia, he never followed his friend Dahl to Norway.

He was in awe of the North. His famous *Polar Sea* (Hamburger Kunsthalle, 1823/24) attempts to show that, even in the eternal ice, God is near. The sheets of ice in the Hamburg picture are similar to the slanting cliffs pointing to the veiled moon. The large bay with its offshore reefs forms a natural harbour. However, a ship trying to navigate into this harbour would be faced by the danger of these reefs, which are the unsettling main subject of this picture. The only sign of life is the group of trees in the right foreground. The eye is led from here over the entry of the bay and the reefs to the moon, whose light magically illuminates the sea. It would help a ship trying to reach the harbour to navigate around the reefs.

In his 1809 commentary on the Tetschen Altar, Friedrich compared the light of the setting sun to the Holy Father, whose son Christ reflects this light on the earth of the New Testament and thus takes over the task of the moon. This light, shining in the night, prevents us from falling off the path of life. The ship steering towards a harbour has this meaning in many of Friedrich's works. There is no ship here, the viewer must visualize it for himself. Only by such visualization does the meaning of this mysterious scene become clear. Friedrich uses a completely different method from that in the landscapes with windmills to lead the viewer to a deeper level of meaning in the picture.

HBS

46

47

Man and Woman Contemplating the Moon, c. 1833

Oil on canvas, 33 × 44 cm
Staatliche Museen zu Berlin, Nationalgalerie,
inv. no. A II 887, NG H 6
Börsch-Supan and Jähnig no. 404

This painting is a variation on the 1819 painting (Gemälde-galerie, Dresden), showing a woman instead of a young boy. According to Friedrich's friend Wilhelm Wegener, the painter portrayed himself and his student August Heinrich (who died in 1822) in the Dresden painting. The woman who takes the place of the boy is probably Friedrich's wife Caroline. She rests her arm longingly on her husband's shoulder. The rocky, sloping path is dangerous in the night. The only light comes from the waxing moon, whose full shape, however, looms in the darkness. To the right is the morning star; the future promises more light.

The couple stand by the hacked-down stump of a tree, a symbol of death, but are covered above by the branches of a mighty spruce, as they gaze at the moon. For Friedrich, the spruce was a symbol of Christian hope and life. Here, it stands in juxtaposition to the bare oak tree with its bizarrely contorted branches. It threatens to topple into the deep, as its roots are

47

already lifting out of the earth, forming a strange ornament under the moon in the centre of the picture. The role of the oak as a symbol of death, which the travellers distance themselves from on the path of life, is emphasized by the large stone in the lower right of the picture. It is one of the dolmens that Friedrich had sketched on 27 May 1806.

Another difference between the two versions is the more euphonic coloration and light application of colour, typical of Friedrich's later work, which amplifies the atmospheric effect. Painting night is always a difficult task, since light, which differentiates objects from one another and gives them colour, is barely present. Friedrich's technique reminds us of the technique our eyes use, compensating for lack of light by increasing sensitivity. The more we become accustomed to the darkness, the better we see. In the painting this is true not only

of physical, worldly sight, but of the spiritual as well. The dark colours are meant both to create a beautiful effect, and also to comfort and encourage us on our journey. The night sky contained special messages for Friedrich, and he always painted it with devotion.

In 1818 the Danish writer and critic Peder Hjort acquired a painting by Friedrich which also showed a man and a woman gazing at the moon. It has been suggested that this painting is identical with the present picture, and that it is an eclipse of the moon they are watching.[1] Hjort's painting was in his possession till his death in 1871. The provenance of the Berlin painting is not known prior to 1922.

HBS

1. See Monrad in Copenhagen 1991, pp. 77 ff.

48

Willow Bush under a Setting Sun, c. 1835

Oil on canvas, 22 × 30.5 cm
Frankfurter Goethe-Museum, Frankfurt am Main,
inv. no. IV–1953–35, Börsch-Supan and Jähnig no. 422
COPENHAGEN ONLY

If we imagine ourselves as wanderers in a landscape such as
this, we will not only realize how lost and hopeless the situation
appears, but also notice the extremely low-angle view and the
details as if in a close-up, as though we have half-sunk into the
earth. We have no chance of gaining an overview of the scene.

In the middle, behind a pond reflecting the blue of the sky,
is a tree stump, an omen of death, flanked by dying willows,
which are arranged in a festive symmetry but are rhythmically
free. Together with the leafless bushes, they enclose the narrow
stage of the foreground like bars. Movement is no longer
possible, only the display of the sublime. In the middle, there
is space between the bars for the sun, an unusual set-up in
Friedrich's oeuvre. Those things joined together on the surface
are endlessly separated from each other in space.

Only a low sun can be worked into the pictorial composition,
but only then is it also possible to stare directly at the sun
without being blinded. The question remains whether it is a
rising or a setting sun. A rising sun would be more in line with
Friedrich's thought, as a symbol for new possibilities at the end
of one's life. In this way, the flowers in the front would be a
sign of hope and life in the confusing tangle of the branches.
Friedrich did not observe this exact scene, but his lengthy
experience in nature stands behind the creation of this picture.

The picture acts as a parable of the animal frailty of human
life and the omnipotence of heaven not only through the
symbolism of tangible objects, but also through the feeling of
an atmosphere in which moisture, coolness and mist fight with
the warming power of the sun. Friedrich always placed the
senses in opposition to reason in his theoretical writings, as
activities of the soul.

Friedrich's manner of painting is masterful and fast. There
are even *pentimenti* in the sky, a rarity in Friedrich's work —
the branches of the right willow originally extended further
to the left.

HBS

49

Eduard Gaertner (1801–1877)

49

Rue Neuve-Notre-Dame, 1826

Oil on canvas, 44 × 33 cm
Signed and dated bottom left: "Ed.Gaertner/Paris 1826"
Stiftung Preussische Schlösser und Gärten Berlin-Brandenburg,
Potsdam, inv. no. GK I 1295

Gaertner does not make the cathedral in Paris the dominant
feature and avoids using its symbolic grandeur to increase the
impact of this picture. Instead, he shows a section of it at the
end of a not very deep picture area. He depicts the atmosphere
of an early morning in a densely built quarter on the Ile de
la Cité when the sun is still low. The light is falling diagonally
into an alleyway and only a few details are highlighted. Coolness and moisture can be sensed here and the cathedral's west
façade, still covered in haze and shadow, cannot be experienced
as three-dimensional. Gaertner has chosen a perspective which
allows only less than half of the façade to be seen. The southern
tower appears to be almost replaced by a four-storey house that
projects into the area and is about as tall as the northern tower.
Thus the cathedral appears as an integral part of the town and
not its centre. Right and left, the pictorial space in which every
detail is registered begins with the fronts of houses which go
beyond the actual picture frame; every single brick, the window
panes with their reflections, the washing hung out to dry, or the
potted plants standing on the balconies are signs of life in this
quarter. In the still rather poorly painted details the young
Gaertner indulges in the narration of daily life which also
includes animals. It is already the artist's main concern to
present the town as the creation of its inhabitants and as their
home, and not just as a collection of sights – in Berlin this
approach had been taken by Johann Georg Rosenberg in his
famous etchings of views dating from 1776 to 1785.

However, the feeling of air and atmosphere is new
in Gaertner's work. In 1826 he sent this painting from Paris
to the exhibition of the Berlin Academy together with four
watercolours titled *Prospects from Paris*. King Friedrich
Wilhelm III purchased them there, probably because they
reminded him of his own stay in Paris in 1814.

HBS

50

View through a Courtyard, 1827

Oil on canvas on hardboard, 46 × 33 cm
Signed and dated bottom right: "E. Gaertner fec:1827"
Staatliche Galerie Moritzburg, Halle, inv. no. I/63

This picture was painted while Gaertner was living in France
from 1825 to 1828. Even in later works he liked to make use of
the view through a gateway which, like a backdrop, formed an
inner frame and intensified the effect of the enclosed main
scene. In this way, however, the artist surprisingly emphasizes a
non-spectacular detail that merges buildings and plants together
and is of interest only as a painting. The arch and the opened
door suggest a development of space into depth, but one cannot
see more than a few metres: up ahead is an impenetrable wall
of overgrown stones, trees and shrubs. Its size suggests the
picture is much more than a study.

This subject was perhaps linked to a personal memory of
Gaertner's, as it is hardly believable that it would have attracted
a buyer, especially as figures have been dispensed with and
no motion other than the play of light and the decay of the
brickwork are apparent. Otherwise, the only disturbing detail
is the broken-off branch still hanging in the tree in the centre.

The foliage of the trees, the shrubs and the brickwork are
depicted meticulously. Certainly, this picture should also be
evidence for the ability to reproduce the power of suggestion
in a piece of experienced reality. It must be remembered that
in the same year that Gaertner painted this picture Nicéphore
Niepce presented his photographic experiments to the Royal
Society in London. Only in France could Gaertner have
conceived the idea behind this painting.

HBS

50

51

Corner in the Eosander Courtyard
of the Berlin Palace, c. 1830

Oil on canvas, 58 × 47.5 cm
Stiftung Preussische Schlösser und Gärten Berlin-Brandenburg,
Potsdam, inv. no. GK I 12003

This painting is one of Gaertner's few unsigned works, which
can perhaps be explained by its unfinished state. The pen marks,
which rendered all details of the baroque architecture with
precision, are still visible. On top of that, a light hand applied
the splashes of colour, so that in many places the white primer
shows through, creating the impression of worn-out plaster, in
which light is captured. Only two tiny figures, apparently
servants, are to be seen.

Gaertner reproduces merely a third of the pompous
Eosander's portal frieze, modelled on the Arch of Septimus
Severus in Rome and named after the architect Johann
Eosander Göthe. He compensates for this reduction with the
astounding idea of splitting the picture plane diagonally. The
parallel wall of the shortened palace wing is in sunlight above,
in shadow below. Moreover, the ordered architecture is brought
to life in two different ways: through the variously treated
curtains behind the windows and through the shadows of the
projecting architectural sections. The sun is in the south-west;
thus it is afternoon.

The trail of smoke rising from a small chimney is as modest
a sign of life as the two small figures. Gaertner sees the awe-
inspiring royal palace with the eyes of a rational citizen, who
is aware of the everyday. At the same time, he also sees it as a
painter, for whom the sensation of forms, colours and light is
important.

HBS

Fig. 24. This page: Eduard Gaertner,
Panorama of Berlin, 1834. Charlottenburg
Palace, Berlin, Schinkel Pavilion

52

Panorama of Berlin from the Roof of the Church of Friedrichswerder, 1836

Surviving third, fifth and sixth of six original pictures
Oil on canvas, 92 × 112 cm, 92 × 93 cm, 91 × 112 cm
The State Museum Reserve "Peterhof", Petrodvorec,
inv. no. PDMP 1143 sh-1145 sh
OTTAWA AND HAMBURG ONLY

Gaertner's main work was his six-piece panorama of Berlin.
The first version, dating from 1834 (this page), was acquired by
Friedrich Wilhelm III (Schloss Charlottenburg, Berlin, Schinkel
Pavilion). No other view of the town from this period is more
authentic. The two triptych-like halves with an almost square
centre panel and two longer side panels folded at an angle of
135 degrees are meant to be hung in diagonally opposite corners

of a room. Then the observer has the impression of standing
on the roof of the church built according to Schinkel's plans.

In 1836 Gaertner painted a second version for the Czarina
Alexandra Fedorovna of Russia, Princess of Prussia by birth,
so that she would have a view of her native city in far-off
St Petersburg. The artist added all the subsequent structural
alterations and as he was able to complete these at a faster
tempo the treatment of the buildings is somewhat looser. The
colouring is paler and the clouds are more dramatic. In what
was originally the third picture (cat. no. 52a, opposite), building
tools are recognizable in the foreground which belong to the
mason depicted in the second picture (see fig. 24, above). He
is occupied with building a pinnacle on which the lightning
conductor, still on the ground, is to be attached. The view
extends over two inner courtyards and the river Spree to
Schinkel's Museum at the Lustgarten, to the cathedral, to the
Church of St Mary and from there to the Palace, which has

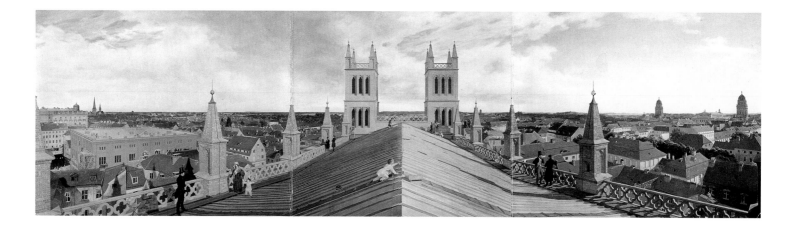

52a

52b, 52c

been moved to the border and is only partially visible, and in no way appears to be the centre of the town which it is in reality. Thus, Gaertner does not show Berlin as the residence of the king, but as the town of its citizens, whose activities on the streets and even through the windows of their homes he narrates with humour. The fifth picture (cat. no. 52b, above), one of the almost square centre panels, shows the church's towers and the roof, which one of Gaertner's two young sons, swinging a stick like a sword, is bravely climbing for a new view (the parents are displayed on the fourth picture, together with the smaller son). His cap has fallen from his head along the way. We should be as curious as the boy. Near the left tower Schinkel and his friend Peter Beuth are standing by the roof balustrade. The following, sixth, picture (cat. no. 52c) shows the view from Kreuzberg with the memorial for the Wars of Liberation, designed by Schinkel, in the distance left of the towers of the

German and French Cathedrals at the Gendarmenmarkt, between which Schinkel's Schauspielhaus is visible. The row of trees in front belongs to the plantation of the opera trenches, originally a part of the city fortifications.

Besides Gaertner's talent for storytelling and interpretation his skill for colouring is noteworthy. When he reproduces the tiles with such varying tones it is not because of pedantry but because of the pleasure he takes in the delicate nuances of this building material, which was more widely appreciated because of Schinkel. He depicts Berlin with unconcealed affection for his birthplace, but always remains truthful to reality. Gaertner's views are less for the tourist than for the townspeople with whom he shares his local patriotism. His preference for new buildings underlines the modernity of the city.

It demands absolute command of perspective to produce such so-called angle panoramas, for the angles may not be

visible. Here, it is not presented as a special virtue – as Hummel liked to do – but with an intense impression of atmosphere that merges into something natural. This is created primarily due to the play of light. It is a summer afternoon. The sun is beginning to set and casts long shadows which intensify the colours, but the atmosphere of a day that is nearing its end is still missing.

When Gaertner painted his picture series the fashion for panoramas was in decline. It began in England at the end of the eighteenth century and spread from there to the continent. The first of such circular paintings was shown in Berlin in 1800 and presented a view of Rome. Painted by Johann Adam Breysig and Karl Ludwig Kaaz, it was displayed in a small circular building erected specially for it, since these panorama scenes were large, due to the desired effect of illusion. They were

influenced more by theatre than by easel painting. Schinkel also created a circular city panorama in 1808, a view of Palermo. The main concern of these paintings was with illusion and the pleasure of recognition. Gaertner moved beyond this by bundling the authentic observation, the picturesque finesse and the humour of his story into a statement that reaches as far as the *genius loci* of the town.

Before the Russian Revolution of 1917, the panorama was kept in the Palace of Znamenka, a country estate not far from Peterhof which was granted to Alexandra Fedorovna by her husband Czar Nicholas I; it then passed into the possession of his son, Grand Duke Nicholas Nicholaievich. During World War II it was stolen. Three of the six pictures were returned from Germany after the war; the remaining three have never been recovered.

HBS

53

Landscape on the Havel River, 1840

Oil on canvas, 39.2 × 64 cm
Signed and dated on boat bottom right: "E. Gaertner 1840"
Angermuseum, Erfurt, inv. no. 8323

More than other veduta painters in Berlin, Gaertner was attracted by the numerous lakes in the surrounding area, which serve as a base for the pictorial space and lead to a unity of top and bottom due to the reflection of the sky in the water. Not only did he depict the scenic charm of these lakes, but he also observed that industrial estates were starting to settle along their shores which focused only on the utility of nature. The group of industrial buildings has been erected according to the rules of utility and does not follow aesthetic principles, leaving only here and there any room for pine trees. Gaertner portrays this very soberly, without making a judgement, but also without any pride in the technical developments. The setting evening sun lends the otherwise dull landscape a colourful appeal by lighting up the buildings and the red roofs and thus intensifying the harmony between colours. A small part of the cloud's blue on the left behind the veil of steam promises brightness.

Despite the picture's symmetry it does not have a proper centre or a main subject. Indeed a steamship in the centre with the Prussian flag on its stern can just be made out, but it is not emphasized as a technical improvement. The barges on both sides of the river take up far more room. The people depicted are occupied with different tasks. They all seem small and of no importance in this picture. It is not just chance that the location of this painting has still not been pinpointed: industry has not given this place any significance, but rather made it anonymous.

HBS

54

**Landscape in the March of Brandenburg,
c. 1845/50**

Oil on canvas, 25.5 × 48 cm
Signed bottom right (scratched): "E Gaertner"
Stiftung Stadtmuseum Berlin, inv. no. GEM 91/6

It has not been possible to determine the location of this place but, according to its dimension, it is perhaps a small town that extends along the shore of two lakes separated from one another only by a dam. Despite the exact reproduction of individual buildings it was obviously not the artist's intention to depict the small village of Kähnsdorf on Lake Seddin, with which it has sometimes been identified. It is even doubtful whether this is a Brandenburg landscape. The extent of the horizon, which is emphasized by the unusually long format and the seagulls, indicates that it could depict a coastal area. It is possible that it is a landscape in West or East Prussia, where the artist spent time in the mid 1840s, the probable period of this picture.

In his oeuvre there is nothing directly comparable. The broad and, in parts, even opaque manner of painting in the foreground and also the light strokes of the luscious green on the near shore of the right lake and, not least, the signature scratched into the wet paint (unusual for Gaertner) lends the painting the character of a study. On the other hand, some details have been included only for the sake of composition – in particular, the small, geologically meaningless elevation to the right front with hastily painted pine trees, the raven, and the viewing direction from right to left which is demanded of the observer. The stroller walks in the same direction as the parabolic curve of the large lake extending into the picture and the same as the movement of the clouds. The centre of this lightly and fluidly painted picture is the black rain cloud, accentuated by the two seagulls. However, the primary focus is the wide sky over the mainland and the dramatic reflection of it in the lake. Air and water have more significance than the mainland and far more than the architecture. In contrast to the parts in the foreground that are only sketched, the meticulously painted details in the distance are meant to draw the eye into the depth.

HBS

Jacob Gensler (1808–1845)

55

Study of Clouds, c. 1830

Oil on paper mounted on cardboard, 23 × 34.6 cm
Hamburger Kunsthalle, inv. no. 2016

A young man of about twenty-two, a budding artist, observes a
hilly landscape and the cloud formations above in the blue sky
of the setting sun from a great distance. After making some
cursory notes in pencil, he paints the shallow hills rolling off
to the left near the sky with a fine brush. He showed so little
concern for the terrain, the path of the eye into the distance,
that he left the study unfinished.

With this study, the young Jacob Gensler turned to a
subject that had preoccupied painters for several decades:
Alexander Cozens, Pierre-Henri de Valenciennes, Thomas
Girtin and the Viennese Michael Wutke (all before the turn
of the nineteenth century), as well as Dahl, Friedrich, Blechen,
Georg von Dillis and John Constable (from the 1820s on).
For all of these artists, clouds were an integral part of their
landscape painting, and not just in preparatory studies.[1] Perhaps
Jacob Gensler knew nothing of this tradition. He probably did
not know the terminology of Luke Howard, who would have
spoken here of cumulus and stratus clouds at the base. It would
be rather unlikely for a student at the Academy in Munich to be
familiar with Howard's essay.

The powerful and yet ephemeral forms of the clouds
apparently attracted Gensler, as well as the fusion of blue and
yellow, from brightly lit to shadowy parts within one shape. He
began by painting the clouds, mixing yellow and grey, and acted
very quickly. He then painted the blue of the sky, filling most of
it in. The blue changes its tone and composition, in some parts
gleaming, in others hazy; the blue becomes more powerful
where the bands of grey clouds float to the top.

What differentiates Gensler's early work from the studies of
clouds by his contemporaries and predecessors is his wide-angle
panoramic view. Perhaps he decided that completion of the
bottom third of the picture would destroy the effect.

HRL

1. Werner Busch, "Die Ordnung in Flüchtigen –
   Wolkenstudien der Goethezeit", *Goethe und die Kunst*,
   Schirn Kunsthalle Frankfurt, Kunstsammlung zu Weimar,
   1994, pp. 519–27.

56

On the Beach at the Baltic Sea near Laboe, 1842

Oil on paper mounted on cardboard, 21.4 × 46.3 cm
Signed and dated lower right (scratched): "Laboe
Septbr. 42. J.G."
Hamburger Kunsthalle, inv. no. 1320

When Jacob Gensler went outside to paint studies from nature,
he had large compositions in mind, which he carefully prepared
through figure and landscape studies. However, as he stood on
the beach of the Baltic near Laboe in the Probstei (a landscape
near Kiel, which he painted often), on 5 September 1842, he
concentrated on the experience of light and air, change and
transience. One imagines that he began with the horizon, with
the forests and the houses in the far-off distance on the other
side of the Kiel Bay, and the shimmering expanse of wavy
water. He captured the changing appearance of the cloudy sky
overhead and the ground under his feet with rapid, occasionally
fleeting brushstrokes: the floating clouds in the blue sky
and their shadows on the mud, the puddles and the sand. He
sketched the bush with many sweeping brushstrokes. He
directed his attention to variations in light above all else.

Even this study might have been useful for one of Gensler's
larger compositions, though its transitory air seems far removed
from the enduring timelessness of his large paintings. The
extended longitudinal format is unusual. Even seascapes have
a less extreme relationship between length and width, for
example in the older French standard format. The experience
of expansive space finds its concomitant expression.

HRL

55

56

Christian Friedrich Gille (1805–1899)

57

In the Park, 1833

Oil on paper, 25.5 × 35 cm
Städtische Kunstsammlung, Chemnitz, inv. no. 410

The choice of the close-up, looking at a small piece of the world, can be found in Gille's paintings as in those of many other northern German and Danish artists of his generation. The painter content with the close-up sees nature in a concise form.

Gille's eye falls on a shallow stream and, above all, on the river's edge lined with flowers, the grass of the meadow, a bush and other plants. The young painter does not stop at mere description, since there are only a few plants to identify. It is the light of the sun that captures his eye, falling brightly on the meadow and emphasizing the blossoms and then moving to the shaded bush.

Gille was concerned with quickly capturing intense experience. His brushwork is fleeting, without disregarding the particular. He does not lose himself in watching, he wants to hold on to what flashes by, and what he sees is nature bathed in light.

HRL

58

View over the Rooftops in a Dresden Suburb, c. 1830

Oil over pencil on paper mounted on cardboard, 17.5 × 20.5 cm
Hamburger Kunsthalle, inv. no. 5396

The radical mode of the sparse pictorial composition joins with the subtle realization of the delicately nuanced moods of light. Three-quarters of the picture shows nothing but the blue sky and puffy white clouds, and the rest is simply horizontal lines, only at second glance identifiable as buildings. A half-dozen short, vertical brushstrokes in the right corner materialize as a group of trees before our eyes.

It is morning. The light of the rising sun fills the sky; the blues increase at the top, below the light shines more diffusely. The roofs in the background pick up the violet from the wisps of clouds floating above the buildings. As he began to paint on the drawing paper, Gille filled the brush with thinned, runny paint and applied it in even, regular short strokes, line by line; the brushstroke is considerably less visible at the end of each line. Until the horizontal strokes at the very bottom, line follows line. The colour changes almost imperceptibly, its bright tone increasing only a little. Gille added the diaphanous clouds later.

This is recognizably a study from nature, but the artist shows so little interest in topography that we do not expect identification of the locality. Helmut Börsch-Supan, with the help of a contemporary map of the city, has ascertained that part of Dresden-Neustadt, near the bank of the Elbe, is depicted here. The long buildings are military supply sheds, the group of poplar trees are on the drilling ground for cadets. Gille's teacher J. C. Dahl knew this view as well; his apartment, at An der Elbe 33, was on the other bank of the river, almost directly across from this view.

In the middle, a pencil sketch shows through the thin paint. On the reverse side, one finds a traditional rendering of a landscape with outlines of trees and the slope of a mountain to the right.

HRL

Louis Gurlitt (1812–1897)

59

Near Esrum on Seeland, 1834

Oil on canvas, 23 × 36 cm
Signed lower left: "L Gurlitt" (initials linked)
Hamburger Kunsthalle, inv. no. 1150

The viewer is invited to enter into this little picture: up a softly rolling hill, into an earthwork-lined lane marked by deep wagon ruts, then past bushes and a house with a high reed roof. Our eye wanders further – over two rows of trees, house roofs towering above some of them – to broad plains where two sails draw our attention to a river, and finally ends up at a range of mountains, which sinks off on the right side. The sky over this landscape radiates brightly; it becomes darker at the top.

The young artist elaborately crosses the view into the distance with a wide-angle perspective. Like the flapping of

60

A Water Mill near Christiania, 1835

Oil on paper, 31 × 31 cm
Signed lower left (scratched): "L Gurlitt"
(initial capitals linked)
Hamburger Kunsthalle, inv. no. 1155

birds' wings, the earth walls on the side spread the field of
vision. The distinctiveness of this picture is its combination of
breadth and depth. As Kasper Monrad has suggested, with this
painting Gurlitt made "an important step on the way to a new
Danish landscape painting."[1]

Gurlitt painted this little picture in the hope of winning
a competition run by the Copenhagen Art Association: a
landscape, showing "a Danish region", would be awarded 150
talers. Gurlitt's entry did receive the citation for best picture,
but he was not awarded the prize, since his picture was deemed
too small. Could that have surprised him? The painting has not
only the dimensions, but also the character, of a study. Although
it is precisely structured, it is not composed in line with the laws
of tradition. Whether or not it was created in the studio or
outdoors it still has the freshness and liveliness of a study of
nature – we need only look closely at the loamy trail or the
two bushes! The light of the sun is seen, not scooped out; it
fills nature with life. Part of this is also the atmosphere, the
intangible element of air; air is discernible where it lets a little
bit of grey appear hazy. In the end, Gurlitt received 100 talers.
The award was not only an expression of respect for his talent,
but also a reluctant acknowledgement of the new.

HRL

1. Kasper Monrad, *Hverdagsbilleder*, Copenhagen, 1989, p. 243.

Gurlitt reproduces an extreme close-up of the strange
construction, in all its detail, of a water mill from three pillars
of stacked logs, including the two dams, the water flowing
behind, the towering poles, and the saturated boards. The
buildings in the back appear poor and decrepit, while in contrast
to the frail man-made work, the sloping, tree-covered hill does
testify to the power of nature, even though this power has
begun to decline; even the tree in the distance is half-dead.
However, the blue, almost cloudless sky outshines everything;
the light of the midday sun shines brightly, letting the water
shimmer, the vegetation flourish and the barn roof light up.
It is light that causes life to flourish.

As an art student Gurlitt ended his second journey through
Norway in 1835 in Christiania (present-day Oslo). Near there
he discovered the unusual canal, from which the miller himself
directed the water on to the mill. The construction became the
inspiration for this study, not the mill itself. Thus Gurlitt chose
a subject which would not have been considered picturesque by
almost any painter of the previous generation.

Gurlitt used the study for a larger composition (above), in
which the sky is dramatically clouded over, and the mill takes
on a big role. The comparison makes apparent the route taken
from a sober depiction of nature to an effective pictorial
composition.

HRL

60

61

View into Mountains near Civitella, 1845

Oil on paper mounted on cardboard, 26.8 × 32.9 cm
Hamburger Kunsthalle, inv. no. 5335

Gurlitt used his ability to join the exactness of the close-up with
the impressive effects of the remote view throughout his career.
While living in Rome from 1843 to 1846, he took trips to the
surrounding area, where he painted studies from nature, such
as this one, time and again. Here, he painted with the Porta San
Francesco in Civitella behind him, where the view extends
north to the Monti Ruffi and the Mammelli in the distance
(Domenico Riccardi established the exact location).

The view passes through a barren, rocky mountain
range, cut by gorges, sparse in vegetation. Brown and ochre
tones predominate, supplemented by green in the shadow to
the left and the light in the front, a small patchwork of blue
and brown further in the middle, and of white and black across
two white areas at the top. This bleak landscape is not devoid of
human presence or the occasional building.

The path into the distance is divided into illuminated and
shadowed zones; the clouds have also been organized by light
and dark. The main scene is created by light from a brightly
illuminated, steeply towering rock formation; a plateau rises
in the middle like a ramp.

In addition to an impressive orchestration of light, the lively
effect of this study comes from the brushstrokes, which are
clearly discernible almost everywhere; especially painterly are
the strokes directly under the peasant woman. Although it looks
as if she has laid many large pieces of cloth out to be bleached
by the sun, it is really only the light colour of the brush that we
perceive. Narrative of any kind is alien to the picture.

HRL

Georg Haeselich (1806–1880)

62

In the Heather, c. 1845

Oil on canvas, 31 × 37 cm
Hamburger Kunsthalle, inv. no. 3191

After spending a long period in Munich studying, Haeselich returned to Hamburg and, when the heather bloomed in early autumn, he went out to the heath, a steppe-like area near Luneburg. Haeselich was probably the first painter ever to see heather as something worth painting.

The hilly landscape, a region formed by glaciers, is framed by a row of bushes. Between these edges the hills roll softly and rise with a path that goes off to the top. The rising curve of the horizon stretches an arch between the bushes on each side. Rain clouds hover in the sky. The open, sketch-like painting in the sky is concomitant with the generous brushwork in the foreground. The earth, the roundness of the worn-down granite, the heather and the bushes are all rendered with the exactness of a superior draughtsman.

The homogenous effect of the subdued colours does not allow the question of transition between sharp and hazy outlines to surface. The sharply subdued light of the cloudy sky is strong enough to let the distant hills appear light between the dark bushes and the ground in the front to appear in various shapes. Despite the railing rising on the right and the paths into the distance, this empty countryside, devoid of human presence, appears abandoned.

HRL

Constantin Hansen (1804–1880)

63

A Company of Danish Artists in Rome, 1837

Oil on canvas, 62 × 74 cm
Originally signed and dated (according
to an old statement): "Roma 1837 C.H."
Statens Museum for Kunst, Copenhagen, inv. no. SMK3226

In March 1837, Constantin Hansen received a commission from the Copenhagen Art Association for a painting of his own choice of subject. He began a picture intended to give an impression of artists' life in Rome. But he chose not to follow the same pattern as several other painters, who portrayed Danish and German artists enjoying themselves in Roman tavernas and surrounded by Romans in picturesque dress (Franz Catel in 1824, Dietrich Wilhelm Lindau in 1827, and Ditlev Blunck in 1836). Hansen consciously sought to avoid the familiar clichés concerning artists in Rome, and was keen to show his friends as serious artists concerned with discussing important questions. Here, the architect Gottlieb Bindesbøll is reclining while he describes the journey he and Rørbye had recently made to Greece, a country that at that time, only a few years after the Greek War of Independence, was still an unknown land for most of those interested in art. There is much to indicate that Hansen was aiming at a psychological portrait of each individual figure, and he has provided a subtle picture of the way in which each of them is listening to Bindesbøll's account. In 1838 – while Hansen was still in Rome – the art historian N. L. Høyen, who knew all the artists portrayed quite well, wrote a searching and sensitive account of this picture, in which he showed that he had read and understood the painter's characterization of the group of artists.[1]

Although Hansen has tried to create a natural grouping for his figures, the picture nevertheless bears the hallmark of a contrived scene. It is not a particular moment observed on the spot. Hansen painted a number of meticulous studies of details before starting on the actual painting – of the empty room (private collection) and of each individual figure (most in the possession of Statens Museum for Kunst). His own figure (far left) has been painted on the basis of a study that Albert Küchler painted for him after he himself had made a rough pencil drawing of the posture he wanted.

Several attempts have been made to interpret this painting.[2] Most fascinating is a suggestion that it was intended as a modern, everyday paraphrase of Raphael's School in Athens. Like the Italian Renaissance master, the Danish artist has grouped his figures around an opening giving access to the light, and in each case the figures represent a cultural élite. But while the portals in Raphael's painting open the way to a superior insight, Hansen's door opens on contemporary reality, and the ancient philosophers are replaced by some quite down-to-earth Danish artists.[3]

The figures represented are, from left to right: Constantin Hansen, Gottlieb Bindesbøll (reclining), Martinus Rørbye (sitting in the doorway), Wilhelm Marstrand, Albert Küchler, Ditlev Blunck and Jørgen Sonne. Some of Hansen's oil studies can be seen on the wall, and on the table at the right there is one of Bindesbøll's first proposals for the Thorvaldsens Museum.

Although the contemporary reception of this picture was fairly mixed, it is now considered to be one of the finest works of the Danish Golden Age.

KM

1. See N. L. Høyen, *Skrifter*, Copenhagen, 3 volumes, 1871–76, I, p. 98 ff.; quoted in English in London 1984, cat. no. 29.
2. See the account in Los Angeles & New York 1993–94, cat. no. 44.
3. This interpretation was first proposed by Søren Kaspersen in 1981, and further developed by him in Copenhagen & Århus 1991, pp. 54–67.

64

The Arch of Titus in Rome, 1839

Oil on canvas, 24 × 29 cm
Signed and dated bottom right: "Const. H. 1839"
Statens Museum for Kunst, Copenhagen, inv. no. SMK3679

A noticeable gap emerged in the 1830s between Eckersberg's art and that of his pupils. While the teacher generally applied the same attitude to all his views of Rome and executed them with the same passionate care, his pupils showed more flexibility when they sought to take up the thread during their visits to Italy. Their approach varied according to their intention in each individual picture. There is a striking difference between the small oil studies they painted outdoors and the large, carefully planned compositions they produced in the studio. There is almost no such distinction in Eckersberg's art. These large compositions by the young artists were intended to capture everything that was typical of Rome, and they often acquired a distinct element of genre painting. In many cases, therefore, the result was quite conventional. In their studies, on the other hand, the young painters retained their fresh and unprejudiced approach.

This applies to Constantin Hansen above all. There is a significant difference between his picture of a few Romans playing *boccia* in front of the so-called Temple of Vesta in Rome (1837, Statens Museum for Kunst) and this study of the Arch of Titus near the Roman Forum. He has portrayed it from a somewhat unusual perspective. The arch is seen not from the front, but from the side, so that the façade appears drastically foreshortened. The picture is not a faithful depiction of the structure and was thus not intended for tourists. It is a study made exclusively for the artist's own use.

The perspective clearly betrays Eckersberg's influence. The foreshortening and the wall surface, which is parallel to the picture surface, are features found in several of Eckersberg's architectural studies of Rome. On the other hand, the use of colour is noticeably different from Eckersberg's clear, almost schematic choice of colours. Hansen has a far greater feel for the fine, varied shades in the sunlight and shadows. In this picture he moves in the direction of Impressionism's treatment of colour more than any other Danish artist of his day.

KM

Carl Hasenpflug (1802–1858)

65

View of the Garrison Church in Potsdam, 1827

Oil on copperplate, 63.3 × 81.3 cm
Signed and dated lower right: "C. Hasenpflug 1827"
Stiftung Stadtmuseum Berlin, inv. no. GEM 80/7

This painting is an example of an *Uhrbild* (clock picture), a genre very popular during the Biedermeier period. The clock tower of the Garrison Church in this painting houses a real clock, the mechanism of which is mounted on the reverse of the copperplate. The painting thus had a practical function in the home, which in that period was not seen as detrimental to its dignity as a piece of art. The Royal and Garrison Church, built in 1730–32 and designed by Philipp Gerlach, was a place of particular dignity, home to the bell chime "Üb' immer Treu und Redlichkeit"[1] as well as the final resting place of Friedrich the Great and the soldier-king Friedrich Wilhelm I. It was severely damaged in 1945 and finally destroyed in 1968. Eduard Gaertner depicted it a second time in 1840 from almost exactly the same position, also as an *Uhrbild* but in a vertical format (Stadtmuseum, Berlin).

Hasenpflug's architectural paintings, when they were not fantasies, usually depicted famous churches, as here. What is unusual and possible to explain only as a patriotic gesture is Hasenpflug's choice of a baroque church. He selected the view so that our line of sight would be directed undisturbed over the Broad Bridge, with its Roman warriors by the Räntz brothers, into the Broad Street and to the castle. On the other side, running parallel to the canal, we see the silhouette of the Garrison Church and the houses on the opposite bank. Our view is finally led by the tower into the sky. The time of day, judging from the south-easterly sun, is late morning. It is apparently Sunday, since the somewhat formal accessory figures, who contribute to closing the deep space, appear to be in part church-goers; no one is working.

The artist's use of light leaves most of the architecture in shadow; only the southern face of the tower and the long house have been brightly illuminated, to emphasize verticality. Just as Schinkel liked to do, Hasenpflug has drawn the architectural details in pen, over which the paint was glazed. The sky takes up a large part of the picture, and the few clouds in the lower part make reference to the silhouettes of the buildings, while the tower reaches into pure blue. The green masses of leaves are spread symmetrically and intensify the festive effect of the picture.

HBS

1. The bell chime "Be ever faithful and honest" enjoyed great popularity well into the twentieth century.

66

Snowdrifts in the Cloister of the Halberstadt Cathedral, 1837

Oil on canvas, 26 × 22.5 cm
Signed at bottom: "C. Hasenpflug"
Städtisches Museum, Halberstadt, inv. no. Kl/294

The frame is inscribed: "South-east Part of the Cloister of the Halberstadt Cathedral painted by C. Hasenpflug 1837." In fact, the painter does render exactly the view from the east wing of the cathedral cloister in Halberstadt, to the south. The Late Gothic relief of the Lamentation of Christ is still there. The large pointed arches, opening into the courtyard, were later subdivided into tripartite arches.

The snow intensifies the light of this bright winter day and separates distinctly bright and dark surfaces of the walls and vaults of this Early Gothic cloister. In the small details of this large building, Hasenpflug expresses deep respect for the concentrated spiritual power created here. A cloister is a closed and ordered world unto itself, where a person can recollect himself in private. Hasenpflug shows here, however, how the snow breaks into this closed-off world and how the wind blows it into all corners and even covers the sculpture. The crumbling retaining wall offers no resistance, and there is no one here to restore order.

A biography of the artist in *Deutsches Kunstblatt* in 1856 stated: "The severe snowy winter of 1837–38, which took over half of spring, quaintly decorated the cloister of the Halberstadt churches, the ruins of Walkenried and Paulinzella. He, who until now just as likely built as painted in his pictures, realized now the especially painterly side of the buildings." We can verify this statement against Hasenpflug's oeuvre. In fact, in 1837 he began an unbroken string of pictures showing ruins in winter, which he probably painted not only for their picturesque appeal, but as an expression of a painfully felt opposition between the medieval world and the present.

Hasenpflug knew the cathedral in Halberstadt well. In the same year in which he painted this picture, Friedrich Lucanus's life work appeared, *The Cathedral of Halberstadt: its History, Architecture, Antiquities and Art Treasures*, to which Hasenpflug contributed illustrations. The goal of Lucanus's book was to garner contributions for the preservation of the structure by emphasizing its high artistic quality. This small picture seems like a resigned commentary on such efforts.

HBS

Johann Erdmann Hummel (1769–1852)

67

Polishing the Granite Basin
for the Lustgarten, 1831/32

Oil on canvas, 64.5 × 87 cm
Stiftung Stadtmuseum Berlin, inv. no. 59/926x

At the 1832 Berlin Academy exhibition, Hummel exhibited three pictures which he described in the catalogue as: "The large Granite-Basin portrayed in different moments: 301. – In the studio, where, by means of a steam machine, it lies polished, completely finished. 302. – How it is being erected at the Kupfergraben in the new warehouse district, which is under construction, and being erected, and being moved, in order to put it in the right position. 303. – How it is displayed in the meantime in the Lustgarten. The view is taken from the Museum in the direction of the palace. Note: It will perhaps be noticed by some, the same basin is depicted in a different colour in each of the three views; I would like to draw your attention to the fact that it is polished, and consequently takes on the colour of the objects which surround it. E.H."

This explanation verifies the desire of the painter that the observer views the picture as a result of artistic as well as scientific activity. He reveals himself to be a representative of that generation shaped by the Enlightenment and affirms technical progress, demonstrated by the manufacture of the 6.9-metre granite basin. Originally, this should have been placed in the rotunda of Schinkel's museum, but because of its size it was erected at the front. The finish – perfected by steam and a demonstration of the beauty that technology can win from natural materials – should be admired no less than the carving of the basin from a huge boulder found near the Fürstenwald and transported to Berlin.

Hummel not only paints with exact precision the speckled structure of the stone, but also presents the carving device and the windows of the workshop. Even the view through the open door behind the painter is reflected distorted in the stone. The value of this work of art contrasts with the mere functionality of the workshop. We do not know its location. The view from the side window leads to buildings, but the reflection of the door shows water, in which trees and the sky are mirrored, referring to the landscape from which the granite block came. We know that the stone was transported on the river Spree, making it necessary to erect the workshop near the water.

The painting cannot be ascribed to any conventional genre. It is easiest to connect it with descriptions of work in Diderot's *Encyclopedia*. However, there is a strange absence of workers. Christian Gottlieb Cantian (1794–1866) made the basin. The first and second of the three pictures made their way from his family to the Stadtmuseum in Berlin; in addition to the third painting, a smaller version of the picture shown here is thought to exist.

HBS

68

In the Park of Buch Castle, c. 1835

Oil on paper mounted on canvas, 44 × 55.5 cm
Staatliche Museen zu Berlin, Nationalgalerie,
inv. no. NG 15/60

In 1836, the sixty-seven-year-old Hummel exhibited three
pictures at the Berlin Academy, numbers 401–3: "Three
Landscapes, Representing Views in Buch. Property of Canon
von Voss." Like *Polishing the Granite Basin* (cat. no. 67), this is
a tripartite cycle. Buch was a village to the north-east of Berlin
which belonged to the Voss family until 1898. The castle
was here, and there was an English garden. Count Wilhelm
von Voss was the owner of the three pictures, which are today
in museums in Essen, Wuppertal and Düsseldorf. All are
60 cm in height, two measure 75 cm in width and one 53 cm;
this last, almost square, was probably the centre of the group.

The picture from Berlin shown here, also from Voss's estate,
is a slightly smaller version of the painting in Wuppertal. It
shows park scenery with buildings probably connected to a
mill – in other words, not a particularly architectural choice
of subject. Also, the other figures suggest something to do with
agriculture. The wagon pulled by three white horses is loaded
with corn. In contrast, a group of two old linden trees is
splendidly presented at the edge of a thicket on a small hill.
Through the branches one's gaze penetrates into the distance
without intending to notice the artistically laid-out garden.
Hummel juxtaposed the compact tops of the lindens with a tall,
slender tree to the right, which lets the sky shine through all
over. His intention was to reproduce, with the greatest precision
and respect for nature, a park with trees, a meadow and water.
He does not shy away from reproducing every single leaf of a
tree. Such love of large trees was expressed above all by Johann
Christian Reinhardt, in his similarly exact paintings and
drawings. He and Hummel were friendly in Rome in the 1790s.
This conscientiousness connects Hummel's rare landscapes with
his sometimes beguiling architectural and genre paintings.

HBS

Just Ulrich Jerndorff (1806–1847)

69

Cliff Landscape in Saxon Switzerland, 1837

Oil on paper mounted on canvas, 28 × 39 cm
Landesmuseum für Kunst und Kulturgeschichte – Schloss
und Augusteum, Oldenburg, inv. no. LMO 15.520
HAMBURG AND COPENHAGEN ONLY

A picture of complete stillness: rugged cliffs, a stream spanned by a wooden bridge, the connection between the two trees on the left and the farm on the right – these are the things we perceive with a cursory glance. Despite the flowing water, it is as though nothing stirs. The cumulus clouds hang still in the light blue sky. The morning light gives this impression, letting the relief of the many-layered cliff face appear clearly defined, as does the bridge's railing and the bright white from the wall of the house between the trees. In the end, the light shows every tree and every shrub with great clarity. It is light that gives nature its manifold shape.

On closer inspection we discover that beyond the sandy path with the turf, beyond the bushes and trees on the bank, the stream is dammed before the bridge. In the water are slats, perhaps some kind of fish trap. At last, we see two people standing in front of a strange hut on the other bank. Despite its stillness, this picture is full of details, and almost has something to tell.

An inscription (not by the artist) on the frame of the canvas on which Jerndorff's paper was mounted gives the reference to Saxon Switzerland. As Helmut Börsch-Supan has discovered, the painting shows the granite cliffs on the river Weisseritz in an area called the Plauenscher Grund (the previous supposition that this is a landscape near Oberstein is incorrect). Jerndorff's 1837 Italian journey apparently took him through Dresden.

HRL

154

Jens Juel (1745–1802)

70

View of the Little Belt from Hindsgavl, c. 1800

Oil on canvas, 42 × 62.5 cm
Thorvaldsens Museum, Copenhagen, inv. no. B 237

71

View of the Little Belt from a Hill near Middelfart, Funen, c. 1800

Oil on canvas, 42.3 × 62.5 cm
Thorvaldsens Museum, Copenhagen, inv. no. B 238

Jens Juel was Denmark's leading portraitist in the final decades of the eighteenth century. As well as his many portraits, however, he also painted numerous landscapes, about seventy-five altogether.[1] The pictures can be divided into three categories: backgrounds to portraits, "Gothic" mountain views and specific Danish localities.[2] These two views, painted near the estate of Hindsgavl outside Middelfart in western Funen, both belong to the last category.

When Juel painted the first view, from the Hindsgavl mansion overlooking Fænø Sound, as this part of the Little

Belt is called, he must have been standing on the southern part of the peninsula, which jutted out like a promontory to the west of Middelfart. To the left we can see parts of Fænø, which almost completely hides the neighbouring island of Fænø Kalv, while Skærbæk and Nørreskoven, each on its own side of the entrance to Kolding Fjord, frame the sound in the distance. The symmetrically constructed scene is a summer's day in the area known as Grønnedal close to Hindsgavl, between two hills enclosed by a white fence in the direction of Fænø Sound. The picture is populated by various groups of figures. There is a couple standing close to the fence, with their backs to the viewer, enjoying the view across the belt, while another couple are sitting on the bench, deeply engrossed in conversation. Then there is a mother with her two children, the daughter playing with a dog and the boy sitting on the grass. However, not everything is pure idyll, as a bailiff can be seen chiding a peasant in the shaded foreground a little away from the other figures.

The second picture, asymmetrical in construction, shows two riders on their way up the winding road leading from the town of Middelfart, which can be seen in the background. To allow them to enter the area in the foreground surrounded by a dry stone wall, a peasant girl is holding the gate open. In the right foreground a farmer sits on the grass, with two children playing beside him. When Juel painted this scene, he was, according to the title, standing on high ground looking out towards the town of Middelfart on the Little Belt. In view of the size of the church and the direction of the road indicated by the green

71

bushes, it is an obvious assumption that the gate in the foreground marks the entrance to the estate of Hindsgavl at the
end of Adlerhusvej, some two kilometres from the mansion
of Hindsgavl in the direction of the town. This spot has been
marked for many years by a red porter's lodge (now used as a
private residence). The countryside jutting into the field of
vision on the left is part of the Jutland coast.

The fact that neither of the pictures shows the mansion
of Hindsgavl or its owners might suggest that they were
commissioned by Christian Holger Adler, the reformist owner of
Hindsgavl, and depict "before and after" scenes of serfdom and
its abolition. The period before this watershed in Danish history
is shown in the first view, partly in the shape of the angry
bailiff and the submissive peasant, and partly in a composition
that clearly separates the social groups from each other. The
time after the change, on the other hand, is brought to life in
the second picture where both groups, peasants and squires, are
now seen in friendly coexistence. Christian Holger Adler was
among the great landowners in Denmark who supported the
agricultural reforms that led to the end of serfdom in 1788. In
1787, Adler himself published a small tract on this subject and
the same year he set about putting his ideas into practice. By
1796, eight years after the formal abolition of serfdom in the
country, all the farmers who had previously belonged to the
estate of Hindsgavl were free.

The scenes from the Hindsgavl estate have traditionally been
dated to c. 1800, a full twelve years after abolition, when the
event was no longer much in the public mind. It is likely,

however, that they were painted some years earlier, perhaps in
1797, when Juel was in Funen in connection with his work on
the large Ryberg family portrait.[3] If they were begun in 1797,
the possibility exists that C. D. Friedrich might have seen them
in Jens Juel's studio before leaving in May 1798. This is
probable, not least because Juel's pairing of pictures consisting
of one centred and one off-centred scene is often encountered in
Friedrich's work.[4]

The pictures of Hindsgavl before and after the abolition of
serfdom were not hung there, although this had presumably
been the intention. Instead, they were bought by the engraver
G. L. Lahde at auction in 1803 after Juel's death. Thorvaldsens
Museum acquired them in 1843 from Lahde's daughter.[5]

Until recently, Juel's landscapes have been seen as a kind
of leisure occupation for the painter and therefore not
characterized by the same seriousness as his extensive work
as a portraitist. This view has now been partially revised.

GW

1. Henrik Bramsen, *Landskabsmaleriet i Danmark
   1750–1875*, Copenhagen, 1935, p. 23.
2. Anders Kold, "Ej blot af lyst og i ledige stunder: to
   landskaber af Jens Juel på Thorvaldsens Museum",
   Meddelelser fra Thorvaldsens Museum, Copenhagen,
   1989, p. 43.
3. Ellen Poulsen, *Jens Juel*, Copenhagen, 1991, no. 682.
4. Kasper Monrad, *Caspar David Friedrich og Danmark*,
   Copenhagen, 1991, p. 189.
5. Anders Kold, op. cit., pp. 42–53.

Georg Friedrich Kersting (1785–1847)

72

Court Preacher D. Reinhard in His Study, c. 1811

Oil on canvas, 47 × 37 cm
Dated lower right on table: "181."
Staatliche Museen zu Berlin, Nationalgalerie,
inv. no. NG 27/63, Schnell no. A 30

Caspar David Friedrich, who walked with Kersting through the Riesen Mountains in 1810, wrote on 26 March 1818 to his brother Heinrich about a portrait Kersting had done of him: "The picture, of my studio, is yours, and I give you a free hand, as you like. However, I expect you not to sell it. There is a similar picture from Kersting available here, the study of the famous preacher Reinhard, of him sitting and reading at his desk. One can see the cliffs through the window: Königstein, Lilienstein, Pfaffenstein, in short all of Saxon Switzerland in the distance."

D. Franz Volkmar Reinhard, a court preacher, who died on 6 September 1812 at the age of fifty-nine, was one of the most famous theologians of the Enlightenment. He strove for the moral uplifting of man through proof of supernatural revelations. Following Friedrich's interiors, Kersting understood the study as a reflection of the state of mind of its user, thus adding a new dimension to the portrait. The picture of Reinhard can also be read in this way. It was possibly intended as a present for the sitter, though it did not remain in his possession; it was exhibited in Dresden in March 1816 where it was for sale. We have no reason to suppose that it is a posthumous portrait, other than the fact that the subject is idealized.

In none of Kersting's thirteen other known interiors with a window view does landscape, through expansion and clarity, play so great a role as here. The windows, rather unconvincing from an architectural standpoint, appear almost as if Kersting added them for the sake of the view, and thus accepted a scaling down of Reinhard's figure. Reinhard lived in the Grosse Brüderstrasse in the centre of Dresden, which means this certainly cannot be the view from his study. The garden where he enjoyed spending his summers was in the suburb of Wilsdruff, set in the opposite direction from Saxon Switzerland. The picture thus contains symbolic elements that intensify reality and cannot be understood as an exact illustration of an interior. The lightness and size of the room are expressions of freedom of thought and enlightenment. Reinhard studies in natural light. The worlds of books and nature are not opposites, the theologian sees them both as God's creation. There are other clues to the painter's free approach to reality. We can verify that in 1808 Reinhard received the bust of Luther from Schadow as a gift and placed it in his study. However, here it has been over-dimensionalized, occupying the width of the entire bookcase as a colossal bust. It is also doubtful that the Christ picture above the desk was actually square.

The bright, open landscape in the background is so similar to Friedrich's paintings of the time that his influence is likely, especially since it has been discovered that Kersting painted the figures in Friedrich's *Morning in the Riesengebirge* (1811, Galerie der Romantik, Berlin) at around the same time.

HBS

73

Wanderer in Saxon Switzerland, c. 1820

Oil on canvas, 22.8 × 32.5 cm
Kunstsammlungen zu Weimar, inv. no. 1749
Schnell no. A 94
HAMBURG ONLY

An unidentifiable man in city clothes has scaled a mountain and now, resting exhausted on the ground, looks at the countryside spread out below him, the Elbsandsteingebirge with the magnificent Lilienstein. This is certainly a portrait. As a city dweller and wanderer, he is a stranger in this area. He does not emphasize his physical achievement, rather he contemplates the landscape under an overcast sky with humility. Hats laid aside by resting wanderers serve repeatedly as a sign of devoutness before nature in Friedrich's paintings and this, combined with the small format, expresses this attitude in Kersting's painting. On the one hand, man is trapped to the earth, but on the other he can, by powers of his intellect and spirit, transcend the earthly and contemplate the world from an almost heavenly perspective. The expression on the wanderer's face of being lost in thought appears to reflect this ambivalence. The seedling of an oak tree, which can barely grow into a tree on the top of the mountain, can be seen as a symbol for fighting bravely despite resistance, but still failing in the end. This meaning of the oak plays a large role in Kersting's work. Kersting abstains from gesture and personal touch, and conscientious recording harmonizes with the streak of resignation in the man. This separates the work from Friedrich's *Wanderer Looking over the Sea of Fog* (Hamburger Kunsthalle), which was probably done somewhat earlier.

In portrait painting, sitting or even reclining figures are a common theme, symbolizing a love of nature (this was especially so in England).

HBS

Friedrich Wilhelm Klose (1804–c. 1874)

74

The New Warehouse District in Berlin, 1835

Oil on canvas, 31 × 35 cm
Signed and dated bottom right: "F. W. Klose 1835"
Stiftung Preussische Schlösser und Gärten Berlin-Brandenburg,
Potsdam, inv. no. GK I 3711

The area today known as "Museum Island" (Museumsinsel),
dedicated solely to art, was originally filled with buildings,
mostly designed by Schinkel, to serve the shipping traffic on
the Spree. Klose considered these newly built complexes worthy
of being painted. The canal in the foreground, leading to the
salt depot which had been built in 1834, was first dug in 1833.
To the right of the salt storehouse the back of the Salt Tax
Building is visible. The large, five-storey building on the right
with the brick wall is a warehouse. To the left, between the
trees, one can make out the dome of the cathedral and the
roof of Schinkel's museum with its statues of the Dioscuri. The
ideas of ennobled and mundane realities collide powerfully with
each other. The diagonal light of the afternoon sun casts long
shadows, creating a strict composition of light and dark surfaces
and a clear perspectival construction of space. Added to that is
the allure of the reflection. The vertical edges of the buildings
are repeated in the ship masts. Figures and vegetation play a
secondary role, while the sky is more important for enlivening
the picture, with its turbulent contour of clouds, its striking
indentation above the museum and upward-moving course. One
feels the wind. Even this man-made world of architecture still
contains an element of the unpredictability of nature.

This painting is probably based on a drawing Klose
completed on site, because he must have had a study of
some kind that he later used to complete a watercolour. The
watercolour was exhibited in 1838 at the Berlin Academy
as number 413 under the title *The Salt Storehouse in Berlin*.

The thin application of paint does not differ substantially
from his watercolour technique. In 1835, Klose painted
another picture showing the opposite side of the warehouse
and the Kupfergraben from the parallel point of view, possibly
as a companion picture; it was acquired by King Friedrich
Wilhelm III.

HBS

Christen Købke (1810–1848)

75

Cloud Study, c. 1833

Oil on paper mounted on board, 17.6 × 26.0 cm
Statens Museum for Kunst, Copenhagen, inv. no. 7506

Købke painted a small number of cloud studies in the early
1830s, but it was only at the beginning of the 1840s that he
seriously turned to them as subjects for his paintings. He was
doubtless inspired in part by his teacher, C. W. Eckersberg,
but also perhaps by J. C. Dahl during his regular visits to
Copenhagen. These studies were preparations for landscape
paintings, but they were also ends in themselves; without
having his mind on anything else, the artist was able to devote
himself to the constantly changing formations and play of
colour in the clouds. Compared to Eckersberg's cloud studies,
Købke's differ in their frequent use of dramatic or atmosphere-
creating effects, as in Dahl's studies. Købke clearly did not have
the same meteorological, almost scientific, interest in clouds as
Eckersberg.

In this study, Købke was fascinated by the contrast between
the clouds' lowest, relatively heavy and dark sections and the
uppermost, light and bright areas that are lit up by the sun,
with a blue sky as their background. At the same time he has
tried to create spatial depth in his picture by varying the
nuances in the clouds. The painting is undated, but it is closely
related to *View from a Window in Toldbodvej Looking towards
the Citadel* (cat. no. 77), which can be dated with some certainty
to the summer of 1833.

KM

76

View of the Citadel Ramparts with the Towers of Our Lady's and St Peter's Churches in the Background, c. 1833

Oil on paper mounted on canvas, 17.0 × 30.7 cm
Den Hirschsprungske Samling, Copenhagen, catalogue 1982,
no. 313

Christen Købke's father, a master baker, had a contract to deliver
bread to the military garrison in the Citadel. From 1816, the
Købke family lived in the Citadel, but beginning in 1832
Christen Købke, together with the painter Frederik Sødring,
rented some rooms for use as a studio in Toldbodvejen (now
Esplanaden) just outside the Citadel ramparts. In *View from a
Window in Toldbodvej Looking towards the Citadel* (cat. no. 77),
he depicted a view of his childhood haunts. In the same year,
1833, he also painted a number of scenes from the Citadel,
including this one, where he is looking *out* from it.

There are considerable compositional parallels between
the view from the window in the Toldbodvej studio and this
painting. In both there is a section in the foreground hiding
much of the background, but whereas a chimney in the
Toldbodvej painting provides a measure of the distance covered
by the picture from the spot on which the painter is standing, in
this picture there is nothing to convey this. Using a quite radical
method of composition, Købke has allowed part of the actual
rampart around the Citadel to rise up and hide the view towards
the back.

This is quite remarkable. Like the three figures he shows
walking on the rampart, Købke could have taken a few steps
and observed the towers of Copenhagen from there. But he
chooses to let the towers and trees appear – slowly, one feels –
as in a film that has just commenced. The day, too, has just
started, and the clouds in the sky are illuminated and taking
on numerous shapes and colours. Everything is fresh and new
and must be captured at this moment. The small walking
figures extend the viewer's range and are looking at what we
shall shortly see. They personify the experience of discovering
it all anew.

75

The radical way in which the picture is cut can be taken as indicating that Købke painted only what he saw from exactly that spot, and this very realism and soberness in the conception of the view are special characteristics of what has been called the "Copenhagen School". But in my view there is no doubt that Købke simply wanted to have the actual Citadel rampart in his picture, that he was entirely conscious of the pictorial potential it provided. To a later age, the radical quality of the composition and the cutting is quite surprising.

With a single exception, Købke did not exhibit his studies of the Citadel. They were not intended for the public, but were the painter's own exercises and observations, which both sharpened his ability to reproduce what he saw, and also constituted an important element in his understanding of the space around him, the nearby Citadel and the world outside its ramparts.

SM

77

View from a Window in Toldbodvej
Looking towards the Citadel, c. 1833

Oil on paper mounted on canvas, 15.0 × 27.5 cm
Statens Museum for Kunst, Copenhagen, inv. no. SMK 3156

In this painting, Købke looks towards his family's home in the Citadel with the yellow houses in the right background, the trees on the surrounding ramparts behind the houses, the spire on the Citadel church to the right of the chimney in the foreground and the Citadel mill on the left. Further away there is a glimpse of the sound and a stretch of the Swedish coast. It is a whole world in a picture of modest proportions, and even then only in its background. The foreground is dominated by a chimney on the roof ridge of a house. Over by far the largest

76

77

part of the surface of the picture, Købke has indulged in painting light, bright clouds illuminated by the rays from a late afternoon sun low in the sky.

This is a view from Købke's studio in Toldbodvej in Copenhagen, where he painted one of his most inspired portraits, that of the artist Sødring with whom he shared the studio. Købke seems to have kept the rooms until 1845, although for a long time he also had a studio and apartment in his parents' large house on Blegdammen, which they bought in 1832.

It is significant that Købke chose a studio from which he could see his *home*. Throughout his entire life as an artist, time and again he chose subjects linked to his own immediate world and to that of his parents and thereby also to the places where he himself lived or had lived. If any of Eckersberg's students painted exactly what they saw in front of them in study after study, it was Købke. In his small studies we often seem to have a feeling of seeing, together with the artist, just that accidental bit of reality that briefly entered his field of vision. It is similar to the element of chance in a photographic snapshot, with the same fortuitous cuts.

But, naturally, Købke's painting is not accidental. Of course he could easily have chosen to have the houses in the Citadel occupy the entire surface of the picture, or simply to study the clouds. But the chimney in the foreground transforms the picture into something unusual. It is from this that the distance into the background can be measured via the reducing sizes of the mill and the church. Concerning the content of the motifs, this chimney is far less important than the church and the mill, but thanks to its position in the picture it acquires a far greater significance. This dualism endows the picture with magic and fascination. At the same time the chimney links the earth and the sky, and keeps the painting together on the vertical plane. On its surface it clearly divides light and shade; it is a crystalline, formal, unambiguous element that seems to cry out for symbolic interpretation, but in view of the immediate and enormously fresh sensual experience that is the very essence of the painting it is unreasonable to expect one.

There is also a further strange characteristic that can be seen in many of Købke's studies: he places a block of some kind in the foreground – here, in the form of the roof ridge, which seems to cut out the view. It is paradoxical to depict something and to hide it at the same time. Metaphorically speaking, this considerably increases the distance to the houses – and thus to his childhood home – in the background.

SM

78

One of the Small Towers on Frederiksborg Castle, c. 1834–35

Oil on canvas, 177 × 162 cm
Det danske Kunstindustrimuseum, Copenhagen, inv. no. 1325

During the first half of the 1830s, Christen Købke frequently painted Frederiksborg Castle, the Renaissance castle outside Hillerød, a market town north of Copenhagen. Købke first stayed in Hillerød in the late summer of 1831 as a result of his sister Conradine's complicated post-natal illness. During his stay, Købke spent some time with the art historian N. L. Høyen, who was spending the summer in Hillerød to evaluate and register the castle's very large and complex collection of national portraits.[1] Høyen was one of the key personalities in the emerging nationalist movement in Denmark. That same wave led to the abolition of absolutism and the introduction of democratic government to the country in 1849.

In a letter to his friend J. F. Schouw, dated 16 August 1831, Høyen describes how Købke was making various studies of the castle: "It is quite overwhelming to see what a building like the castle, or indeed even simply a part of it, can contain in the way of variety and wealth of shapes; you really only feel yourself to be alive when you see the artist bring out on his paper one interesting feature after another."[2] Købke studied the castle from both quite conventional and more unusual perspectives. In order to paint this picture, he crawled up on the roof of the castle and observed the spire on the great north-eastern corner tower and the view down across the adjoining fields and wooded areas as seen from above. The main focus of the picture, the large spire of the corner tower with the flag at the top, stands out with its light and shade, as a mighty, almost organic shape. The shape is repeated, but in miniature, in the spire of the stair turret and is counterbalanced in part by the square chimneys of various sizes.

Købke recreated the view from the roof of Frederiksborg Castle in another painting entitled *View across the Roofs of Frederiksborg Castle*. Both paintings came to form part of the decorations in Købke's parents' dining room in their country house on Blegdammen, which in those days was still a short distance from Copenhagen. In addition to the paintings from the roof of Frederiksborg Castle, the dining room, the most splendid room in the house, was adorned with two grisaille copies of Thorvaldsen's most popular reliefs, *Day* and *Night*, done by Købke.

78

79

Both views from the roof of the castle were done in two versions, which differ mainly in size. To this can be added the fact that the first set are considerably smaller and, moreover, painted on canvases of varying size. This, together with the independent nature of the pictures, might suggest that the idea of using them as part of the decorations in the dining room was conceived only after Købke had painted the first pictures.[3] Another view is that the genesis of the pictures was a plan according to which, on the background of drawn sketches (one of this version was made as early as July 1831),[4] the artist was to make painted studies and finally finished paintings.

The two paintings from Frederiksborg Castle for Købke's parents' dining room were severely criticized by art critics at the time. The art historian Emil Hannover wrote of them in 1893: "These decorations are without any particular artistic value, the scale having been too enormous for Købke's brush and for the quite insignificant views."[5] This view has now been revised, and today they are seen as examples of the contemporary fusion of pictorial art and architecture – but examples in which the subjects, in contrast to the others we know of, are not taken from antiquity, but refer to places with which the painter had a personal affinity.[6]

GW

1. Hans Edvard Nørregård-Nielsen, *Christen Købke*, volume I, Copenhagen, 1996, pp. 182–83, n. 37.
2. Hans Tybjerg, *Omkring Købkes Frederiksborg Slot ved Aftenbelysning*, Copenhagen, 1996, p. 8.
3. Kasper Monrad in Copenhagen 1996a, pp. 187–91.
4. Hans Edvard Nørregård-Nielsen, op. cit., volume II, p. 15, n. 13.
5. Emil Hannover, *Maleren Christen Købke*, Copenhagen, 1893, p. 71.
6. Kasper Monrad, op. cit., p. 191.

79

Frederiksborg Castle Seen from Jægerbakken, Study, c. 1835

Oil on paper mounted on cardboard, 22.2 × 33.5 cm
Den Hirschsprungske Samling, Copenhagen,
catalogue 1982, no. 316

This is the study for Købke's submission for a competition announced by the Art Association of Copenhagen in March 1835 with the theme "A public place or building". The competition, the second of its kind, was arranged at the suggestion of the

80

enterprising art historian N. L. Høyen and was aimed at increasing the knowledge and awareness of the country's historical buildings, as part of an overall increase in national sentiment. One result was that architectural studies of historical buildings became popular motifs among the painters of the Danish Golden Age. The Renaissance castle in Hillerød, north of Copenhagen, which was rebuilt by Christian IV in 1602–25, was anything but a random choice on Købke's part. He had on various occasions made both drawn and painted studies of it, as well as making finished pictures from various angles (see cat. no. 78).

The preparatory work for the competition was undertaken in the summer of 1835. During this work, Købke met up with the artist Jørgen Roed who had also chosen to depict the castle for the competition, but from a slightly different angle. Købke's drawn proposal formed the starting point for this painted study, which was subsequently increased to a large format almost without alteration. The difference between the sketch and the final painting is seen only in the appearance of more boats on the castle lake, the changed character of the cloud formations, the greater detail in the windows in the castle and adjacent buildings and the clearer reflection of the castle in the water. From Jægerbakken, Købke has captured Frederiksborg Castle from an imposing angle, from which two of its great wings can be seen, along with some lower adjacent buildings, all

surrounded by a vast expanse of sky. This spreading sky with its floating clouds and the shapes of the castle reflected in the dark waters of the surrounding lake reveal the building in an evocative, almost fairy-tale light.

Such a sense of atmosphere in a picture of an important historical building was anything but typical of the time. Instead, it was customary to record the subjects by daylight in accordance with the principles taught by Eckersberg. In this painting, Købke was probably inspired by the Romantic landscape art that was emerging in Dresden. His knowledge of such painting might have come via Høyen, who had met Caspar David Friedrich in Dresden in 1822–23, or through Dahl, who lived in Dresden from 1821.[1]

It can be seen from several letters from Købke that this painting created considerable problems for him, problems so great that at one time he started all over again. He was far from finishing the second version when the deadline for submissions was reached. His friend Jørgen Roed won the competition with *The Circus at Frederiksborg Castle* (National Historical Museum, Frederiksborg). The Art Association, however, also purchased Købke's contribution to lend to its members.[2]

GW

1. Kasper Monrad in Copenhagen 1996a, pp. 195–96.
2. Ibid., p. 195.

80

Morning View at Østerbro, 1836

Oil on canvas, 106.5 × 161.5 cm
Statens Museum for Kunst, Copenhagen, inv. no. 844

Købke's painting is seen from Østerbrogade looking towards Trianglen, roughly at the turning to present-day Willemoesgade.[1] When sketching the subject, Købke was presumably sitting on the parapet along Sortedamsøen, one of the three large lakes in Copenhagen, visible on the left of the picture. The painting provides an excellent picture of everyday life in the first decades of the nineteenth century on one of the main avenues leading north from Copenhagen. Here we can see how horse-drawn carriages were carrying peasants in their Sunday best into the city, the men in dark clothes and top hats, the women in characteristic white bonnets. Behind them can be seen a horse-drawn cart and various carriages driving in the opposite direction. The traffic on the gravelled road proceeded at a moderate pace, since the road was also used by cattle on the way from the city to the common to graze. Along the row of houses on the right side of the street are representatives of the bourgeoisie, while on the opposite side are so-called *skovser* women standing or sitting as they take a rest. These women, named after the fishing village of Skovshoved, where they lived, walked some fifteen kilometres every day to sell their fish at stalls along Gammel Strand in the centre of Copenhagen.

The land in this area had formerly belonged to the Crown, but was now privately owned. Rosendal, the large, yellow two-storey house in the centre of the picture, was owned by the merchant J. F. Tutein, and the land belonging to it stretched right down to the sound. To the left of it there was a relatively wild area known as Classens Have after the industrial magnate and landowner J. F. Classen, who founded it. The property next to Rosendal on the right was I dalen, owned by the physical education teacher V. V. F. F. Nachtegall who rented out accommodation in it to those in need of convalescence or simply needing to get away from the city. One of the house's permanent residents, Signe Læssøe, gathered many of the young artists, authors and painters of the day in her rooms, including Hans Christian Andersen, Constantin Hansen and J. T. Lundbye. The yellow building on the opposite side of the road was a market garden owned by a man named Danchert. Right at the back of the picture we can just glimpse Trianglen and beside it Nordre Frihavnsgade, where Købke's father had once had his bakery.[2]

Købke made two pencil drawings of this view but, contrary to his habit, apparently no painted studies. By means of a system of squaring, the second compositional drawing was transferred directly to the large canvas. In a letter to his friend, the painter Jørgen Roed, Christen Købke describes the work process with this large and demanding picture: "I have at last come so far, my dear comrade-in-arms, that I have gained peace enough to collect my thoughts for you. I am sitting here among all my studies for my painting of the view of Østerbro which I managed to set out yesterday. I have changed several things in it, it has cost me a good deal of time to collect the necessary studies, and before finally making up my mind. Now, I hope that it will on the whole remain as it is. The figures in it I have admittedly made up in my head, but I lack the necessary studies, which, however, I hope soon to have, as I know how I want them. As I have also felt the need here to be able to paint animals, I have begun to make a rather keen study of them, and I believe I have such an excellent opportunity to do this on the Common that I shall learn it in time. Now that I have collected the studies for the figures for the Østerbro I mentioned and arranged them on the canvas, I will leave them for a time so as to be able to start on it with fresh eyes when I begin to paint; then it will come straight from the heart.[3]

The Common to which Købke refers consisted of large areas of grass surrounding Copenhagen at the time (parts of it still exist in Fælledparken). About a thousand head of cattle used to graze on it, kept in various cattle sheds in the city during the night. As he says to Roed, Købke undertook a large number of studies of animals here. Later, he extended these to include the various human figures walking or sitting in the horse-drawn carriages.

GW

1. Hans Edvard Nørregård-Nielsen, *Christen Købke. Dosseringen og Frederiksberg*, volume II, Copenhagen, 1996, p. 94.
2. Ibid., pp. 93–94.
3. H. P. Rohde, *Kun en maler*, Copenhagen, 1993, p. 48.

81

View from the Limekiln with Copenhagen in the Background, 1836

Oil on canvas, 34.0 , 55.0 cm
Nivaagaards Malerisamling, Nivå

Apart from the pictures he painted during his journey to Italy in 1838–40, the geographical range of Købke's subjects was not great. Most of his landscapes were done in the immediate vicinity of his home in Blegdammen just outside Copenhagen. Generally speaking, he went only a few hundred metres before settling down to draw or paint. His longest excursions were to the bay near the limekiln (Kalkbrænderi), roughly a kilometre north of Copenhagen, where he found subjects for two pictures including this view. It was painted on a meadow near the sound coast with a strandrider's house in the foreground and Copenhagen harbour and Nyholm in the distance (a strandrider was something between a wreckmaster and a customs official).

While Købke's physical horizon was very limited, his artistic outlook was considerably wider. The painting testifies to how familiar he was with the classical European models and how fully aware of his artistic effects. When he chose the subject, he was in all probability, consciously or unconsciously, modelling himself on an etching by Rembrandt, the *Landscape with a Cottage and Hay Barn* from 1641.[1] Like the Dutch master, he

positioned himself so that the view across the flat landscape was divided in two by the building in the middle of the picture, and a contrast is created between the near and the far. The parallels are especially striking if we compare Rembrandt's etching with the compositional drawing Købke made on the spot before starting to paint (Statens Museum for Kunst).

However, there is no doubt that this landscape is one that Købke was looking at as he painted. This is indirectly confirmed by a note in Eckersberg's diary for 16 October 1836: "Visited Købke on Blegdamsveien, he had done some paintings, from there to the limekiln and back." Eckersberg took a keen interest in his former students' work and wanted to see the paintings Købke had just completed. His highest expectations were undoubtedly for Købke's major work *Morning View at Østerbro* (cat. no. 80), which was almost finished. But there is no doubt that he also saw this picture, and so he went out afterwards to the bay near the limekiln to see the view for himself. Neither Eckersberg nor his pupils would ever think of painting a landscape that could not be seen in reality.

KM

1. Christopher White and Karel G. Boon, *Hollstein's Dutch and Flemish Etchings, Engravings and Woodcuts. Vol. XVIII–XIX: Rembrandt van Rijn*, Vangendt and Co., Amsterdam, 1969, cat. no. B225; see Erik Fischer in Copenhagen 1981c, pp. 28 ff.

82

The Forum in Pompeii, Study, 1840

Oil on paper mounted on canvas, 36.6 × 44.4 cm
Dated: "10 Juli 40"
Fyns Kunstmuseum, Odense, inv. no. 645

Købke was in Pompeii in September 1839 and during the
summer of 1840. He made both a compositional drawing and
an oil study of the forum on the same day, 10 July 1840, and
back in Copenhagen he was commissioned by the Copenhagen
Art Association to do a large-scale painting of this study. The
painting was to be part of the annual lottery of works of art
organized for the members of the Association.

However, even in Pompeii, Købke must have been thinking
of this study as the starting point for a larger painting. The
apparently casual nature and immediacy of composition that

is characteristic of Købke's studies from the years he spent in
Copenhagen before setting out for Italy have here been replaced
by a carefully thought out and harmonious composition with
a clearly defined foreground, middle distance and background.
The picture is thus divided into distinct planes, with a
perspective sloping from both sides towards a point in the
background; at the same time, there is a carefully planned
colour perspective running from the shaded foreground to the
golden light in the middle distance and the complementary
bluish haze of the background. The harmoniously positioned
pillar at the start of the middle distance stands exactly on the
golden section and creates a sense of calm. The study is ready
to be transformed into a major painting, suitable for showing
in the official exhibition at the Academy in Copenhagen; the
larger painting has since been acquired by the J. Paul Getty
Museum (Malibu, California).

SM

83

Cloud Study, c. 1840–45

Oil on paper mounted on board, 15.5 × 24.3 cm
Statens Museum for Kunst, Copenhagen, inv. no. SMK7438

After his return from Italy, Købke turned seriously to painting studies of clouds. To judge by the posthumous catalogue of his effects, he painted more than twenty studies at this time. In this one, he has looked at the sky on a grey day when it was dominated by a thick covering of cloud. He was thus unable to play on the correlation between clouds and clear sky, but has painted a study of grey against grey. The challenge to the painter here was to express the different shades of grey and to make the clouds appear sculptural without the use of sharp contrasts.

The cloud studies were made alongside the landscape studies that Købke painted near his home. In a painterly sense they are closely related, and occasionally all there is to distinguish the two types is a different perspective. The present study has measurements identical to *View near Copenhagen* (c. 1840–45;

Statens Museum for Kunst),[1] where a narrow strip of landscape is seen beneath an overcast sky, and where a couple of mills break the sharp distinction between landscape and sky. The clouds in this picture are also closely related to the cloud formations in *View of Østerbro Seen from Dosseringen, Overcast Sky* (c. 1841–45; Statens Museum for Kunst).[2] Købke might also have inspired several younger landscape artists to paint cloud studies, especially Lundbye, who painted his first study of this type as early as 1837. After Købke's early death in 1848, a large number of his cloud studies – including those exhibited here – were bought by P. C. Skovgaard, confirming the great significance of Købke's art for a narrow circle of artists.

KM

1. See Copenhagen 1996a, cat. no. 163.
2. See ibid., cat. no. 158.

84

The Garden Gate of the Artist's Home
on Blegdammen, c. 1841/45

Oil on paper mounted on canvas, 29.5 × 24.5 cm
Statens Museum for Kunst, Copenhagen, inv. no. 6827

The imposing country property on Blegdammen, which Købke's parents acquired in 1832, housed most of the family: the artist himself, his wife and child, his parents, several of his brothers, his unmarried sisters and an unmarried aunt.[1] Blegdammen was at that time virtually a suburb of Copenhagen. The name (literally "the bleaching pond") arose because from the seventeenth century the area was used to bleach cotton materials. As late as the first decades of the nineteenth century there were still such bleaching areas among the industrial factories and properties that had been built in the meantime.[2]

In the summer of 1845, two years after the death of the artist's father, the family had to relinquish the house. Købke's mother moved to Kvæsthusgade, while he and his family settled in an apartment in Frederiksborggade in central Copenhagen. Shortly before leaving, Købke painted a series of pictures in which he expressed his personal impressions of the familiar places in and around the house. The picture of the garden gate opening on to Sortedam Dosseringen was part of this sequence. The other pictures in the series show the stairs leading up to his studio, the courtyard in front of the house with the gate leading into Købke's part of the garden, and finally the view from the basement kitchen looking up towards the courtyard. A feature common to all the pictures is that they depict gates or stairs that must be passed in moving from one place to another. Just as the

four pictures depict four different localities in and around the house, they are also painted at four different times of day and show the changes in light during the course of the day.

The picture of the garden gate was done in the afternoon, when the sun no longer stood out so sharply against the sky. The sun is casting light on the left side of the fence and providing a warm glow on the tall, slender tree trunks, framed in a multitude of leaves in greenish brown shades with the path leading out on the other side of the fence. The open gate denotes the transition from the secure family home to Sortedam Dosseringen, which Købke painted on various canvases over the years, and to the city alluded to by Trinity Church in the background. The church and the small ship framed by the gateposts have been interpreted as the meeting between two essential sets of norms in Købke's oeuvre – the ship being the symbol of movement, desire and the possibility of resolution, and the church the symbol of the Christian faith that characterized Købke's view of life.[3]

GW

1. Kasper Monrad, *Købke på Blegdammen og ved Sortedamssøen*, Copenhagen, 1981, p. 20.
2. Ibid., pp. 5–6.
3. Mikael Wivel in Copenhagen 1996a, pp. 318–23.

Johan Thomas Lundbye (1818–1848)

85

A Sunken Road near Frederiksværk, 1837

Oil on paper mounted on board, 22.1 × 24.9 cm
Signed and dated: "Frdsksv. April 37 Joh. Lundbye"
Statens Museum for Kunst, Copenhagen, inv. no. SMK 6471

Lundbye was only eighteen when he painted this motif of two young men seated on a slope, with part of a roof, a short stretch of road, a glimpse of a patch of water and, in the background, a rather higher hill surmounted by a burial mound. It is a revised version of a subject he had already painted a month before and immediately exhibited at the Academy but which, in his own words, he "rubbed out" in 1841.[1] The now vanished painting was called *View of Frederiksværk before Sunrise, Late Autumn*.

It is possible that the present variant of the subject shows the scene before sunrise, but the shadows behind the two men and the light in the sky could also indicate that the hour is a little later. It is difficult to know whether this uncertainty is characteristic of the painting in general. It is as though the individual layers hide each other: the slope hides the road, and the house and the slope on the right hide the water and the landscape beyond. The picture veils rather than displays its subject. But it is, of course, this very factor that makes it so fascinating.

Meanwhile, it is certain that this view is from the edge of Denmark's biggest lake, Arresø near Frederiksværk, and the landscape in the background is the Auderød headland stretching out into the lake and crowned by a burial mound. It is likely that Lundbye has depicted two of his six brothers in the picture, though they are not exact likenesses. Lundbye's father was appointed head of a military detachment in Frederiksværk in 1836 and had an official residence to the north of the town with a view across Arresø. Although Lundbye still continued to live in the Citadel in Copenhagen when his family moved to northern Zealand, he often went there and painted a large number of subjects in Frederiksværk and the surrounding area.

The similarity between this painting and those of Christen Købke has been demonstrated before.[2] This can be seen especially in relation to the easy manner of painting and the apparently haphazard way in which the subject is truncated. But Lundbye's study is nevertheless quite different – far more

enclosed, and with the individual pictorial elements more sharply distinguished from each other.

SM

1. Karl Madsen, *Johan Thomas Lundbye*, Copenhagen, 1895, p. 248, cat. no. 28.
2. Kasper Monrad, *The Golden Age of Danish Painting*, New York, 1993, p. 178.

86

Dolmen at Raklev, 1839

Oil on canvas, 66.7 × 88.9 cm
Signed and dated: "JTL Mai 1839"
Thorvaldsens Museum, Copenhagen, inv. no. B 255

There are three important, carefully executed paintings by Johan Thomas Lundbye in Thorvaldsens Museum, all from 1838–39. This is one of them, which Lundbye sold to Bertel Thorvaldsen shortly after finishing it in May 1839. As is clear from a diary entry of 1845, Lundbye would have liked to donate yet another painting from July 1839 to the future museum (Thorvaldsens Museum opened as Denmark's first purpose-built museum in September 1848), and there was even a plan for displaying all four paintings in the museum. They were presumably to have hung in the same room, a clear indication of a national awareness and a sense of patriotism in a museum with a national purpose, although Thorvaldsen's own art and his collection of paintings were decidedly international.

The subject in this painting is a burial mound near Raklev, not far from the north-west Zealand town of Kalundborg where Lundbye was born. The significance of the past for the present that Jørgen Roed painted into his motif in a treatment of 1832 (cat. no. 93) is merely a gentle hint compared with Lundbye's treatment of the theme. Here, the past speaks loud and clear,

85

86

dominating the entire landscape and literally towering into the present. We are not for a moment in any doubt that we are faced with an example of programme painting, with a work that seeks to embody a specific view of the relationship between a country's past, its landscape and its nature. Together they form a framework for the lives of past generations, the present and the special character of a people.

This kind of landscape and the relationship between Lundbye's Denmark and the traces of past generations are central themes in Lundbye's art. The burial mound as an important visual element in this theme is obvious; among Lundbye's spiritual mentors were both the museologist and historian of ancient Scandinavia, Christian Jürgensen Thomsen, and the art historian Høyen, both of whom were intensely preoccupied with national character. In concrete terms, Lundbye could also have seen a burial mound represented just as monumentally in a drawing by Caspar David Friedrich, which was in the Danish Crown Prince Christian Frederik's collections in Copenhagen. The Crown Prince had acquired

the drawing *Dolmen at Gützkow* (c. 1837–38) directly from Friedrich, and Lundbye doubtless knew it.[1]

But it is typical that Lundbye should give his Romantic painting a different twist from Friedrich. Friedrich's themes are the absolute, the eternal, the non-national; and the experience of landscape is quite fundamental to the individual human being. For Lundbye, the message and the relationship are concrete: "What I as a painter have set myself as the object in my life is to paint my beloved Denmark . . . what beauty there is in these fine lines in our hills, undulating so charmingly that they seem almost to have arisen from the ocean, the mighty ocean by whose shores the steep, yellow dunes stand, and in our forests, fields and heaths," wrote Lundbye in 1842.[2]

SM

1. Kasper Monrad in Copenhagen 1991, p. 73.
2. J. T. Lundbye, diary entry for Maundy Thursday 1842, in *Et Aar af mit Liv*, introduction by Mogens Lebech, Copenhagen, 1967, p. 47.

87

Fields near Aagerup South of Vejby, 1843

Oil on canvas, 15.5 × 26 cm
Ny Carlsberg Glyptotek, Copenhagen, inv. no. 3112

In June and July 1843, Lundbye stayed in the small village of
Vejby in northern Zealand, together with his close friend and
fellow painter Peter Christian Skovgaard. They wanted to
discover the simple life in the country, in the place where
Skovgaard's mother lived. A few months before this trip,
Lundbye finished his largest painting to date, *A Danish
Coastline. View from Kitnæs near Isefjord*, which he had worked
on intensively for more than a year. And immediately before
Lundbye left for Vejby, the painting was sold to the Royal
Gallery of Paintings at Christiansborg Palace in Copenhagen.

In his diary, Lundbye tells of the great sense of liberation he
felt at getting away from the large painting. And we clearly feel
this sense of freedom in the many studies he made in Vejby and
the surrounding area in the summer of 1843. In this painting
he looked from Vejby towards the nearby village of Aagerup
and painted a picture that is amazingly light and bright, the
essence of everything that is lovely in the Danish summer.

It is often the case with Lundbye that his paintings assume
the character of "images of the world", appearing to encompass
an enormous vista of everything from close up and far away and
equally often occupying a very small surface, as is the case here.
From the flowering and meticulously painted burdock in the
foreground we are led across a fairly large area; from the fields
between Vejby and Aagerup, which Lundbye has only sketched
with paint, to a hedgerow filled with rich vegetation, and from
there to a group of trees and houses in the background,
Aagerup. But far away one catches a glimpse of the shifting
sand dunes near Tisvilde, and in our thoughts we are already
well beyond them, drawn in by the light and expansive
atmosphere of the painting.

One might think that Lundbye would have to make use of
every single square millimetre of the small surface in order to
depict so much, but that is not at all the case. In the foreground
of the picture he has left a fairly large area empty. And the sky,
too, contains only a touch of blue, so the canvas can be seen
through the paint. It is this very paradox – endowing the view
with such a powerful effect in light, space and colour within the
space of such a small surface and with so few devices – that is
the essential fascination of this painting.

Although in a painting such as this, Lundbye seems to have
forgotten to be programmatic in paying homage to the Danish
landscape, it is naturally here, more than in carefully conceived
paintings, that we fall completely in love with the gentle,
undulating Danish countryside.

SM

Ernst Meyer (1797–1861)

88

Teatro Marcello, Rome, 1830s (?)

Oil on paper mounted on canvas, 26.7 × 35.9 cm
Signed: "EMEYER"
Den Hirschsprungske Samling, Copenhagen,
catalogue 1982, no. 393

Ernst Meyer lived for most of his life outside Denmark, mostly in Germany and Italy. Among both German and Danish artists in Rome he became something of an institution. This painting is rather unusual in his work as a whole. He principally painted genre scenes, and his portrayals of Roman street life, often containing tiny narrative scenes, attracted a large following among visitors to Rome. He himself made numerous copies of a few of his pictures in order to satisfy demand. And naturally, there is also an element of genre in this painting of a section of the ancient Teatro Marcello's curved wall, which is still a prominent structure in Rome (the shops, however, which had presumably been in the lower level of the ruin from the Middle Ages on, are no longer there).

The theatre was started under Julius Caesar and completed by the Emperor Augustus in memory of his nephew Marcus Claudius Marcellus. It is naturally not without significance that it is an ancient building, for the very fact that buildings dating back to antiquity were quite happily being used as dwellings or shops by Italians of his own day is something Meyer found particularly interesting.

In terms of colour, Meyer kept to a limited scale of predominantly brown shades – no feast of colour this – but a few touches of green in the beam above the entrance to the wine-seller's and in the plants growing above the small tiled roof brighten it up.

There is considerable doubt about the date of the painting. A daguerreotype taken in 1865 only four years after Meyer's death shows an almost identical section of this view, apparently without any alterations to what is described above. This has given rise to a suggestion that the painting should be dated to the 1850s.[1] A dating in the middle of the 1830s has also been suggested, and this seems far more likely in relation to Ernst Meyer's main oeuvre.[2]

SM

1. *Künstlerleben in Rom. Bertel Thorvaldsen. Der dänische Bildhauer und seine deutschen Freunde*, Nuremberg, 1992, p. 454.
2. Harald Olsen, in *Roma com' era nei dipinti degli artisti danesi dell' Ottocento*, Rome, 1985, p. 86.

Christian Morgenstern (1805–1867)

89

**Beech Trees in Frederiksdal
near Copenhagen, 1828**

Oil on paper mounted on cardboard, 25.4 × 33.1 cm
Hamburger Kunsthalle, inv. no. 1131
Mauß no. 28

Four mighty beech trunks are the main subject of this picture.
Morgenstern has depicted them up close; he was not interested
in the whole trunk, and we see only the sweeping branches of
the last beech. However, the painter's true theme is light, the
light in shadows too. The sunlight hits the left trunk from the
side, the half sand-, half grass-covered field from the front,
and the strips of grass from behind; the wooden fence is in the
shade. Light shines even where the sun's rays do not hit. The
two large trunks in front are hit indirectly; the sunshine comes
through the leaves and is reflected green, allowing the trunks
in the shade to appear light in front of the dark wall of leaves.
Morgenstern, a careful observer, turned his attention and his
artistic ability to the nuances of light turning to dark. The
young artist discovered his second theme in the half-dark
of the penumbra, where the roots snake in the foreground,
somewhat like the underworld of the towering trunks.

Morgenstern spent the summer of 1828 in Frederiksdal
on the estate of the painter Johan Ludvig Lund, one of his
professors, who gathered many young artists around him.
Beech Trees was born in this milieu.

HRL

90

View of Mount Brocken, 1829

Oil on paper mounted on canvas, 28.5 × 32.5 cm
Hamburger Kunsthalle, inv. no. 1123
Mauß no. 40

The Brocken is the highest mountain in the Harz range in central Germany. These mountains attracted several artists from northern Germany. The peak of the Brocken can be seen far in the distance, and two other tree-covered mountains have pushed their way up to the front. The trees on the closest slope are highly differentiated, especially along the ridge.

Only at second glance does our eye wander into the distance. First we notice the sloping countryside with the occasional pine tree. Boulders rest on the grass; in front they are toppled over, in the middle lie single rocks, and further to the back between the trees the boulders tower like a monument. Our attention is drawn to the leafless trunks of the pines, to the first two which are cut off at the picture's edge, to the three whose high tops stand against the light blue sky and, finally, to the two trees next to the four round stones, whose tops barely rise above the green of the forests in the distance. The tall, thin trunks are emphasized by lateral highlights. The grassy incline is composed of diagonal ground waves, producing stripes of light and shadow. The grass struck by the bright light and the illuminated cliffs are the attractions of this study and create the effect of a single moment.

HRL

91

An Entrance Gate to a House
in Partenkirchen, 1831

Oil on canvas, 31.1 × 27.5 cm
Signed and dated lower left: "C M 1831"
(initials linked, above a star)
Bayerische Staatsgemäldesammlungen, Munich,
inv. no. 10778; Mauß no. 58

Like a ship being pulled into a maelstrom, our gaze is pulled into the picture although on a sideways path, constrained above and below and in clearly defined steps, like backdrops one behind the other. At first our gaze is drawn quickly to the sunlit courtyard wall past the domed tavern, after that it finds the wall with the arched entrance, the brightly lit vaulting with the unequal depressions, the pail to the left, the wagon and other equipment to the right, and finally moves to the shadowy back wall, to the lonely guest in front of the barred windows. On the other side of the courtyard, our gaze penetrates deeper into the distance, passing through a barn to a second courtyard, towards a pile of wood and a dark door. The view in the distance is directed by the changes of light and dark.

Morgenstern effortlessly mastered perspectival construction of space, allowing him to dedicate his attention completely to the portrayal of a variety of tones of reflections of the light. The attraction of this picture is the differentiation of tones, and this in a sketch-like style – the brushwork is constantly visible.

The date next to the initials can only point to the date of completion, since it was sold in January 1831, and nothing in it suggests winter. So this study, from a former cloister in Partenkirchen, a village in the Bavarian Alps between Munich and Innsbruck, is a painting away from nature, done in the artist's studio. However, it has not lost any of its freshness in the painterly translation.

HRL

Ludwig August Most (1807–1883)

92

View of Berlin from the Roof of the Museum, 1830

Oil on canvas, 79 × 105.5 cm
Signed and dated lower left: "18 LM 30"
Muzeum Narodowe, Poznán, inv. no. Mo 1790

Time and again, a significant new building inspired a nineteenth-century Berlin painter. This is the case with *View of Berlin from the Roof of the Museum*, which Most created for the opening of Schinkel's most important building in the centre of the city. The museum officially opened on 3 August 1830; Most exhibited his picture shortly thereafter on 19 September at the Academy. One feels the pride and enthusiasm that inspired the painter as well as all the people of different backgrounds and ages, men and women, who are depicted here. They mull about and chat with each other, except for the two workers who are concerned with the building, giving the impression that the structure is not yet quite finished. The city is bathed in the glow of the evening. One has the impression of a leisurely Sunday atmosphere.

At the same time, the picture matches the passion of the time for panoramas, which guaranteed an overview and put the city in the context of the nature around it. Most also shows Friedrich Tieck's group of Castor and Pollux, which

was designed to be seen from far away and was a self-conscious play on the antique Dioscuri who stood on the Roman capitol. In including these statues, shown from the rooftop perspective, Most shows us something we would not otherwise see.

Nevertheless, Most does justice to Schinkel, who conceived his museum as more than just a showcase for works of art. It should be a building that teaches how to see and allows us to view the city as a shared space. Sight should bring insight. This pedagogical task is served by the entrance hall, which opens out to the castle across the way and to the whole city. On the left of Most's picture, the Lustgarten can be seen. The Church of Friedrichswerder, another newly completed building by Schinkel, rises in the middle. In the distance is the Memorial to the Wars of Liberation in Kreuzberg. The view is completed by the armoury in front, the two domes of the Hedwig Church, the German and the French Cathedrals at the back, and the dome of the Church of the Trinity on the side.

HBS

Jørgen Roed (1808–1888)

93

An Artist Resting by the Roadside, 1832

Oil on canvas, 58 × 48 cm
Signed and dated: "I.ROED. 1832."
Statens Museum for Kunst, Copenhagen, inv. no. SMK 2063

Jørgen Roed's painting of the thoughtful artist sitting outside in the countryside is extremely uncommon in the art of the Danish Golden Age, especially when we consider that it was painted in 1832 and not ten to fifteen years later, when it would not have been unusual to see such a scene in the paintings of, say, Johan Thomas Lundbye.

By the side of a path leading away from a wider road, a young artist with a painter's stool and his portfolio tied firmly to the knapsack on his back sits in the shade of an overgrown burial mound. He is deep in thought, has picked a red flower and is holding it up to his face as he absentmindedly draws in the soil with a stick – a face, perhaps. He appears not to sense that a storm is brewing and it will soon be raining. A coach drawn by four horses is just passing a milepost on the road out in the sunlight, and as far as the eye can see there is a view across the landscape towards a rather bigger town and beyond.

The painting is imbued with a melancholy, thoughtful atmosphere. The lovely sunny weather will soon be gone, and the past represented by the burial mound is also gone. But what does the flower in the painter's hand signify? Love? Or is that, too, gone? Is his beloved in the coach that is driving past? Have they taken leave of each other? There are many questions to be asked, but they are not to be answered in such concrete terms,

because the painting does not tell a concrete story. Rather, it evokes a mood and the potential for the viewer to think about things that last and those that pass.

The identity of the artist portrayed is also not a necessary key to an understanding of the painting's message. Based on the figure's similarity to those in other paintings,[1] it is probably a portrait of Roed himself. The town in the background is probably the central Zealand town of Ringsted, where Roed had his childhood home, and he often visited it while a student at the Academy in Copenhagen, sometimes accompanied by his close friend Constantin Hansen. But Roed is not illustrating a private story here, in this carefully planned and – for its time – fairly large painting, which was exhibited in Charlottenborg in 1833. It is rather a painting of the lonely wanderer in natural surroundings full of spirit, where the past speaks clearly to anyone listening and at the same time gives rise to deep introspection. This was unusual in contemporary Danish art, though the German parallels to it are well known (see cat. no. 73).

SM

. 1. Hanne Jönsson, in *C. W. Eckersberg og hans elever*, Copenhagen, 1983, pp. 127–28.

94

The Cathedral of Ribe, c. 1836

Oil on canvas, 30.0 × 38.8 cm
Statens Museum for Kunst, Copenhagen, inv. no. 3798

In March 1836, the Art Association of Copenhagen arranged a competition to be won by the artist who was best able to reproduce either the exterior or the interior of the cathedral in the small town of Ribe, close to the North Sea coast in the south-west corner of Denmark. The cathedral is one of the great examples of Romanesque architecture in Denmark, built at the beginning of the twelfth century. The tall clock tower was built in the mid-thirteenth century and later rebuilt. The idea behind the competition was to direct attention to the legacy of historical architecture from Denmark's past, in this case the Middle Ages. The art historian Niels Laurits Høyen, in particular, was campaigning for an effort to be made to preserve historical structures. He was convinced that artists could play a part in attempts to create an awareness of the country's past and its monuments by making pictures available to the public via the annual exhibitions in Copenhagen. The paintings were to become part of the debate on cultural policy and a tool for forming public opinion. In 1829 Constantin Hansen, Jørgen Roed and Christen Købke produced architectural paintings of some of the greatest works of architecture in Denmark (see cat. nos. 79, 97).

Høyen had been appointed Professor of Art History in the Academy of Fine Arts in 1829, after which he undertook a series of journeys around Denmark to examine and record medieval and Renaissance architectural remains. He spent several weeks in Ribe in 1830, noting the cathedral's poor state of preservation. Roed took part in the Art Association competition and was awarded the prize for a picture of the interior; while in Ribe, he also made on-the-spot sketches for paintings of both the interior and exterior. It is interesting that Roed re-created the interior of the church as he wished to see it restored, and not as it actually looked when he painted it. Here, too, we sense Høyen's influence.

Such a point of view – reproducing the historical building in its supposed original state – might also have been of significance for Roed in this painting of the exterior. He viewed the building from the south-west, looking towards the apse and the great transept. He saw the church as fashioned in one piece, like a sculpture, to which nothing could be added or taken away. The painting is a study, done in the thinnest of oil paints, almost like a watercolour, but it is nevertheless noticeable that almost all decorative figures and narrative elements have been removed. Only at the south-western corner is there a man standing and two children sitting, apparently engaged in conversation, and a close look reveals a stork on the roof of the transept. Otherwise, the picture is sober, factual and fresh as a daisy in the clear daylight.

SM

Martinus Rørbye (1803–1848)

95

View from the Artist's Window, c. 1825

Oil on canvas, 38 × 29.8 cm
Statens Museum for Kunst, Copenhagen, inv. no. SMK 7452

We see a view through the window of an apartment in Amaliegade in Copenhagen, with part of the city's harbour in the background. Rørbye's parents moved to this area in about 1816, and Martinus Rørbye was still living at home when he painted this picture around 1825.

This painting is one of several fairly small, very detailed and quite spontaneous representations of the reality staring artists in the face in the early Danish Golden Age (see also cat. no. 1). These were quite clearly paintings that were examining, somewhat cautiously and like an exercise in seeing, the possibility of understanding reality anew. This one was in many respects "nothing", at least in relation to the kind of painting that still officially dominated the Academy of Fine Arts with its historical, mythological and religious themes and its academic approach to painting embedded in formal schemes and stylistic ideals.

The very possibility of painting spontaneously and without inhibition, and the idea that nothing was too insignificant to be painted, provided the most important tools en route to the new artistic experiences which C. W. Eckersberg gave to his students. But Eckersberg was also preoccupied with the potential for creating pictures and thus recreating reality offered by the use of linear perspective. This, too, seems to emerge from Rørbye's little picture, where the depiction of the base of the birdcage with its parallelogram turns into a geometrical exercise. Rørbye did not construct his perspective lines quite convincingly. In particular, the line in the open window on the left appears to be drawn incorrectly, and thus becomes so obvious that he has actually made an effort to do it properly.

But the painting contains far more. Rørbye seems to have been very preoccupied with depicting the light. The sun is directly to the east, and the early morning light is coming in low through the window. Rørbye has meticulously shown light and shade in every single tassel in the thin curtain at the top and in every upright in the railings in front of the window. And the light is naturally of great significance for the most important subject in the painting: the relationship between inside and outside.

What makes this work so unusual in early Golden Age painting is that the artist has to relate to and convey a much greater complexity when portraying both the relative darkness of the room and the white light in the sky as well as all the shades in between. Rørbye has not made the task any easier for himself in aiming to paint the window ledge tightly packed with potted plants, with the shiny surface of a sloping table as a reflector for the light outside, and a host of details of harbour life painted in the subdued colouring of the middle ground. Some thick bushes or a group of trees block part of the view, but they provide a quieter background for the pots in the window ledge and allow us to focus on them.

It is, of course, striking that it should be precisely the potted plants that are accorded such a dominant position in the painting. And in view of the inside–outside theme it is tempting to see an allegory in this. It has been suggested that the growth of the plants from the seed assumed to be in the little pot on the right, via the shoots in the protective growth tubes to the sprouting agave, as well as the quietly flowering globe amaranth and the abundantly flowering hortensia, are all intended to symbolize the cycle of life, and even to be seen in relation to Rørbye's own situation at the time, when he was soon to leave home.[1] The small child's foot in the window ledge is setting off a movement in contrast to the solidly planted adult foot, and to this symbolism we can naturally also add the bird in the cage, which is both inside and outside at the same time.

SM

1. Anne-Birgitte Fonsmark, "Udsigter og indsigter – Martinus Rørbye: 'Udsigt fra kunstnerens vindue'", *Kunstværkets Krav*, Copenhagen, 1990, pp. 67–77.

96

Norwegian Landscape with Cliffs in the Foreground, 1830

Oil on paper mounted on card, 18.0 × 30.2 cm
Statens Museum for Kunst, Copenhagen, inv. no. SMK7280

When Rørbye went to Norway in 1830, his main object was to make studies for genre paintings. He arrived in Oslo in the middle of July and from there continued on a tour of the southern part of the country for the next two months. He sketched eagerly all along the way, but during his stay in Telemarken at the end of August he also spent time painting a series of landscape studies. Among them, presumably, was this study, the genesis of which is possibly documented. It might have been made on 24 August, when Rørbye noted in his diary: "Spent the morning painting a view high in the valley."[1]

From a relatively high vantage point Rørbye looks out across the valley and the distant mountains. The perspective is quite typical for a devoted pupil of Eckersberg: Rørbye has not positioned himself in such a way as to be able to paint a panoramic view across the valley; on the contrary, we scarcely derive any impression of the valley, as the view is limited by the outcrop of rocks on the right. On the other hand, he has shown all the more interest in this. He has also been more concerned to catch the many bluish shades in the mist shrouding the distant mountains. It is a long way from Rørbye's picture to the panoramic Norwegian mountain landscapes that J. C. Dahl regularly showed in the Academy exhibitions in Charlottenborg. However untraditional the subject might seem, Rørbye nevertheless, probably unconsciously, had a classical pattern at the back of his mind in choosing it – that is to say, Allaert van Everdingen's Norwegian landscape *River with Cliffs* from 1647. This picture could be seen in the Royal Gallery of Paintings (now Statens Museum for Kunst) in Copenhagen. There are striking similarities between the two works, both in the actual subject and in the asymmetrical composition.

Rørbye sat painting in front of his subject, presumably with the paper fixed to the lid of his painter's box (the holes made by the drawing pins with which he fixed it are still visible). When he removed the still damp painting, he happened to make a fingerprint in the blue of the sky near the top edge. However, as this was a study for his own private use, he did not take the trouble to make good the damage.

The painting is possibly identical to one sold in 1849 in the auction of Rørbye's personal effects entitled *Norwegian View with Rocks in the Foreground*.

KM

1. See Martinus Rørbye, *Rejsedagbog 1830*, Georg Nygaard, Copenhagen, 1930, p. 95.

97

Vester Egede Church with Gisselfeld Convent in the Background, 1832

Oil on canvas, 23.7 × 34.2 cm
Dated bottom right: "1832"
Ny Carlsberg Glyptotek, Copenhagen, inv. no 3249

Rørbye painted strictly architectural pictures only to a limited extent. As a student of Eckersberg, he could not avoid having his attention drawn to the architecture of earlier ages. But he did not consistently devote himself to Danish medieval and Renaissance architecture, as Købke and Roed did in several pictures (see cat. nos. 79, 94). On the other hand, he did not avoid depicting a typical Danish village church, as when he sat down to paint a view of the village of Vester Egede in southern Zealand in 1832.

The starting point for Rørbye and his fellow artists was not the religious significance of the churches, but their status as historical monuments. So it is significant that Rørbye placed himself neither in the middle of the church nor in front of the western façade, but at a certain distance. In this way, the church simply becomes one building among several – although more dignified and striking – and no special emphasis is placed on its role as a place where people could seek spiritual comfort. Nor has Rørbye depicted the road leading to the church. Entirely in

accordance with Eckersberg's principles, he has chosen to look at the church from an unexpected angle, entirely from the side, so that it does not play any particularly representative role.

Rørbye has given the church a part corresponding to the one village churches were given in pictures by landscape artists in later years. They did not make them their principal subjects, but often chose to portray then from a considerable distance, rather as landmarks than as the houses of God.[1] There is a crucial difference between the significance given to churches by the Danish painters and that accorded by German artists such as Friedrich and Schinkel, whose Gothic cathedrals often had a visionary quality. For the Danes, religion was a private matter.

Rørbye painted this picture in the summer of 1832 while in southern Zealand, where he was also energetically making a large number of drawn and painted sketches of the area, mainly landscapes and figure studies of peasants and rural workers, but also a few architectural pictures.[2]

KM

1. See Jørgen I. Jensen, "Den afsondrede, fjerne kirke. En kirkehistorisk udfordring hos guldaldermalerne", *Meddelelser fra Thorvaldsens Museum*, 1994, pp. 149–58.
2. See Jens Peter Munk, "'Den følende Beskuer'. Rørbyes rejse til Sydsjælland sommeren 1832", *Meddelelser fra Ny Carlsberg Glyptotek*, 1993, pp. 5–36.

98

View of the Roman Campagna with the Tiber and Monte Soracte in the Background, 1835

Oil on paper on canvas, 32 × 41 cm
Signed and dated bottom right: "ROM 1835"
Göteborgs Kunstmuseum, inv. no. 1929

During his stay in Italy, Rørbye regularly left Rome to go and paint in the mountains, and in the middle of the Italian winter, in January 1835, he painted this picture of a lonely man wrapped in a cloak in the Roman Campagna. There is undoubtedly an actual experience behind the painting – perhaps Rørbye observed a fellow artist resting during a walk in the Campagna. But with this picture he has turned to one of Friedrich's most essential themes: the lonely individual's confrontation with and experience of nature. The depiction of the cold, windswept landscape powerfully contributes to the melancholy atmosphere of the picture, and the cross formed by the bars of the fence adds a religious dimension to the view. As Rørbye had scarcely seen works by Friedrich other than those to be seen in Denmark before he painted the picture, the qualities reminiscent of Friedrich merely serve to show how widespread his idiom was. In contrast to most other Danish pictures showing signs of borrowing from the German master, there seems to be a symbolic element in Rørbye's picture in line with that in Friedrich's pictures: the cloaked man's faraway look suggests a longing for the hereafter (compare the sombre mood); this is underlined by the way in which the line of the horizon in the picture divides the figure so that his body is of this world and his spirit (his head) of another.[1] Friedrich incorporated a similar division into earthly and heavenly spheres in several pictures, most clearly in *Landscape with a Lone Tree in the Light of Morning* (Nationalgalerie, Berlin).

KM

1. See Anne-Birgitte Fonsmark, "Udsigter og indsigter. Martinus Rørbye: 'Udsigt fra kunstnerens vindue', c. 1825", in E. J. Bencard, A. Kold and P. S. Meyer, eds., *Kunstværkets krav. 27 fortolkninger af danske kunstværker*, Fogtdal, Copenhagen, 1990, pp. 73–76.

Karl Friedrich Schinkel (1781–1841)

99

Bank of the Spree near Stralau, 1817

Oil on canvas, 36 × 44.5 cm
Signed and dated lower left: "Schinkel 1817"
Staatliche Museen zu Berlin, Nationalgalerie,
inv. no. Schinkel Museum A 15
HAMBURG AND COPENHAGEN ONLY

This is the only one of Schinkel's landscape paintings to come
close to Caspar David Friedrich in composition and mood, as
well as in the lacquered, smooth, immaculate application of
colour. He painted it for General Neidhardt von Gneisenau.
This is the later version of an 1815 painting (destroyed in 1945),
which showed two women and two men, one of whom played a
lute. Instead of the vaults, there was a summer house entwined
in vines. This picture has a deeper, more serious and energetic
feel. The cool evening wind, tousling the hair of the men, and
the music of the horns creates a melancholy atmosphere at
sunset. Palpably, the lustre will soon grow dull and fade away.

Stralau was a village on the Spree south-east of Berlin.
Schinkel depicts it with fantastic intensity. The silhouette of the
tall trees, the two villas and the house did not exist as they are
shown here. Not even Berlin, visible in the distance, has been
rendered faithfully. Stralau was known to the people of Berlin
for its fair, the *Stralauer Fischzug*. However, instead of the
merriment of a crowd at a country fair, Schinkel gives us an
atmosphere of farewell in an aristocratic park landscape. The
strict composition plays a role in this. The muscular boatman,
pushing the boat away from the shore with his strength, creates
a conspicuous triangle. This figure conjures up images of the
mythical Charon, who ferries boats to the underworld. The lines
of perspective, which become clear in the vaults, point exactly
to the horizon and, in a way, replace the sunbeams of the
setting sun, which is somewhat right of centre. Evening light
is depicted as exactly as muted nature is rendered suggestively.
One recognizes the deliberate composition by an artist who, as a
painter, worked primarily for the theatre, directing a production
and devising architectural compositions in reference to a plot.
The arch is not only an inner frame, but like a backdrop directs
our view into the painting.

HBS

Fig. 26. Franz Louis Catel, *Schinkel in Naples*, 1824. Staatliche Museen zu Berlin, Nationalgalerie

Julius Schoppe (1795–1868)

100

The "Emperor's Pine" in the Park of Kleinglienicke, 1827

Oil on canvas, 25 × 40 cm
Stiftung Preussische Schlösser und Gärten
Berlin-Brandenburg, Potsdam, inv. no. GK I 8804

In 1825 Schoppe painted a continuation of an Italian panorama wall painting in the Kleinglienicke castle, home to Prince Karl of Prussia since 1824. Schoppe followed a preliminary study by Schinkel, which showed the view from a terrace over the sea on the island of Capri. Two men standing on the terrace contemplating the countryside are seen from the back. This mural was not Schoppe's first. In 1817 he had painted a view of the Alps from the Kanzel in Aigen near Salzburg (Gemälde-galerie Neue Meister, Dresden), in memory of his stay in the Salzkammergut. In the foreground, he enjoys the view with his fellow painters Carl Friedrich Zimmermann and Carl Gropius, as well as with the poet Alois Weissenbach.

This painting supposedly relates to one Schoppe did in September 1827 and exhibited at the Berlin Academy, *View from the Park of Glienicke near Potsdam*, which showed a pulpit in a tree. The view goes from the steep east bank of the Havel to the Jungfernsee north to Sacrow. Beneath the top of a massive pine growing on the slope, a platform of wooden slats has been fashioned around the trunk, allowing the opportunity to experience the view around the tree. Several branches were, as we see, sawn off in order to give the pine a more appealing look. The tree-top, branches, pulpit and the path in the foreground have all been composed into a harmonic picture by the landscape designer, which Schoppe only needed to pick up and paint from the right place. The trunk of the pine appears exactly where the horizon sinks into the low hills. Schoppe carefully drew all details, his fine brushstroke captured all structures and emphasized them against the air and calm surface of the water. Corresponding to his disciplined manner of painting, the work gives the impression that everything has been formed by necessity.

The name "Emperor's Pine" refers to a visit of Czar Nicholas I of Russia, who was married to Princess Charlotte of Prussia.

HBS

Peter Christian Skovgaard (1817–1875)

101

Oat Field near Vejby, 1843

Oil on canvas, 25.5 × 28.5 cm
Dated bottom left: "1843"
Statens Museum for Kunst, Copenhagen, inv. no. 4950

The parish of Vejby was somewhat isolated when Skovgaard visited it, with Gribskov, the largest forest in Denmark, to the south, and the bleak Zealand coast to the north. The number of inhabitants in the parish was put at 1,143. People in the area in those days lived mainly on the land. In the village of Vejby, the largest in the parish, there was both a church and a school. P. C. Skovgaard's parents had formerly owned farms near Ringsted in central Zealand and at Græsted close to Vejby, but for financial reasons had been obliged to give up both. His mother had run the store in Vejby since 1823.[1]

That summer, Skovgaard stayed in his mother's house, while his friend Lundbye lodged with Morten Jensen, one of the local farmers. The two friends spent their days painting and drawing the farms, fields and roads in and around Vejby. They often painted the same views, but seen from slightly different angles. We can trace their activities closely over these months because Lundbye carefully noted in his diary what each of them had been painting and when. Lundbye, who came to the place with fresh eyes, was untiring in discovering new subjects, while Skovgaard, who knew all the localities beforehand, appears not to have made quite the same number of studies.[2]

Skovgaard's picture of an oat field near Vejby shows a fertile landscape in which the light-coloured blades of oats stand gently waving in the wind, surrounded by grass and yellow dandelions in the foreground and trees and bushes in the background. At the very back we can glimpse the top of a thatched roof with a chimney, probably belonging to the owner of the field. The sky is done in a shade of light grey, imparting a lyrical quality to the picture. This is not a carefully planned study, but rather a snapshot, taken at close quarters, of a typical Danish locality.

The characteristic Danish landscape was a much-loved subject from the middle of the 1830s onwards. This so-called national Romantic landscape painting established itself in earnest in the Charlottenborg exhibition in 1838. Like Lundbye, Skovgaard was taken with these ideas and filled with the urge to picture the Danish landscape.

GW

1. Bente Skovgaard, *Sommerrejsen til Vejby 1843: J. Th. Lundbye og P. C. Skovgaard*, Copenhagen, 1989, pp. 10–13.
2. Ibid., pp. 11, 22, 54–58.

Frederik Sødring (1809–1862)

102

The Rear Courtyard of Charlottenborg Palace, 1828

Oil on canvas, 26.3 × 28.2 cm
Signed and dated: "F.Sødring 1828, pinxit"
Statens Museum for Kunst, Copenhagen, inv. no. SMK 7442

Sødring was only nineteen when he painted this picture. That same year he had made his first appearance in the Charlottenborg exhibition with copies of two paintings by Dahl. This subject could scarcely be more unpretentious: a rear courtyard predominantly painted in reddish brown and greyish brown shades, with a couple of slightly stronger and brighter colours in the moss on the roof above the water pump and the articles of clothing on the clothes lines. The subject is seen from the south-facing rear courtyard of the Academy in Copenhagen, and it suggests to us that the painter is hardly yet ready to venture out. He stays inside the nest – the secure walls of the Academy – and does not yet dare to move outside.

Sødring painted what he saw. At the same time, he inscribed his subject in a wider context, as is often seen in paintings from the Danish Golden Age. It is natural in a rear courtyard to expect wash tubs, water pumps, clothes lines with garments hanging out to dry, a shed containing straw, a cat in a window, some rickety brickwork and sunlight that can penetrate only with difficulty to light up part of the yard. And it was good practice for Sødring to attempt to paint what he could see just in the rear courtyard, undisturbed by others. But at the same time the subject has also provided him with an occasion for continued studies in the correct use of linear perspective. If we look carefully at the corner of the protruding length of wall to the right of the picture, we can find a row of vertically placed holes pricked in the canvas with a needle. It can be assumed that Sødring tied a thread between a needle placed in the perspective vanishing point right out to the left of the picture or immediately beyond its left edge and extending to a needle fixed at intervals in a vertical line on the right side of the picture. These were lines to help him construct the mathematically correct perspective.

Since linear perspective was one of Eckersberg's passions, it is naturally interesting that the windows seen above the tall basement are those of Eckersberg's own apartment. Sødring was never actually a student of Eckersberg, but he knew the circle around him, in particular Købke, with whom he shared a studio a few years later in Toldbodvej (see cat. no. 77). Equally interesting is the fact that Sødring exhibited a second version in the Charlottenborg exhibition in 1830. So it created neither offence for its realism nor indifference for its choice of subject, but reflected self-understanding in the broad public for whom the ordinary and the everyday were a virtue.

SM

103

View of the Marble Square with the Uncompleted Frederik's Church, 1835

Oil on canvas, 77.5 × 98 cm
Signed and dated: "1835. F. Sødring"
Statens Museum for Kunst, Copenhagen, inv. no. SMK 263

During the reign of the absolutist King Frederik V, the decision was taken to construct a completely new district in Copenhagen. It was to be given the name Frederiksstaden (Frederik's City) and was to have a monumental church – Frederik's Church – at its centre. Several architects, including the avant-garde Frenchman Nicolas-Henri Jardin, worked to bring the church project to fruition in the second half of the eighteenth century. But the undertaking became too expensive; the church was left standing unfinished until the end of the nineteenth century, when it was completed according to an altered design and funded by a private financier, C. F. Tietgen.

For most of the nineteenth century this ecclesiastical torso stood in a very central position in the Copenhagen panorama. It was conceived on the grand scale and inspired by the latest in European neoclassical architecture. It was naturally inevitable that it would itself prove an interesting subject for painters, and several artists – including Eckersberg, Bendz and Sødring – painted the unfinished cathedral. For a time Lundbye lived in a house directly opposite it and he, too, was naturally fascinated by its vast proportions and romantic aspect.

Classical antiquity was almost reincarnated here in the middle of the city, as a picturesque ruin and a piece of contemporary architecture closely linked to antiquity. It was inevitable that it should give rise to thoughts on the part of some people about the survival of antiquity and grandiose architecture in the midst of a city that was anything but classical, but nevertheless vibrant. The ideal and the real were thriving side by side. And Sødring certainly appears to have been conscious of this dualism. He divided the composition of the painting into two almost equal parts. With churchyard calm, the unfinished cathedral is standing almost entirely in shadow. It is contrasted with the row of houses which seem to be pulsating with life in the clear sunshine, their windows open to the fresh air, laundry hanging out and smoke merrily billowing up from the chimneys, while water is being heated for wash-day. The dualism is further underlined by the two trees in the centre of the picture – one alive and one dead. And with humour Sødring has juxtaposed some unused stone slabs for the church and some mattresses out to air as though they were on parade.

A few years before Sødring's picture was painted, in 1833, the Art Association of Copenhagen arranged a competition for suggestions as to how the unfinished church could be completed and used as a museum for works of sculpture. The idea behind this was to take steps to establish a museum for Thorvaldsen's works in Copenhagen.

SM

Adolph Vollmer (1806–1875)

104

Landscape in Holstein, 1827

Oil on paper mounted on cardboard, 22 × 30.8 cm
Signed and dated lower left: "AV d 13 July 1827.
Neversdrf" (initials linked)
Hamburger Kunsthalle, inv. no. 1159

The sky is overcast but the meadows, bushes and trees appear strong and fresh in the clear air. A body of water stretches into the background, the Grosse Binnen Lake. Behind a small strip of land, with two forests and a small settlement, the Baltic Sea spreads out – more precisely, Hochwacht Bay – and behind the water one sees land again (Ulrich Pietsch succeeded in pinpointing the location).

The twenty-two-year-old Vollmer chose one of northern Germany's most attractive points, beloved by two generations of painters and writers. Vollmer, however, remained below on the plain, while the other artists – such as Louis Gurlitt (right) – always stood on the hill near Stöfs. His is a more prosaic view.

Vollmer was especially concerned with the mixing of light and dark tones in the green of the vegetation. Light should take shape in the trees, fields, water and sky. He attempted to differentiate the various levels of light. He worked with short, stiff brushstrokes, which became more condensed at the top and bottom.

Three weeks after 13 July 1897, the day he dated this picture, Vollmer wrote to a friend, "I began a small picture in bad weather. Maybe I'll get it finished while I'm on the road."[1] Despite this specific reference, one cannot connect it to this study, since nothing indicates that Vollmer did more work on it. Vollmer must have meant another picture, and he himself did not see this work as a finished painting.

HRL

Fig. 27. Louis Gurlitt, *View over the Grosse Binnen Lake to Hochwacht Bay*, c. 1861. Altonaer Museum in Hamburg

1. Gerhard Kegel, "Ein Brief des Hamburger Malers Adolph Friedrich Vollmer an Otto Speckter aus dem Jahre 1827", *Zeitschrift des Vereins für Hamburgische Geschichte* 83, 1997, p. 349.

105

Near Aumühle, c. 1830

Oil on paper mounted on cardboard, 27.5 × 38.1 cm
Hamburger Kunsthalle, inv. no. 1161

More than the character of the area, light seems to have decided Vollmer's choice of subject. The reflection of the trees from the other river bank in the dammed up Bille creek, the blue sky with its small clouds in yellow, white and grey, and the reflections of light on the fish trap (with a head on the top) and tiny wicker branches first capture the eye. The viewer perceives what the light emphasizes on the other river bank as well: a half-hidden house, the birch trunks, three cows on a little bridge and even the two people under the large tree. It is the atmosphere of a peaceful autumn afternoon.

It was not far for Vollmer from Hamburg by way of Bergedorf to the Sachsenwald, at the edge of which is Aumühle. We can assume that he began and finished this painting in nature in one sitting. He painted mostly with a fine-tipped brush, but sketched effortlessly. This helped him to capture a direct impression, but at the same time he went beyond an exact depiction of reality to imbue the landscape with a special mood.

HRL

Friedrich Wasmann (1805–1886)

106

**Evening Atmosphere in the Tyrol:
the Rose Garden near Bozen, 1830/31**

Oil on paper mounted on cardboard, 15.3 × 32.7 cm
Hamburger Kunsthalle, inv. no. 1376
Nathan no. 193

The last light of the setting sun accentuates two mountains,
which appear in a warm pink colour, while the rest of the
mountains are submerged in increasing darkness. Wasmann
painted from a high point; between the artist and the mountain
known as the Rose Garden east of Bozen (Bolzano) on the edge
of the Dolomites lay mountains sloping to the middle with a
valley further in the distance.

The growing dusk forced him to work quickly. He painted
the sky and mountains in quick, long strokes. With a fine brush
he added structure and light to the jagged mountain range.
He led the brush in alternating directions, set darker lines and
finished the outline in yellow. In this manner he translated his
impression of the light on the two mountains, which reflected
it differently.

HRL

107

107

Wreath of Clouds in the Tyrol, 1830/31

Oil on paper, 14.3 × 26.4 cm
Hamburger Kunsthalle, inv. no. 1379
Nathan no. 206

Were it not for the clouds, we would speak of a clearly
organized picture, composed in stripes: bushes and trees over
the meadow, underneath two poplars and a pine forest, then
the mountain range as the main subject, the highest peak in the
middle, and over that the sky. However, Wasmann gives ample
attention to the clouds, which wrap around the mountains like
a wreath. The clouds crawl into the depths and shroud the
peaks. They appear compact or dispersed into mere wisps, and
their tonal variation scales from greyish blue to yellowish white.
Wasmann thus sets the finite against the infinite and the
sublime nature of the Alps against the intangibility (and, no
less, divinity) of the clouds. At the left edge of the picture, the
clouds allow a view into the distance, to a snow-covered peak
and a glacier; it becomes especially evident how the artist works
with opposites, those of above and below, of heaven and earth.

Draughtsmanship and precision combine in Wasmann's
equally sketch-like and decisive painting. At the front, several
strokes of the tip of the brush expose the paper, without
transforming these lines into renderings of objects.

HRL

108

View of the Campagna, 1832

Oil on paper mounted on cardboard, 24.1 × 19.3 cm
Hamburger Kunsthalle, inv. no. 1389
Nathan no. 241

The view through an open window stretches into rocky
countryside, which drops steeply to the right; our eye then
jumps into the distance where, through the hazy light, a hilly
landscape appears, ending finally in a blue chain of mountains.
Our gaze then wanders upward to the light-filled sky.

Close-up the viewer sees not only a path pulling us into the
painting (with a little fantasy we can make out three standing
figures and a donkey), but also the single, long house next to a
tree. The overgrown slopes and the cliffs are brightly lit by the
sun, and tucked next to them are islands of colourful shadow.
The hills in the background are divided by many valleys and
ravines. Smoke from two fires makes it clear that this is an
inhabited place. The countryside appears completely in a
greenish-blue lit from behind, much darker than the pale
blue of the distant mountains. Our view to the light is limited
by the dark to the right and above. The open windowpane and
bank are lighter. Wasmann, in choosing the location in the
room, placed himself almost unnoticeably to the left, and thus
avoids bland symmetry.

The rendering of the window betrays this as a spontaneous
sketch. The stone frame to the right has been painted in a dark

108

brown brushstroke, scorning a natural straightness. The naturalness of the study of nature is specific to this little picture, and it is possible that Wasmann knew nothing of this theme's tradition. The preliminary pencil marks have not been hidden by the thin wash of paint, especially in the sky. The picture lives from its naturalness, whether from the wider brushstrokes in the window frame or from the delicate strokes in the countryside. However, Wasmann did succeed in giving it a concrete construction and tension. The view stretches from Cervara, where Wasmann lived for five months, to the Aniene Valley north-east of Subiaco.

HRL

109

The Brick Hut Valley with the Serpentara near Olevano, 1832

Oil on paper mounted on cardboard, 26.8 × 43.7 cm
Hamburger Kunsthalle, inv. no. 1394
Nathan no. 240

From above the view goes to a mountain crest, from which the terrain drops away, precipitously at the cliffs, then more softly, until it rises again to the viewer. Where the crest sinks lightly to the right, a new, soft, tree-covered hill is formed. While the crests on the left appear far away, the mountain on the right is obviously closer. The trail leads to the floor of the valley; a second, further away, runs where the steep ascent begins.

More than half the landscape lies in shadow. The sun must have been so low that its light could not shine over the mountain crest. The valley is completely submerged in shadow. Where the countryside rises again, it is in beaming light. The bushes and the trees are virtually lit up. Wasmann seems to have been most concerned with how shadows in a landscape can be perceived as a reduction, not as the absence, of light. The depth of the shadow increases gradually, until the light appears in its full radiance. The tonal differentiation is so subtle that it is noticeable only after longer study of this picture.

The painting itself is done with the greatest liberty. The brushstrokes, short stripes, long lines, patches and arches are energetic, meaning placed quickly as in a sketch. Such fast painting was needed to finish this powerfully organized picture, in order to capture the wandering light.

As Domenico Riccardi has pointed out, Wasmann chose a point on the way to Roiate, Olevano at the back, with a view over the Brick Hut Valley (*Valle delle Fornaci*) to the peak of Monte Guadagnolo at the left and Monte S. Arcangelo in the middle. On the hill at the right is the grove called the Serpentara. Wasmann scorned both the romantic view of Civitella as well as the typical one of the Serpentara, which is seen here more or less from the back.

HRL

109

Select Bibliography

Major books, exhibition catalogues and catalogues raisonnés are abbreviated in the notes to the text as follows, with full details in the relevant section of the bibliography.

Aubert 1893: *see under* J. C. Dahl
Bang 1987: *see under* J. C. Dahl
Berlin 1990: *see under* Carl Blechen
Börsch-Supan and Jähnig 1973: *see under* C. D. Friedrich
Cologne 1995: *see under* General
Copenhagen 1901: *see under* General
Copenhagen 1981a: *see under* Christen Købke
Copenhagen 1981b: *see under* Martinus Rørbye
Copenhagen 1981c: *see under* Christen Købke
Copenhagen 1983a: *see under* C. W. Eckersberg
Copenhagen 1983b: *see under* C. W. Eckersberg
Copenhagen 1983–84: *see under* C. W. Eckersberg
Copenhagen 1991: *see under* C. D. Friedrich
Copenhagen 1994: *see under* J. T. Lundbye
Copenhagen 1996a: *see under* Christen Købke
Copenhagen 1996b: *see under* Wilhelm Bendz
Copenhagen & Århus 1991: *see under* Constantin Hansen
Hamburg 1996: *see under* General
Hamburg, Flensburg & Nivå 1997–98: *see under* Louis Gurlitt
London 1984: *see under* General
London 1990: *see under* C. D. Friedrich
Los Angeles & New York 1993–94: *see under* General
Luxembourg 1997: *see under* General
Madrid 1992: *see under* C. D. Friedrich
Monrad 1989: *see under* General
Munich 1985: *see under* General
Munich 1988–89a: *see under* J. C. Dahl
Munich 1988–89b: *see under* General
New York & Chicago 1990–91: *see under* C. D. Friedrich
Oslo 1988: *see under* J. C. Dahl
Paris 1984–85: *see under* General
Rave 1940: *see under* Carl Blechen
Wirth 1979: *see under* Eduard Gaertner

General

Aubert, Védastine, "Breve fra Thomas Fearnley til J. C. C. Dahl", *Kunst og Kultur*, vol. 12 (1925), pp. 1–27

Busch, Werner, "Die autonome Ölskizze in der Landschaftsmalerei. Der wahr- und für wahr genommene Ausschnitt aus Zeit und Raum". *Pantheon*, 41 (1983), pp. 126–33

Cologne 1995: Monrad, Kasper, and Götz Czymmek, *Aus Dänemarks Goldener Zeit. Landschaftsmalerei des früheren 19. Jahrhunderts aus dem Statens Museum for Kunst, Kopenhagen*, exh. cat., Wallraf-Richartz-Museum, Cologne, 1995

Copenhagen 1901: *Raadhusudstillingen af Dansk Kunst*, exh. cat., 3rd edn., Copenhagen, 1901

Gunnarsson, Torsten, *Friluftsmåleri före friluftsmåleriet. Oljestudien i nordiskt landskapsmåleri 1800–1850*, Acta Universitatis Upsaliensis. Ars Suetica 12, Uppsala, 1989 (English summary, "Open-Air Sketching in Scandinavia 1800–1850")

Gunnarsson, Torsten, *Nordic Landscape Painting in the Nineteenth Century*, Yale University Press, New Haven and London, 1998

Hamburg 1996: Leppien, Helmut R., et al., *Mit klarem Blick. Hamburger Malerei im Biedermeier*, exh. cat., Hamburger Kunsthalle, Junius Verlag, Hamburg, 1996

Høyen, N. L., *Skrifter*, Copenhagen, 3 vols., 1871–76

Jensen, Jørgen I., "Den afsondrede, fjerne kirke. En kirkehistorisk udfordring hos guldaldermalerne", *Meddelelser fra Thorvaldsens Museum*, 1994, pp. 149–58 (English summary, "The Remote, Isolated Church")

Johansson, Ejner, *De danske malere i München. Et ukendt kapitel i dansk guldalderkunst*, Spektrum, Copenhagen, 1997

Kaspersen, Søren, "Fra Skolen i Athen til Via Sistina nr. 64 øverste sal", *CRAS*, xxix (1981), pp. 28–36

Kent, Neil, *The Triumph of Light and Nature. Nordic Art 1740–1940*, Thames and Hudson, London, 1987

Klose, Olaf, and Lilli Martius, *Skandinavische Landschaftsbilder. Deutsche Künstlerreisen von 1780 bis 1864*, Neumünster, 1975

London 1984: Monrad, Kasper, *Danish Painting: The Golden Age*, exh. cat., introductions by Henrik Bramsen and Alistair Smith, National Gallery, London, 1984

Los Angeles & New York 1993–94: Monrad, Kasper, et al., *The Golden Age of Danish Painting*, exh. cat., Los Angeles County Museum of Art and the The Metropolitan Museum of Art, New York; Hudson Hills Press, New York, 1993

Luxembourg 1997: Sillevis, John, ed., *Peintures de l'Age d'or du Danemark*, exh. cat., Musée national d'histoire et d'art, Luxembourg, 1997

Martius, Lilli, *Die schleswig-holsteinische Malerei im 19. Jahrhundert*, Neumünster, 1956

Monrad, Kasper, "Privatsamlingernes betydning for kunstmuseerne – historisk set", *Kunst og Museum*, vol. 19 (1984), pp. 7–17

Monrad 1989: Monrad, Kasper, *Hverdagsbilleder. Dansk Guldalder – kunstnerne og deres vilkår*,

Christian Ejlers Forlag, Copenhagen, 1989 (English summary, "Pictures of Everyday Life. The Golden Age of Danish Painting and Sculpture. The Artists and their Circumstances")

Munich 1985: Fischer, Erik, and William Gelius, *Von Abildgaard bis Marstrand*, exh. cat., Neue Pinakothek, Munich, 1985

Munich 1988–89b: Himmelheber, Georg, ed., *Kunst des Biedermeier 1815–1835*, exh. cat. Bayrisches Nationalmuseum, Prestel Verlag, Munich, 1988–89

Munk, Jens Peter, "'Den følende Beskuer'. Rørbyes rejse til Sydsjælland sommeren 1832", *Meddelelser fra Ny Carlsberg Glyptotek*, vol. 49 (1993), pp. 5–36 (English summary)

Norman, Geraldine, *Biedermeier Painting 1815–1848*, Thames and Hudson, London, 1987

Novotny, Fritz, *Painting and Sculpture in Europe 1780–1880*, Penguin, Harmondsworth, and Baltimore, 1960; 2nd edn., 1971

Paris 1984–85: Monrad, Kasper, *L'Age d'or de la peinture danoise, 1800–1850*, exh. cat., introductions by Henrik Bramsen and Palle Lauring, Grand Palais, Paris, 1984–85

Wirth, Irmgard, *Berliner Malerei im 19. Jahrhundert*, Siedler Verlag, Berlin, 1990

By artist

WILHELM BENDZ

Copenhagen 1996b: Saabye, Marianne, ed., *Wilhelm Bendz 1804–1832. A Young Painter of the Golden Age*, exh. cat., The Hirschsprung Collection, Copenhagen, 1996

Johansson, Ejner, *Wilhelm Bendz*, 1992

Saabye, M., ed., *Wilhelm Bendz 1804–1832. Et ungt kunstnerliv*, exh. cat., The Hirschsprung Collection, Copenhagen, 1996

CARL BLECHEN

Berlin 1990: Berlin Nationalgalerie, *Carl Blechen. Zwischen Romantik und Realismus*, exh. cat., Prestel Verlag, Munich, 1990

Rave 1940: Rave, Paul Ortwin, ed., *Karl Blechen. Leben. Würdigung. Werk*, Deutscher Verein für Kunstwissenschaft, Berlin, 1940

CARL GUSTAV CARUS

Prause, Marianne, *Carl Gustav Carus. Leben und Werk*, Deutscher Verlag für Kunstwissenschaft, Berlin, 1968

JOHAN CHRISTIAN DAHL

Aubert 1893: Aubert, A., *Professor Dahl. Et Stykke ar Aarhundredets Kunst- og Kultur-*

historie, H. Aschehoug, Christiania (Oslo), 1893; 2nd edn., *Maleren Johan Christian Dahl, etc.*, V. Aubert, A. Krogvig, and C. W. Schnitler, Christiania (Oslo), 1920

Bang 1987: Bang, Marie Lødrup, *Johan Christian Dahl 1788–1857. Life and Works*, Norwegian University Press, Oslo, and Oxford University Press, Oxford, 3 vols., 1987

Munich 1988–89a: Heilmann, Christoph, ed., *Johan Christian Dahl 1788–1857. Ein Maler-freund Caspar David Friedrichs*, exh. cat., Neue Pinakothek, Munich, 1988–89

"Nature's Way": Romantic Landscapes from Norway. Oil Studies, Watercolours and Drawings by Johan Christian Dahl (1788–1857) and Thomas Fearnley (1802–1842), exh. cat., The Whitworth Art Gallery and Fitzwilliam Museum, Cambridge, 1993

Oslo 1988: Lange, Marit, ed., *Johan Christian Dahl 1788–1857. Jubileumsutstilling 1988*, exh. cat., Nasjonalgalleriet, Oslo, and Bergen Billedgalleri, 1988

CHRISTIAN DANKVART DREYER

Ludvigsen, Suzanne, and Henrik Bramsen, *Dankvart Dreyer 1816–1852. Malerier og tegninger*, Kunstforeningen and Fyns Kunstmuseum, 1989

Swane, Leo, *Dankvart Dreyer 1816–1852*, Copenhagen, 1921

C. W. ECKERSBERG

Copenhagen 1983a: Skovgaard, Bente, Hanne Westergaard and Hanne Jönsson, *C. W. Eckersberg og hans elever*, exh. cat., Statens Museum for Kunst, Copenhagen, 1983 (English translation of articles, 1984)

Copenhagen 1983b: Fischer, Erik, Jan Garff, Vibeke Knudsen, Jan Würtz Frandsen and Bjørn Westerbeek Dahl, *Tegninger af C. W. Eckersberg*, exh. cat., Department of Prints and Drawings, Statens Museum for Kunst, Copenhagen, 1983 (2nd edn., 1983, with English translation of the introduction)

Copenhagen 1983–84: Helsted, Dyveke, Eva Henschen and Bjarne Jørnæs, *C. W. Eckersberg i Rom 1813–16*, exh. cat., Thorvaldsens Museum, Copenhagen, 1983–84

Eckersberg, C. W., *Forsög til en Veiledning i Anvendelsen af Perspektivlæren for unge Malere*, Copenhagen, 1833; repr. 1973

Eckersberg, C. W., *Linearperspektiven anvendt paa Malerkunsten*. Text by G. F. Ursin. Copenhagen, 1841; repr. 1978

Fischer, Erik, *Tegninger af C. W. Eckersberg*, Den Kgl. Kobberstiksamling, Copenhagen, 1983

Fischer, Erik, *C. W. Eckersberg. His Mind and Times*, Bløndal, Copenhagen, 1993

Funder, Lise, and Claus Hagedorn-Olsen, eds., *C. W. Eckersberg*, exh. cat., Århus Kunstmuseum, 1983

Hannover, Emil, *C. W. Eckersberg*, Copenhagen, 1898

Jönsson, Hanne, ed., *C. W. Eckersberg og hans elever*, exh. cat., Statens Museum for Kunst, 1983

Saabye, Marianne, ed., *Den nøgne guldalder. Modelbilleder C. W. Eckersberg og hans elever*, exh. cat., The Hirschsprung Collection, 1994

THOMAS FEARNLEY

Gunnarsson, Torsten, *Friluftsmålerie före friluftsmåleriet*, Uppsala, 1989, pp. 207–30

"Nature's Way": Romantic Landscapes from Norway. Oil Studies, Watercolours and Drawings by Johan Christian Dahl (1788–1857) and Thomas Fearnley (1802–1842), exh. cat., The Whitworth Art Gallery and Fitzwilliam Museum, Cambridge, 1993

Willoch, Sigurd, *Maleren Thomas Fearnley*, Oslo, 1932

Willoch, Sigurd, "Thomas Fearnley og de danske malere i Italia", *Kunst og Kultur*, vol. 64 (1981), pp. 249–57

Willoch, Sigurd, *Thomas Fearnley, 1802–1842*, exh. cat., Stiftelsen Modums Blaafarveværk, 1986

Willoch, S., and H. Alsvik, *Thomas Fearnleys tegninger fra reiser ute og hjemme, 1824–1840*, Oslo, 1952

CASPAR DAVID FRIEDRICH

Börsch-Supan, Helmut, *Caspar David Friedrich*, Prestel Verlag, Munich, 1990

Börsch-Supan and Jähnig 1973: Börsch-Supan, Helmut, and Karl Wilhelm Jähnig, *Caspar David Friedrich. Gemälde, Druckgraphik und bildmäßige Zeichnungen*, Prestel Verlag, Munich, 1973

Copenhagen 1991: Monrad, Kasper, and Colin J. Bailey, *Caspar David Friedrich og Danmark / Caspar David Friedrich und Dänemark*, exh. cat., Statens Museum for Kunst, Copenhagen, 1991 (essays in Danish and German)

Leppien, Helmut R., *Caspar David Friedrich in der Hamburger Kunsthalle*, Hamburg, 1993

London 1990: Leighton, John, and Colin J. Bailey, *Caspar David Friedrich, Winter Landscape*, exh. cat., National Gallery, London, 1990

Madrid 1992: Hofmann, Werner, ed., *Caspar David Friedrich. Pinturas y dibujos*, exh. cat., Museo del Prado, Madrid, 1992

New York & Chicago 1990–91: Rewald, Sabine, ed., *The Romantic Vision of Caspar David Friedrich. Paintings and Drawings from the U.S.S.R.*, exh. cat., The Metropolitan Museum of Art, New York, and Art Institute of Chicago, Harry N. Abrams, New York, 1990–91

EDUARD GAERTNER

Wirth 1979: Wirth, Irmgard, *Eduard Gaertner. Der Berliner Architekturmaler*, Propyläen Verlag, Berlin, 1979

JACOB GENSLER

Reuther, Silke, *Johann Jacob Gensler. Ein Maler aus Hamburg (1808–1845)*, LIT Verlag (Monographien 15), Hamburg, 1995 (Ph.D. thesis)

CHRISTIAN FRIEDRICH GILLE

Spitzer, Gerd, *Christian Friedrich Gille. 1805–1899*, Staatliche Kunstsammlungen Dresden – Gemäldegalerie Neue Meister, exh. cat., E. A. Seemann, Leipzig, 1994

LOUIS GURLITT

Hamburg, Flensburg & Nivå 1997–98: Schulte-Wülwer, Ulrich, and Bärbel Hedinger, eds., *Louis Gurlitt 1812–97. Porträts europäischer Landschaften in Gemälden und Zeichnungen*, exh. cat., Altonaer Museum in Hamburg, Museumsberg Flensburg and Nivaagaards Malerisamling, Nivå, 1997–98; Hirmer Verlag, Munich, 1997

CONSTANTIN HANSEN

Copenhagen & Århus 1991: Jørnæs, Bjarne, and Stig Miss, eds., *Constantin Hansen 1804–1880*, exh. cat., Thorvaldsens Museum, Copenhagen and Aarhus Kunstmuseum, Århus, 1991

Hannover, Emil, *Constantin Hansen*, 1901

Ragn Jensen, Hannemarie, "Constantin Hansen. A 19th-century Danish classicist", *Hafnia. Copenhagen Papers in the History of Art*, no. 10 (1985), pp. 73–104

JOHANN ERDMANN HUMMEL

Morton, Marsha Lee, "Johann Erdmann Hummel. A Painter of Biedermeier Berlin", Ph.D. thesis, New York, 1986; U.M. Dissertation Services, Ann Arbor, 1995

JENS JUEL

Monrad, Kasper, *Jens Juel*, Søren Fogtdal, Copenhagen, 1996

Poulsen, Ellen, *Jens Juel*, 2 vols., Christian Ejlers, Copenhagen, 1991 (with an introduction in English)

GEORG FRIEDRICH KERSTING

Schnell, Werner, *Georg Friedrich Kersting. Das zeichnerische und malerische Werk mit Oeuvrekatalog*, Deutscher Verlag für Kunstwissenschaft, Berlin, 1994

Picture Credits

CHRISTEN KØBKE

Copenhagen 1981a: Nørregård-Nielsen, Hans Edvard, *Købke og Kastellet*, exh. cat., Ny Carlsberg Glyptotek, Copenhagen, 1981

Copenhagen 1981c: Monrad, Kasper, *Købke på Blegdammen og ved Sortedamssøen*, exh. cat., essays by Kasper Monrad and Erik Fischer, Statens Museum for Kunst, Copenhagen, 1981

Copenhagen 1996a: Nørregård-Nielsen, Hans Edvard, and Kasper Monrad, eds., *Christen Købke 1810–1848*, exh. cat., Statens Museum for Kunst, Copenhagen, 1996 (English, French, German, and Danish versions)

Hannover, Emil, *Maleren Christen Købke*, 1893

Monrad, Kasper, "Tyske forbilleder. Frederik Sødring og Christen Købke og München-skolens malere", *Meddelelser fra Thorvaldsens Museum*, 1994, pp. 61–73

Nørregård-Nielsen, Hans Edvard, *Christen Købke*, 3 vols., Copenhagen, 1996

Wivel, Mikael, *Christen Købke 1810–1848*, Copenhagen, 1986 (repr. 1993, text in English)

JOHAN THOMAS LUNDBYE

Copenhagen 1994: Henschen, Eva, Torben Melander and Stig Miss, eds., *Johan Thomas Lundbye 1818–1848 … at male det kjære Danmark*, exh. cat., Thorvaldsens Museum, Copenhagen, 1994 (summaries in English)

Madsen, Karl, *J. Th. Lundbye 1818–1848*, 1949

Saabye, Marianne, ed., *Tegninger & Huletanker. Johan Thomas Lundbye 1818–1848*, exh. cat., The Hirschsprung Collection, 1999

ERNST MEYER

Johansson, Ejner, *De danske malere i München*, 1997

CHRISTIAN MORGENSTERN

Mauß, Martina, "Christian E. B. Morgenstern (1805–67). Ein Beitrag zur Landschaftsmalerei der ersten Hälfte des 19. Jh", Ph.D. thesis, Marburg, 1969

JØRGEN ROED

Nyblom, Helene, *Maleren Jørgen Roed. I: Blade af Dansk Kunst Historie*, Udgivne af Foreningen for National Kunst, 1904

Monrad, Kasper, ed., *Danish Painting. The Golden Age. A Loan Exhibition from the Statens Museum for Kunst, Copenhagen*, The National Gallery, London, 1984

Munk, Jens Peter, ed., *På sporet af Jørgen Roed i Italien 1837–1841*, exh. cat., Ny Carlsberg Glyptotek, 1991

Munk, Jens Peter, "Billeder af et venskab. Constantin Hansen og Jørgen Roed i København og Ringsted", *Meddelelser fra Ny Carlsberg Glyptotek*, 1994, pp. 118–46

MARTINUS RØRBYE

Copenhagen 1981b: Dyveke Helsted, Eva Henschen, Bjarne Jørnæs and Torben Melander, *Martinus Rørbye 1803–1848*, exh. cat., Thorvaldsens Museum, Copenhagen, 1981

Fonsmark, Anne-Birgitte, "Udsigter og indsigter. Martinus Rørbye: 'Udsigt fra kunstnerens vindue', c. 1825", E. J. Bencard, A. Kold and P. S. Meyer, eds., *Kunstværkets krav. 27 fortolkninger af danske kunstværker*, Fogtdal, Copenhagen, 1990, pp. 67–77

Munk, Jens Peter, "'Den følende Beskuer'. Rørbyes rejse til Sydsjælland sommeren 1832", *Meddelelser fra Ny Carlsberg Glyptotek*, 1993, pp. 5–36

Rørbye, Martinus, *Rejsedagbog 1830*, Georg Nygaard, Copenhagen, 1930

KARL FRIEDRICH SCHINKEL

Karl Friedrich Schinkel 1781–1841, exh. cat., Altes Museum, Berlin, 1981

Karl Friedrich Schinkel. Architektur Malerei Kunstgewerbe, exh. cat., Orangerie des Schlosses Charlottenburg, Berlin, 1981

PETER CHRISTIAN SKOVGAARD

Bramsen, Henrik, *Malerier af P. C. Skovgaard*, 1938

Munk-Jørgensen, Wivian and Th. Bullinger, *P. C. Skovgaard, J. Th. Lundbye, Lorenz Frølich*, exh. cat., Skovgaard Museet, 1996

Skovgaard, Bente, ed., *Sommerrejsen til Vejby. J. Th. Lundbye og P. C. Skovgaard*, exh. cat., Statens Museum for Kunst, Copenhagen, 1989

FREDERIK SØDRING

Vestergaard, Lillian, "Landskabsmaleren Frederik Sødring", *Kunstmuseets Årsskrift*, 1981, pp. 48–82

Monrad, Kasper, "Tyske forbilleder. Frederik Sødring og Christen Købke og München-skolens malere", *Meddelelser fra Thorvaldsens Museum*, 1994, pp. 61–73

FRIEDRICH WASMANN

Nathan, Peter, *Friedrich Wasmann. Sein Leben und sein Werk. Ein Beitrag zur Geschichte der Malerei des neunzehnten Jahrhunderts*, F. Bruckmann, Munich, 1954